www.wadsworth.com

www.wadsworth.com is the World Wide Web site for Thomson Wadsworth and is your direct source to dozens of online resources.

At *www.wadsworth.com* you can find out about supplements, demonstration software, and student resources. You can also send email to many of our authors and preview new publications and exciting new technologies.

www.wadsworth.com
Changing the way the world learns®

Guide to Criminal Law for Texas

Guide to Criminal Law for Texas

Third Edition

BARBARA A. BELBOT
University of Houston—Downtown

THOMSON
WADSWORTH
Australia • Canada • Mexico • Singapore • Spain • United Kingdom • United States

Executive Editor: Sabra Horne
Development Editor: Julie Sakaue
Assistant Editor: Jana Davis
Editorial Assistant: Elise Smith
Marketing Manager: Terra Schultz
Marketing Assistant: Annabelle Yang

Project Manager, Editorial Production: Jennifer Klos
Print Buyer: Emma Claydon
Permissions Editor: Kiely Sexton
Cover Designer: Yvo Riezebos
Cover Image: Donovan Reese/Getty Images
Text and Cover Printer: Thomson West

Printed in the United States of America
1 2 3 4 5 6 7 08 07 06 05 04

Library of Congress Control Number: 2001012345

ISBN: 0-534-64418-X

Thomson Wadsworth
10 Davis Drive
Belmont, CA 94002-3098
USA

Asia
Thomson Learning
5 Shenton Way #01-01
UIC Building
Singapore 068808

Australia/New Zealand
Thomson Learning
102 Dodds Street
Southbank, Victoria 3006
Australia

Canada
Nelson
1120 Birchmount Road
Toronto, Ontario M1K 5G4
Canada

Europe/Middle East/South Africa
Thomson Learning
High Holborn House
50/51 Bedford Row
London WC1R 4LR
United Kingdom

Latin America
Thomson Learning
Seneca, 53
Colonia Polanco
11560 Mexico D.F.
Mexico

Spain/Portugal
Paraninfo
Calle/Magallanes, 25
28015 Madrid, Spain

TABLE OF CONTENTS

Guide to Criminal Law
for Texas

Introduction to the Texas Supplement

The Texas Criminal Law Supplement is to be used with Joel Samaha's *Criminal Law,* Eighth Edition. The titles and contents of the Supplement's chapters match the titles and contents of the chapters in Samaha's book. The Supplement's chapters focus entirely on the criminal law in Texas. By reading the two books together, students can develop a deeper and more thorough understanding of the criminal law.

The Chapters

Each chapter in the Supplement follows a fairly standard presentation, beginning with an Introduction. The chapters are divided into two or more sections, each of which consists of an overview of a certain area of the law, including quotes from pertinent statutes, followed by descriptions or edited versions of Texas court opinions that have interpreted those statutes. Some sections have review questions at the end of the section. In other chapters the review questions are placed at the end only certain sections or towards the end of the entire chapter. Each chapter ends with a few concluding thoughts.

The chapters do not cover the full breath of material that is covered by Joel Samaha. They focus more narrowly on specific areas. Students will find that not only is a particular chapter limited to Texas law, it will generally not cover all of the items covered by Samaha in his matching chapter. Students will also find that some chapters cover material that Samaha does not address. The Supplement highlights those things about Texas criminal law that make it unique or especially interesting.

Chapter One introduces students to the Texas Penal Code, a bit of its most recent history and its organization. The Penal Code will make a lot more sense for students who read Chapter One. The chapter also explains how Texas court cases are located and cited. It briefly explains the structure of the Texas court system and how legal precedent works. Chapter One provides an important foundation for the rest of the Supplement.

The Review Questions

The review questions try to help students apply what they have read in the Supplement. Some questions are about the Texas court opinions in the chapters and are designed to make sure students understood what the court decided and why. Other questions are about the Texas statutes, many of which are quoted in the Supplement. There are also questions that will require students to consult a copy of the Texas Penal Code. Finally, there are many hypothetical fact situation questions that take students beyond the reading and ask them to apply the law. These are the fun questions and the most important part of the review process. They simulate the real world. They challenge the students' critical thinking skills, helping them identify the differences and similarities in fact settings and how the law responds accordingly. The questions are meant to be debated and open a topic up for further discussion. By the way, the answers to the review questions are located in the Appendix at the end of the Supplement.

Why study criminal law? For some students the answer is obvious. They aspire to go to law school. Others are or will become law enforcement officials or work in an area of criminal justice where knowing the Penal Code is important. The value of studying criminal law, however, transcends both of those reasons.

The criminal law takes human conflicts and behavior and "translates" them into a formalized structure that categorizes events in fairly complex ways. It categorizes conduct according the act that was performed and, with a few exceptions, according to the intent by which the act was performed. In some instances, the act is further categorized by the type and amount of harm it inflicted. What began as a story about what a person or persons did and how the event unfolded and what resulted from what they did is torn down and reconstructed into legal concepts, described with legal language. Through that reconstruction, valuable information can be lost. It sometimes feels as though the human dimension is set aside. The real people involved, offenders, witnesses, and victims, take a back seat to the newly translated legal description of what occurred and why. On the other hand, the process helps identify and clarify valuable information. It helps eliminate details that are not or should not be central to deciding blameworthiness and punishment. It focuses on those aspects of the event that are most critical. Studying criminal law helps us better understand human behavior and helps us develop critical thinking skills that can be used in any profession, and in our personal lives as well.

The other reason to study criminal law? It's just plain fun.

Chapter One

The Nature, Origins, and Purposes of Criminal Law

INTRODUCTION

This chapter introduces you to the Texas Penal Code, how it classifies criminal offenses and provides for their punishment, specifically:

(1) some of the more important general provisions of the Code,
(2) how the criminal law of Texas can be located and how cases interpreting the law can be accessed,
(3) the Code's scheme for classifying offenses,
(4) the Code's punishment philosophy and provisions for punishment.

You will learn more if you follow along with the discussion in this chapter and throughout the Supplement by consulting the relevant provisions of the Texas Penal Code (often referred to as the T.P.C.). This supplement will describe and quote portions of the T.P.C., but there is no substitute for actually reading the code. Sometimes Code provisions get convoluted enough to warrant a reading out loud. Only by working through and finding provisions of the statute on your own, will you appreciate the complexities, frustrations, and fun (yes, fun) of the law. Purchase a Texas Penal Code and begin a journey into the creative, ever-changing study of the criminal law as defined and enforced in the Lone Star State!

Section 1: LIMITS OF THE CRIMINAL LAW

Texas is one of 25 states that have abolished common law crimes and is considered a code jurisdiction. According to section 1.03 of the Texas Penal Code (T.P.C.), conduct is not an offense unless it is so defined by statute or other legislative act. The codified Penal Code supersedes all common-law offenses and establishes the legality principle – there can be no crime without a law.

> **Penal Code Section 1.03 (a)**
> Conduct does not constitute an offense unless it is defined as an offense by statute, municipal ordinance, order of a county commissioners court, or rule authorized by and lawfully adopted under a statute.

The T.P.C. was first enacted in 1856, and was revised for the first time in 1974. The 1974 revised code is the Penal Code still in use although it has been significantly amended over the last two decades to include new offenses, changed definitions, and different punishment schemes. It retains, however, the organization and structure of the 1974 revisions. Although the 1974 revisions were substantial, they did not radically change the criminal law in the state of

Texas. The revised Code introduced greater clarity, simplicity and order to the law. The T.P.C. does not include all Texas penal law. There are provisions scattered throughout the civil statutes that impose criminal fines and punishment, most of which involve regulatory type offenses. For example, section 195.004 of the Texas Health and Safety Code makes it a Class C misdemeanor to fail, neglect, or refuse to fill out a birth or death certificate. Section 13.007 of the Texas Election Code makes it a Class B misdemeanor to make false statements on an application to vote. Juveniles who engage in unlawful conduct are adjudicated under the provisions of the Texas Family Code. The Penal Code makes clear in Section 1.03, however, that any state penal statute, municipal ordinance, or administrative rule or regulation is of no effect to the extent it overlaps, duplicates, or conflicts with a T.P.C. provision.

Jurisdiction

Section 1.04 of the Texas Penal Code establishes that Texas has jurisdiction over:

(1) offenses any element of which occur in the state;
(2) out-of-state attempts to commit offenses within the state;
(3) out-of-state conspiracies, if an act in furtherance of the conspiracy occurs inside the state;
(4) any offense under the law of another state that is also an offense in Texas, if any conduct including attempt, solicitation, conspiracy or other conduct that establishes criminal responsibility for its commission occurs in Texas;
(5) any offense based on an omission to perform a duty imposed on an actor by state law regardless of the location of the actor at the time of the offense;
(6) if the offense is criminal homicide and the body of the victim is found in Texas, it is presumed that the victim's death occurred in Texas.

Purpose of the Criminal Law

The Texas Legislature states in Section 1.02 that the general purpose of the criminal law is to deal with conduct that causes harm to individuals or public interests the state should be protecting, however, criminal responsibility should attach only to conduct that is unjustifiable or inexcusable, that is, guilty conduct. In the language of the statute is seen the age-old controversy surrounding criminal law. Should the law emphasize a subjective theory of criminal liability and focus on the offender's moral guilt or should it focus on the harm done to the victim and the offender's objective manifestation of criminality?

The Legislature states that the Code is intended to achieve certain objectives, including deterring the public from committing crime, deterring the convicted offender from committing further crimes, and rehabilitating offenders. The Legislature also states that the law is designed to provide for penalties that are proportionate to the seriousness of the offense and that recognize that individual offenders have different potential for rehabilitation. Nowhere in Section 1.02 is retribution listed as an objective of the Texas Penal Code.

Definitions

Key terms found throughout the Penal Code are defined in Section 1.07. The definitions are applied whenever that particular term is used in the Code. The definition section is crucial to understanding the meaning of different criminal offenses. Take for instance the term "person." If an offense proscribes certain behavior by a person, Section 1.07 tells us that a person may include individuals *and* corporations and associations. Prior to September 1, 2003, individual was defined as a human being who has been born and is alive; a definition that still applies to offenses committed before that date. The Texas Legislature, however, enacted legislation that applies to crimes committed after September 1, 2003.

> **Penal Code section 1.07 (26)**
> "Individual" means a human being born alive, including an unborn child at every stage of gestation from fertilization until birth.

The new definition is an important revision that allows prosecutors to charge offenders who have harmed or killed unborn children with crimes they could not charge them with prior to the change. The term "deadly weapon" is defined as:

> **Penal Code section 1.07 (17)**
> **(A)** a firearm or anything manifestly designed, made, or adapted for the purpose of inflicting death or serious bodily injury, or
> **(B)** anything that in the manner of its use or intended use is capable of causing death or serious bodily injury.

Chairs, baseball bats, vases, bottles, and slingshots – the list of deadly weapons is endless! Section 1.07 does not include definitions of all the important terms found in the Code. Some are defined in the specific section of the Code where they are used.

Legislative Changes

The Texas Legislature meets every two years, and, among many other things, it debates and passes amendments to the Penal Code. There are proposals every legislative session for the enactment of new criminal offenses, changes in the scope and definitions of offenses already on the books, and changes in the classification of specific offenses or their punishment. It is important to remember that the Penal Code will change every two years. Sometimes the changes are numerous. Sometimes they are a dramatic departure from the past. Sometimes the changes provide better organization and structure the Code to make it easier to use. New criminal offenses reflect changes in society. When computers became a part of our daily personal and commercial lives, it was necessary to create statutes that addressed crimes that could only be committed with or because of computer technology, such as Section 33.02 of the T.P.C. that defines the crime of breaching computer security. On the other hand, stalking statutes were enacted during the past ten years to deal with behavior that was not new. Stalking laws resulted from a change of attitude that reflected a greater sensitivity and understanding toward victims of stalking behavior, and recognized that stalkers often turn dangerous.

Section 2: CLASSIFYING AND GRADING CRIMES

Every state classifies its crimes into more and less serious offenses. How a crime is classified determines the type and length of punishment. The more serious offenses that involve spending time in the Big House for a year or longer are felonies. The less serious crimes that involve incarceration in the county jail for less than one year or no incarceration, just a fine are misdemeanors. Beyond that common distinction, the states differ considerably in their classification schemes.

Once convicted of a specific crime, the offender's punishment must be within the parameters defined by the Penal Code. Judges and juries do not have the discretion to go outside the law and devise punishments that are not provided for in the criminal laws. Texas is unique in that the law allows the jury that convicted the offender to decide how the offender should be punished. Many states allow only the judge who presided at the trial to decide punishment. According to the Texas Code of Criminal Procedure, it is the offender's choice as to whether punishment is assessed by the judge or the jury, with the exception of capital felony cases when the State seeks the death penalty. In cases where the death penalty is sought, the jury that convicted the offender must participate in the sentencing process.

Punishment Provisions

The type and length of punishment for each offense depends on the classification ascribed to the offense. Once you know a crime's classification you know the punishment facing an offender convicted of that crime. Toward the end of each section that defines a criminal offense, there is a subsection that defines how that particular crime is classified. Chapter 12 of the Texas Penal Code lays out how the various levels of misdemeanors and felonies are sanctioned.

Misdemeanors

Class A misdemeanors are the most serious of this level of offense and are punished by a fine not to exceed $4000.00, confinement in jail for a term not to exceed one year, or both the fine and the confinement. Notice that the statute provides for a range of punishment. The judge or jury need not impose the entire $4000 fine. No fine has to be imposed at all. A jail term of up to one year is available, but an entire year need not be imposed. The range gives the judge or jury the ability to exercise a certain amount of discretion in the sentencing decision, allowing them to consider the circumstances of the case before them.

Class B misdemeanors can lead to a fine of up to $2000.00 and jail time not to exceed 180 days. By jail time, the statute means incarceration in the county jail facility as opposed to the state's correctional institutions. The least serious Class C misdemeanor can be sanctioned only by a fine not to exceed $500.00.

Felonies

The most serious felony is a capital felony. There is only one capital felony offense and that is for certain kinds of homicide as defined in Chapter 19 of the T.P.C. If the State seeks the death penalty for a capital murder, the convicted offender must be punished either by death or life in prison. If the State does not seek the death penalty for a capital murder the only punishment available is life imprisonment. The State is not required by law to seek death for a capital murder.

First-degree felony: imprisonment for life or for any term not more than 99 years or less than five years. A fine not to exceed $10,000.00.

Second-degree felony: imprisonment for a term of not more than 20 years or less than two years. A fine not to exceed $10,000.00.

Third-degree felony: imprisonment for a term of not more than 10 years or less than two years. A fine not to exceed $10,000.00.

Imprisonment for first, second, and third-degree felonies takes place in the Texas Department of Criminal Justice - Institutional Division. Convicted offenders are sent to whatever state correctional facility suits their particular prisoner classification and the needs of the agency.

State jail felony: confinement in a state jail for a term of not more than two years or less than 180 days. A fine not to exceed $10,000.00.

State jail felonies were created by the Texas Legislature in 1993, amid much controversy as part of the most sweeping sentencing reform legislation in the history of the state. The Legislature made many non-violent property and drug offenses state jail felonies. It also doubled the time to be served by most violent offenders by limiting the amount of good time credits they could earn. The rationale for the reform was to balance the need to "get tough on crime" with the need to "get smart on crime." Getting tough involved increasing convictions, the number of offenders in prison and the length of time offenders stay incarcerated. "Getting smart on crime" involved finding less expensive alternatives than prison to protect the public.

Beginning on September 1, 1994, numerous offenses in the Penal Code were assigned to a punishment range called the state jail felony, sometimes referred to as a fourth-degree felony. If a state jail felon is incarcerated, they serve their time in a state jail felony facility without the opportunity to acquire good time credits. After a judge or jury assesses punishment, the judge may suspend the sentence and place the defendant on community supervision. As a condition of community supervision, the judge may order the defendant to serve short periods of time in a county jail or a state jail, or confine the felon to a community restitution center, a substance abuse treatment center, or a local boot camp. If an offender on community supervision for a state jail felony violates a condition of supervision, the judge may revoke the supervision and order the defendant to serve time in the state jail facility.

Effective September 2003, The Texas Legislature made significant changes to the punishment available for offenders convicted of a state jail felony under certain provisions of the Texas Health and Safety Code. Those offenses include possession of certain controlled substances in limited amounts. In those cases, the judge is required to suspend the sentence and place the defendant on community supervision, unless he or she has previously been convicted of a felony. While on supervision, the offender must undergo substance abuse treatment

State jail felonies largely include previous third-degree felonies that involved low level property offenders. Examples of state jail felonies include theft of property valued at $1500.00 or more but less than $20,000.00 and unauthorized use of a vehicle. A few state jail felonies were formerly first and second-degree felonies: burglary of a building, possession or delivery of less than one gram of a penalty 1 controlled substance. Other state jail felonies were formerly misdemeanors: criminally negligent homicide, criminal nonsupport, injury to a child, elderly person or a disabled person by criminal negligence.

State jail felony facilities are different than the state correctional institutions where convicted felons are sent. State jails are also not the same as the county jails that house convicted misdemeanants and pretrial detainees. State jails are unique institutions that are part of the state's correctional apparatus and were created at the same time the legislature created the state jail felony classification. The state jail division of the Texas Department of Criminal Justice works in conjunction with community justice agencies to develop and adopt work, rehabilitation, education, and recreation programs within the state jails.

A state jail felony becomes a third-degree felony if it is shown at trial that the offender used or exhibited a deadly weapon during the commission of the offense or while fleeing from the crime. If the offender who is convicted of a state jail felony has been previously convicted of murder, capital murder, indecency with a child, aggravated kidnapping, aggravated sexual assault, or aggravated robbery, his or her state jail felony conviction is automatically enhanced to a third-degree felony.

Repeat and Habitual Offenders

From a convicted felon's perspective, perhaps the most important part of Chapter 12 addresses penalties for repeat and habitual offenders. Continuing to commit and be convicted of crimes has serious consequences. The argument against habitual offender statutes is that offenders are punished more than once for their crimes: the first time when they are convicted and serve their sentence and a second time when the punishment for a new and different conviction is enhanced because they are repeat offenders. An argument in favor of habitual offender statutes is that repeat offenders obviously did not learn their lesson the first time and need the threat of enhanced punishment. Secondly, repeat offenders are a greater threat to society and deserve enhanced punishment. The courts have upheld the constitutionality of habitual offender statutes.

The Texas Penal Code provides that punishment for a second-degree felony conviction shall be enhanced to punishment for a first-degree felony conviction if it is shown that the offender has been convicted once before of a prior felony. This means that instead of facing a sentence of 2 to 20 years in prison, the convicted habitual offender faces imprisonment of between 5 and 99 years. If it is shown that the convicted offender of a first-degree felony has been once before convicted of a prior felony, his or her punishment shall be enhanced to any term of not more than 99 years or less than 15 years. Instead of facing 5 to 99 years, he or she faces 15 to 99 years.

During the "get tough on crime" era of the 1990s, legislators responded to the public's concerns by making the habitual offender statutes even tougher, especially for repeat sex offenders. The Texas Legislature has mandated automatic life sentences for persons convicted of:

- sexual assault
- aggravated sexual assault,
- aggravated kidnapping with the intent to violate or abuse the victim sexually,
- burglary with the intent to commit a sex offense or indecency with a child

and

If the defendant had been previously convicted of:

- indecency with a child,
- sexual assault,
- aggravated sexual assault,
- prohibited sexual conduct,
- sexual performance by a child,
- possession of or promotion of child pornography,
- aggravated kidnapping with the intent to violate or abuse the victim sexually,
- or burglary with the intent to commit a sex offense.

Not only can the punishment for third, second, and first-degree felonies be enhanced, penalties for repeat misdemeanors can be enhanced as well. Offenders who repeat state jail felonies can also find themselves facing more serious sanctions: third and, in certain circumstances, second-degree felonies.

Interestingly, a life sentence in Texas does not mean that the convicted offender will never see the "free world" again. Texas does not have a life without parole sentence. A prisoner who is serving a life sentence for a capital felony must serve at least 40 calendar years without consideration of good conduct time. If he or she is a habitual offender and is serving an automatic life sentence for one of the crimes described above, they must stay in prison for at least 35 calendar years without consideration of good conduct time.

The Penal Code does not address the availability of community supervision as an alternative punishment to incarceration. Article 42 of the Texas Code of Criminal Procedure describes under what circumstances a judge can suspend a sentence of incarceration and place a convicted offender on community supervision. Article 42 also provides for the award of good time credit to inmates who are incarcerated. Good time credits can significantly reduce how much of a sentence the offender actually serves. Finally, Article 42 describes the parole eligibility process. In order to appreciate fully the sentencing scheme in Texas, you have to link together the various provisions of the Penal Code and the Code of Criminal Procedure.

Section 3: LOCATING TEXAS CRIMINAL LAW

How the Penal Code is Organized

As already mentioned, with the exception of certain regulatory offenses, the criminal law is found in the Texas Penal Code. Each separate offense is assigned a section number. Section numbers are also assigned to other important criminal law concepts such as self-defense, the insanity defense, and criminal responsibility for the conduct of another. If you know the section of the Code that addresses the offense or concept you want to look at, turn to that section. For instance, if you know that aggravated robbery is defined in Section 29.03, turn to that section. Since there are many versions of the Penal Code available, each with their own format and pagination, offenses are located by section number. Code sections are arranged numerically, starting with Section 1.01 through Section 71.05.

The sections are also arranged into chapters. Each chapter includes those sections of the Code that address a particular type of offense. When a new crime is enacted, it is placed in the chapter that best describes the nature of the offense and is given a section number that is not currently assigned to a crime already in the chapter. For example, Chapter 19 includes all the sections of the T.P.C. that deal with criminal homicide. The scheme is sometimes less than perfect. Chapter 22 includes all the sections that deal with the crime of assault: assault, sexual assault, aggravated assault, aggravated sexual assault, and injury to a child, elderly individual, or disabled individual. Chapter 22 also includes crimes that are less obviously assault-like: abandoning or endangering a child, deadly conduct, terrorist threat, aiding suicide, tampering with a consumer product, and leaving a child in a vehicle.

If you do not know the section number of an offense or the chapter in which it is located, look at the topic index in the back of the version of the Code you are using. Use it like any other topic index, look for key words and a section number will be provided. If the key word you chose is not listed, brainstorm and look for other key words.

If the offense you are looking for was enacted after the version of your Penal Code was published, you will not find it! Seek out the most recent Penal Code! The law changes every two years. Even if the offense is listed in your older version, **be careful**. There may have been changes to the definition of that offense during the last legislative session. You may be referring to old law.

Do not forget to refer to Section 1.07 to define important terms in the offense you are researching. Statutes are written in legalese, which is a stilted, formal language. Read the statutes carefully and understand that **every** word in the statute has been placed there for a reason. Be mindful of words like "and," "or," "either," "including but not limited to."

Every state has an official publication of its statutes. In Texas, the official publication of the criminal law is found in Vernon's Texas Code Annotated, a set of three volumes labeled "Penal Code," which is a part of a large multi-volume set that includes all the state's laws. Vernon's is an especially useful place to research the criminal law because in addition to the text of the laws, there are annotations following the text that include extremely helpful information. The text of each section of the Penal Code is followed by notes about the legislative history of the section, when the section was passed and when and what amendments have been made to the section. The annotations also include a listing of law review articles and legal treatises about the particular section. Most importantly, under the heading "Notes of Decisions" the annotations include brief descriptions of cases decided by courts who have interpreted the section, the names of the cases, and where they can be located (citations).

Precedent and Stare Decisis

Not all court opinions carry equal weight in terms of precedential value. The court of last resort in Texas for criminal matters is the Texas Court of Criminal Appeals. The decisions of that court are the final say. The Court of Criminal Appeals has jurisdiction over the entire state. Once that court has spoken about a particular matter, every court in the state must follow its interpretation of the law.

The Texas Court of Appeals is really composed of 14 different appeals courts that serve different parts of the state. Each Court of Appeals has jurisdiction in a specific geographical region of the state. Their decisions are precedent only for the state district and county courts located within their jurisdiction. When using the Vernon's statutes, the researcher will obviously pay close attention to the opinions rendered by the Texas Court of Criminal Appeals. The researcher will also look for the cases decided most recently. If the Texas Court of Criminal Appeals has not rendered an opinion about a particular provision of the code, the researcher will look at opinions rendered by the Texas Court of Appeals. He or she will first look for opinions rendered by the appeals court that includes the jurisdiction where the case is located. If that Court of Appeals has not rendered a decision on the matter, the researcher looks to the other intermediate courts of appeal to see if they have entertained the issue.

Finding Texas Cases

For lawyers, reading the text of the law is only the beginning of understanding what the law means. The next step is to read case opinions that have interpreted the law. Vernon's is one way to locate the names and citations of those cases. After each Penal Code section, there are lists of cases interpreting the provision. Of course, the more important or controversial the section, more cases will be listed. In Texas, the state district courts are the trial courts that sit over the trial of criminal felony cases. Judges in the state district courts do not issue written opinions about their rulings. If a criminal case is appealed to the Texas Court of Appeals, however, the intermediate court of appeals that heard the appeal will often write an opinion. Many of those written opinions are published. Published opinions have citations that designate where in the law books the opinions can be found. If the decision of the Texas Court of Appeals is appealed to the Texas Court of Criminal Appeals, an opinion will usually be written and published. Vernon's Penal Code is one way for researchers to find the opinions of the intermediate Texas Courts of Appeal and the Texas Court of Criminal Appeals. Brief abstracts describe a bit about what the case decided so the researcher can determine whether the case is worth reading.

Because hard cover law books are extremely expensive, every year publishers put together all the recent changes in the law in a paperback version to update the most current hard cover volume. The yearly update is called a pocket part because it literally slips into a pocket placed in the back cover of the hardbound volume that it updates. The pocket not only updates the statute, it also contains the abstracts, names, and citations of court opinions that have been rendered since the hardbound volume was printed. It is essential to check the pocket parts in order to find the most recent law and court cases.

There are other ways to find court opinions about Texas criminal law. One important research tool is the Texas Digest. The Digest is a comprehensive listing of cases that have interpreted all the provisions of the Texas statutes. By looking under those volumes in the Digest for criminal law, you will find cases that interpret the Code's various provisions. The Digest is also updated each year with pocket parts that list the cases decided since the hardbound volume was published. In the front of the Digest's volumes that pertain to the criminal law, you will find an outline of topics. Next to each topic is a symbol in the shape of a key and a number. The number is called the key number. Find the topic you want to research and note its key number. Turn to the key number in the criminal law volumes to find an exhaustive listing of cases interpreting that topic.

If you are lucky enough to have access to a computer database of court cases, your research will be considerably facilitated. There are two commercial electronic (WESTLAW and LEXIS) databases that allow research to be conducted using key words and phrases. The electronic databases are very expensive to use and access is typically limited to persons who are affiliated with the firm or academic institution that has purchased access to the data.

Locating a Specific Case

Once you have the name and citation of a case that sounds like it deals with the issue in which you are interested, the next step is to find the case and read it. Opinions issued by the Texas Courts of Appeal and the Texas Court of Criminal Appeals are found in the South Western Reporters, a multi-volume set of published court cases, both civil and criminal. The South Western Reporter is published by West Publishing Company and is a unit of West's national reporter system. Texas criminal cases decided between 1892 - 1931 are found in the set called South Western Reporters. Criminal cases decided between 1932 - to the current date are found in the set called South Western Reporters 2d. Volumes are numbered, beginning with number one. As new cases are published, new volumes are added and the numbers increase.

Case citations are easy to understand. After the name of a case, there is a string of numbers. That string is known as the case citation. For example, *State of Texas v. Johnnie BadGuy*, 690 S.W.2d 789 translates into:

Case name – State of Texas v. Johnnie BadGuy
Case Citation – volume 690 of the South Western Reporters 2d, page 789

There will be other information following the citation in parentheses, such as (Tex. App. – El Paso 1995). The parentheses tell us that the Texas Court of Appeals in El Paso decided this case in 1995. You may see something like (Tex. Crim. App. 1988) which tells us that this case was decided by the Texas Court of Criminal Appeals in 1988. Case citations often include other information about the history of the case as it was appealed through the Texas court system, but that information is not important for us to master here.

FINAL COMMENTS ON THE NATURE, ORIGINS, AND PURPOSES OF CRIMINAL LAW

The criminal law is society's last resort for exercising social control. It offers the most extreme and powerful set of sanctions. It is important to think about that power as you study the elements of various offenses and the grounds for various defenses. The State can exercise enormous influence over its citizens. Criminal defendants face the most serious of threats to their lives, liberties, and pocket books. The study of criminal law will not feel like a Perry Mason show. It will be exact and sometimes tedious. Details of offenses are important. Shades of meaning in interpreting the law are critical. It may seem as if courts are splitting hairs over the definitions of words and phrases. In the background, however, is the power of the State. When is the exercise of that power appropriate? Under what circumstances do we as a society want the State to take away an individual's freedom? What is the best punishment for a particular offense? Hard questions. No easy answers.

REVIEW

Questions 1-10 require you to practice looking up criminal laws in the Texas Penal Code.

1. Serious bodily injury as defined in the Texas Penal Code would include:
   a. any injury that results in the victim's hospitalization.
   b. any and all harm to the victim's body.
   c. loss of limbs or permanent disfigurement.
   d. only injuries that are of a permanent nature.

2. Public servants as defined by the Penal Code do not include:
   a. jurors.
   b. persons performing governmental functions under a claim of right even though they are not legally qualified to do so.
   c. a college professor at a state university.
   d. employees of private companies that produce products for the U.S. military.

3. According to the Texas Penal Code, to possess something, a person:
   a. must actually have the object in his or her physical possession.
   b. can still possess an object even though it is not in his or her possession if they have a written agreement that states the object belongs to them.
   c. does not have to have actual physical possession of the object as long as they control how the object is used or what happens to it.
   d. can only possess an object if there is identifying marks or features on it that allow it to be traced to that specific person.

4. Effective consent under the Penal Code does not include:
   a. a 12-year-old child who allows his adult next-door neighbor to take his family's car.
   b. a seriously mentally retarded woman who has a sexual relationship with a family friend.
   c. a man who agrees to commit a burglary with his friends because they have threatened to harm his sister if he fails to cooperate.
   d. all of the above.

5. Under the Texas Penal Code, assaulting a family member:
    a. is always punished the same way as assaulting a stranger.
    b. is punished less severely than assaulting a stranger because the offender is considered less of a risk to society at large.
    c. can be punished more severely than assaulting a stranger if the offender has a prior record of assaulting family members.
    d. is not considered a crime unless there is severe bodily injury to the family member.

6. Corporations in Texas:
    a. cannot be found guilty of criminal offenses.
    b. can be found guilty of offenses that provide for penalties consisting of only fines.
    c. can be found guilty of offenses that provide for imprisonment.
    d. can be found guilty of no greater than a third degree felony.

7. Aiding suicide in Texas:
    a. is not a crime.
    b. is a crime only if the person aided actually commits suicide.
    c. is no more than a Class C misdemeanor.
    d. can be a state jail felony if the aid causes suicide that results in serious bodily injury.

8. An offender can admit at the time of sentencing that he is guilty of another unadjudicated offense and ask the court to consider that offense in determining the sentence for the offense for which he has been adjudged guilty. If the court takes the unadjudicated offense into consideration:
    a. prosecution of the unadjudicated offense is prohibited.
    b. prosecution of the unadjudicated offense is not prohibited.
    c. the unadjudicated offense is deemed adjudged because of the offender's admission.
    d. the unadjudicated offense can have no bearing on the Judge's sentencing decision.

9. Criminal solicitation of a capital murder:
    a. is not a crime.
    b. is a second-degree felony if the murder never occurred.
    c. is a first-degree felony only if the murder occurred.
    d. is a first-degree felony.

10. A person found guilty of threatening to commit an act of violence to a another person with the intent to interrupt the public transportation system is guilty of a:
    a. a Class B misdemeanor.
    b. a Class A misdemeanor.
    c. a first-degree felony.
    d. a third-degree felony.

11. Wayne Wierdo had sent a letter to the headquarters of Texas Pharmacy Drugstore Co. stating that he intended to break into one of the company's 100 chain stores operated in Texas and put poison in some of the aspirin bottles sold on over the counter. If the authorities apprehend Wayne before he was able to carry out his threat, he could be charged with a crime under the Texas Penal Code. What's the appropriate crime and its classification level?
    a. tampering with a consumer product, third-degree felony
    b. terroristic threat, third-degree felony
    c. deadly conduct, Class A misdemeanor
    d. tampering with a consumer product, first-degree felony

12. Bad Boy Blue went on a rampage and destroyed his enemy's favorite hot rod, smashing it with a tire iron. The damage amounted to $8000.00. Blue is facing:
    a. third-degree felony
    b. first-degree felony
    c. state jail felony
    d. second-degree felony

13. Joe, the serial burglar, decided to make several hits in one night. First, he burglarized the neighborhood shoe warehouse. A few hours later, he burglarized the residence of a wealthy lawyer. Joe was apprehended by the police. He could be charged with:
    a. state jail felony and a second-degree felony
    b. two second-degree felonies
    c. two state jail felonies
    d. a first and a second-degree felony

14. Timothy Trespasser could not stay away from "visiting" the downtown homeless shelter without the permission of the shelter authorities. Timothy was not homeless and did not want to spend the night. He was nosey. Timothy is guilty of:
    a. a third-degree felony
    b. a Class A misdemeanor
    c. a Class B misdemeanor
    d. no crime because it is not illegal to trespass a homeless shelter

15. Timothy also liked to remove railroad rails and use them as support beams for his cabin in the woods. The railroad company estimated that a rail is worth $300.00. For each rail he stole, Timothy could be charged with:
    a. a Class C misdemeanor
    b. a Class B misdemeanor
    c. a Class A misdemeanor
    d. no crime since no one has been injured and the rails are out in the public

Chapter Two

Constitutional Limits on Criminal Law

INTRODUCTION

Most constitutional challenges are based on the U.S. Constitution. State courts, however, can interpret state constitutions as giving citizens of that state more rights than are provided under the federal constitution. More and more frequently, plaintiffs are arguing that their rights under a state constitution have been violated. Often, their argument is based on both the federal and state constitutions.

This chapter discusses some of the more common constitutional challenges to criminal statutes and examines pertinent sections of the Texas Constitution that impact on the constitutionality of criminal statutes. It relates sections of the state constitution to parallel clauses in the U.S. Constitution. For each section of the state constitution, the discussion also looks at recent cases decided by Texas courts, and a few from the U.S. Supreme Court, that have interpreted that section. The constitutional provisions discussed include:

(1) ex post facto clause
(2) void-for-vagueness
(3) equal protection of the laws
(4) free speech

Section 1: THE EX POST FACTO CLAUSE

OVERVIEW

Article I, section 16 of the Texas State Constitution
No bill of attainder, ex post facto law, retroactive law, or any law impairing the obligation of contracts, shall be made.

Section 16 parallels Article I, section 9 of the U.S. Constitution, which forbids the enactment of bills of attainder and ex post facto laws. A bill of attainder is a legislative act that inflicts punishment without a judicial determination. In a bill of attainder, the legislature decides an individual is guilty without any of the protective safeguards extended in a trial, such as representation by an attorney and rules of evidence. The framers of the Constitution were especially sensitive to bills of attainder because the British used them extensively before and during the American Revolution. The British Parliament would charge an individual with treason, pronounce his penalty, and confiscate his estate.

An ex post facto law makes an action that was innocent and performed before the passage of the law subject to criminal sanctions. The ex post facto clause also prohibits laws that aggravate a crime or make it greater than it was when it was committed; that change the punishment and inflict a greater punishment than what was provided at the time the crime was committed; and which change the rules of evidence that the law required at the time of the commission of the offense, making it easier to convict the offender.

The reasons for prohibiting ex post facto laws is imbedded in our history, however, the clause is far from being only of historic interest. It is alive and spawning new and creative grounds for appeals in criminal cases. Appellants who challenge their convictions under the ex post facto clause generally bring the challenge under both federal and state constitutions because, for the most part, both constitutions provide the same type and level of protection.

CASES

1. *Lynce v. Mathis,* 519 U.S. 443, 117 S.Ct. 891 (1997)
Article I, section 9 of the U.S. Constitution

The issue in *Lynce v. Mathis* involved Florida statutes that authorized the award of early release "provisional" credits to prison inmates when the state prison population exceeded predetermined levels. In 1992, the Florida legislature canceled such credits for certain classes of inmates, including those convicted of murder or attempted murder. Kenneth Lynce was convicted of attempted murder in 1986 and received a 22-year prison sentence. He was released in 1992 after accumulating early release credits; including credits awarded as a result of prison overcrowding. Shortly after his release, the state attorney general issued an opinion interpreting the 1992 statute as having retroactively canceled all provisional credits awarded to inmates convicted of murder and attempted murder. Lynce was rearrested and returned to prison. He argued that the 1992 statute violated the ex post facto clause of the U.S. Constitution.

The U.S. Supreme Court held for Lynce and decided that the 1992 state statute was clearly retrospective and disadvantaged Lynce by increasing his punishment even though the credits had been issued as a way to alleviate prison overcrowding. The motivation behind the award of credits was irrelevant. The Court relied heavily on a prior case it had decided concerning good time credits. In *Weaver v. Graham,* 450 U.S. 24 (1981), the Court ruled that a Florida law violated the ex post facto clause because it retroactively decreased the amount of good time available to an inmate who had been receiving a more generous amount of good time under the law in effect at the time of his conviction. By curtailing the availability of future credits, applying the new good time laws to the inmate postponed his eligibility for parole. It made the punishment for crimes committed before its enactment more onerous.

2. *Kansas v. Hendricks,* 521 U.S. 346, 117 S.Ct. 2072 (1997)
Article I, section 9 of the U.S. Constitution

A second case decided by the Supreme Court in 1997 involving the ex post facto clause was *Kansas v. Hendricks,* which concerned an offender convicted of child molestation with a long history of violent sex offenses. Right before Hendricks was to be released from prison, Kansas enacted the Sexually Violent Predator Act that provided for involuntary civil commitment of persons who due to a mental abnormality or personality disorder are likely to engage in predatory acts of sexual violence. Kansas filed a petition to civilly commit Hendricks under the new law after he was released from prison. He argued that the application of the law was in violation of the ex post facto clause because it resulted in the extension of his confinement and was punitive in nature. The U. S. Supreme disagreed and ruled against Hendricks. The Court found that the state statute did not establish criminal proceedings and was not intended to punish. Since it was a civil proceeding that had no punitive purpose or result, the ex post facto clause was not implicated.

The United States Supreme Court recently examined Washington State's Community Protection Act, which similar to Kansas law, authorizes civilly committing violent sexual predators if their mental abnormality or personality disorder makes them likely to engage in sexual violence. Young challenged his commitment on the grounds that the state statute was punitive *as it was applied to him* because the conditions under which he was confined were punitive in effect. Because he was being subjected to punishment, not treatment, he asserted that the law violated the ex post facto clause. In *Seling v. Young,* 531 U.S. 250 (2001), the Court rejected Young's claim and decided that a civil statute cannot be considered punitive as applied to a single individual so as to violate the ex post facto clause. If individuals committed under the law want to challenge the conditions under which they are held, the Court stated they should pursue a lawsuit to improve their confinement conditions.

3. *French v. State,* 830 S.W. 2d 607 (Tex. Crim. App. 1992)
Article I, section 16 of the Texas State Constitution

In *French v. State*, the Texas Court of Criminal Appeals considered instructions that were given to a jury that had convicted Mr. French of attempted murder and was to decide his sentence. Under a Texas law that went into effect after French committed his crime, the jury was advised that good time credit and parole do exist, but they were not permitted to consider how the parole law might be applied to the defendant. French argued that this new law violated the ex post facto clause because it tainted the jury against his interests during their sentencing deliberations. The Texas Criminal Appeals Court disagreed and ruled that application of the new parole law instruction did not violate the Texas Constitution's ex post facto clause. Wrote the court:

> The inclusion of the parole instruction under Article 37.07, section 4, simply informs the jury that good conduct time and parole exist, and admonishes the jury that it may not consider the manner in which the parole law may be applied to the defendant. The instruction does not punish as a crime an act previously committed which was innocent when done; it does not make punishment for a crime more burdensome after its commission; and it does not deprive appellant of a defense available to him at the time the act was committed.

The Texas Court of Appeals did not agree with Vernon Cooper in *Cooper v. State*, 2 S.W.3d 500 (Tex. App. – Texarkana 2000). Mr. Cooper was convicted of indecency with a child and placed on community supervision on deferred adjudication without having to plead guilty. When he failed to live up to several requirements of the sex offender registration act, his sentence was revoked, he was deemed guilty by the court and placed on regular community supervision. He argued that the sex offender registration requirements were not in effect when he committed his crime. The appeals court ruled that the requirements were not punishment and, therefore, there were no problems with the ex post facto clause.

REVIEW

1. The Supreme Court decided the U.S. Constitution did not require the Kansas Sexually Violent Predator Act be struck down even though the law allows some predatory violent sex offenders to be confined after their prison terms have been served because:
    a. the law did not violate the ex post facto clause because the confinement was civil not criminal in nature.
    b. the law did not violate the ex post facto clause because it did not apply to persons incarcerated before it went into effect.
    c. it did not violate the equal protection clause because all violent, predatory sex offenders are treated alike.
    d. it did not violate the equal protection clause because it creates a special class of sex offenders, which is reasonably related to a legitimate government purpose.

2. The Supreme Court ruled the U.S. Constitution prevents Florida from taking away the good time credits Lynce was awarded because of prison overcrowding because:
    a. Florida was violating the equal protection clause by treating its prisoners differently than other states.
    b. the state statute was so vague as to makes its provisions debatable.
    c. due process required that taking away credits be done after a hearing.
    d. the retraction of his credits violated the ex post facto clause.

3. In *French v. State*, the Texas Court of Criminal Appeals interpreted the ex post facto clause in the Texas Constitution so as:
    a. to require the jury to consider good time and parole in making sentencing decisions.
    b. to require the jury to discuss parole before making a sentencing decision.
    c. to allow the judge to tell the jury that parole does exist but it is not permitted to consider how parole will impact the defendant when it decides his sentence.
    d. to allow the jury to consider when French might be eligible for parole.

4. The ex post facto clause in the Texas Constitution is:
    a. very similar to the ex post facto clause in the U.S. Constitution.
    b. totally different than the ex post factor clause in the U.S. Constitution.
    c. there is no such clause in the Texas Constitution.
    d. has never been interpreted by the Texas courts.

5. The ex post facto clause in both the Texas and U.S. Constitutions is of historical interest only:
    a. true because all the important cases about this clause have been decided.
    b. true because the reason the clause resulted from what the British did before the Revolution. We don't need the clause now.
    c. false because the clause is confusing and no one knows what it means.
    d. false because laws change regularly, introducing new issues that arguably trigger the clauses protections.

Section 2: VOID-FOR-VAGUENESS

OVERVIEW

Article 1, section 19 of the Texas Constitution
No citizen of this State shall be deprived of life, liberty, property, privileges, or immunities or in any manner disenfranchised, except by the due course of the law of the land.

Article 19 parallels the due process clause of the Fourteenth Amendment of the U.S. Constitution. In addition to providing procedural due process, Article 19 also requires substantive due process; laws and their enforcement may not be arbitrary, unreasonable, or unrelated to a legitimate concern of the state.

Defendants who challenge a criminal statute as vague under the due process clause of either the Texas or U.S. Constitutions must show that the operation of the statute is unconstitutional *to him or her in their situation*. Unlike challenges of vagueness under the First Amendment and Article 1, section 8 of the Texas Constitution, the fact that the statute may be unconstitutional as applied to other persons is *not* sufficient. A criminal statute is vague when persons of common intelligence must guess at its meaning and differ about how it should be applied. The language of a statute is not unconstitutionally vague if it conveys a sufficient warning about the proscribed conduct, as measured by common understanding and practices. Words in a statute are to be read in context and construed according to the rules of grammar and common usage. The word or terms in a statute do not have to be specifically defined.

Much like the freedom of speech and vagueness inquiry, the issues under the due process clause are: 1) is an ordinary, law-abiding person put sufficiently on notice by a criminal statute that his or her conduct violated the law, and 2) did the statute gave sufficient notice to law enforcement authorities to prevent arbitrary or discriminating enforcement.

CASES

1. *Parr v. State,* 575 S.W.2d 522 (Tex. Crim. App. 1979)
Article 1, section 19 of the Texas State Constitution

J.D. Parr challenged the involuntary manslaughter statute, Section 19.05(a)(2) of the Texas Penal Code, arguing that his conviction for involuntary manslaughter should be reversed because the statute as then written failed to define intoxication sufficiently to avoid vagueness problems. Parr struck and killed a child while intoxicated. A blood sample revealed his blood contained .23 percent alcohol.

Parr maintained the law failed to give notice of which substances are prohibited. He contended the statute might prohibit a person driving an automobile while that he or she is voluntarily taking prescription medicine. The statute stated that:

> For purposes of this section, 'intoxication' means that the actor does not have the normal use of his mental or physical faculties by reason of the voluntary introduction of any substance into his body.

The court ruled the statute was not unconstitutional because,

> [T]he statute condemns only that conduct when, having involuntarily introduced a substance (albeit a legally prescribed drug) into his body, a person does not have the normal use of his mental or physical faculties and such person operates a motor vehicle *which* results in the death of an individual due to his impaired condition. ...Consequently we hold that Sec. 19.05(b)... is sufficiently definite to give a person of ordinary intelligence fair notice of what conduct is forbidden by statute and that such statute does not reach constitutionally protected conduct.

2. *McCarty v. State*, 616 S.W.2d 194 (Tex. Crim. App. 1981)
Article 1, section 19 of the Texas Constitution

McCarty argued that the Texas statute prohibiting prostitution was unconstitutional because it was so vaguely worded. Section 43.02(a)(1) of the Texas Penal Code stated:

> (a) A person commits an offense if he knowingly:
> (1) offers to engage, agrees to engage, or engages in sexual conduct for a fee

McCarty alleged that the word "offer" was so vague it did not give fair warning of what is illegal conduct, violating the due process clause. The Texas Court of Criminal Appeals noted that the prohibition against excessive vagueness does not invalidate every statute a court believes could have been drafted more precisely. Due process requires only that a law give sufficient warning to allow people to conduct themselves so as to avoid unlawful behavior, and that a law not lull people into a false sense of security. The court concluded that the Texas law gave people sufficient warning of what is prohibited, and the word "offer" is not so vague as to raise speculation about its meaning.

REVIEW

6. In *Parr v. State*, the Texas Court of Criminal Appeals decided the involuntary manslaughter statute:
    a. was confusing and, therefore, void.
    b. should explain which substances are prohibited.
    c. was not void because Parr was clearly intoxicated.
    d. was not void because ordinary people are put on notice about what is prohibited and constitutional conduct is not threatened.

7. In *McCarty v. State*, the Texas Court of Appeals decided that:
    a. the term "offer" is too vague.
    b. even if the statute could have been written more precisely, the term "offer" is sufficiently clear to put people on notice.
    c. the law is fine because everyone knows when prostitution is committed.
    d. the crime is only a misdemeanor and the issue of vagueness isn't important.

8. When a void-for-vagueness challenge alleges that a statute violates constitutionally protected freedom of speech, the courts:
    a. generally rule against the law.
    b. are willing to strike it down even if it is not unconstitutional as applied to the appellant in the particular case before the court.
    c. are unwilling to strike it down unless it is unconstitutional as applied to the particular appellant before the court.
    d. are mostly concerned with whether the law provides sufficient definitions of all the important terms.

9. When courts examine laws that are allegedly void-for-vagueness they:
    a. strike down all laws that do not carefully define every word.
    b. assume that the laws are vague and put the burden on the government to prove they are not vague.
    c. assume that all laws are clear and easy to understand if only the citizens would read them more carefully.
    d. examine the law to see if it provides sufficient warning of the prohibited conduct, based on a common understanding.

Section 3: THE EQUAL PROTECTION CLAUSE

OVERVIEW

Article 1, section 3a of the Texas Constitution
Equality under the law shall not be denied or abridged because of sex, color, creed, or national origin.

Article 1, section 3a parallels the equal protection clause found in the Fourteenth Amendment of the U.S. Constitution. Section 3a was added to the Texas Constitution in 1972. When a challenge is made to a criminal statute based on the equal protection clause, the Texas courts begin with the presumption that the purpose of the statute is constitutional. If the statute does not impinge on fundamental rights or does not involve a suspect classification, the burden of proof is on the party challenging the statute to show that the classification created by the law is not rationally related to a legitimate state interest. This is a heavy burden, and the courts are careful to examine what interest a statute is designed to serve and whether it actually serves that purpose.

A good example of how the equal protection clause has to adapt to changes in society is found in *Finley v. State*, 527 S.W.2d 553 (Tex. Crim. App. 1975). Finley was convicted of attempted rape and made the argument that the rape laws in effect at the time were unconstitutional under the state constitution's equal protection clause. He argued that the state constitution prohibits a statute that constrains men but not women. At the time, the rape laws were written in such a way that only a man could be found guilty of perpetrating the crime. The Texas court admitted that the laws set up a classification on the basis of sex. The judges, however, decided that the rape law served a legitimate state interest. They reasoned that men perpetrate most sexual assaults against women; the state has an interest in preventing unwanted pregnancies; and there are other provisions of the Penal Code to protect men from sexual assaults by women. Finley's argument was ahead of its time. Several years after his case was decided, the state legislature created sexual assault statutes that are gender neutral.

CASE

***Smith v. State*, 898 S.W.2d 838 (Tex. Crim. App. 1995)**
Article 1, section 3a of the Texas Constitution

This is an interesting and important case in the equal protection area. Defendant Smith was convicted of capital murder and sentenced to death. Under Texas law, at the time of Smith's conviction, parole was not a matter that a jury could consider in a capital murder trial. When the jury assessed punishment, they were not informed that a defendant convicted of capital murder who was given a life sentence was not eligible for parole for at least 40 years. Smith contended that Texas law violated both the equal protection clauses of the U.S. and Texas Constitutions because juries trying non-capital cases are given information about the possibility of parole. He alleged that Texas law created a separate classification for capital murder offenders that did not serve a legitimate state interest. During punishment deliberations Texas jurors are asked whether the defendant represents a continuing threat to society. Without being informed that a life sentence means no eligibility for parole for at least 40 years, the jury must answer that question without knowing all the legal consequences of a capital murder life sentence.

The Texas Court of Criminal Appeals rejected Smith's contention. They wrote:

> The party challenging the statute on equal protection grounds has the burden to show that the statutory classification is not rationally related to a legitimate state interest where interests other than fundamental rights or suspect classification are affected. However, the classification must discriminate against *similarly situated individuals*. In this instance appellant's equal protection complaint is not among similarly situated individuals, that is, he is treated the same as all capital defendants.

Soon after the *Smith* decision, the Texas legislature responded to mounting pressure to change what many saw as a fundamentally unfair law. Effective for homicides committed after September 1, 1999, the amended statute requires the judge to inform the jury during the punishment phase of a capital murder trial that if the defendant is sentenced to imprisonment instead of death, he or she will not be eligible for parole until they have served 40 years without any good time credit.

REVIEW

10. In *Finley v. State,* the Texas rape laws in effect at that time (1975) were ruled:
    a. unconstitutional because of the state's equal protection clause.
    b. constitutional even though they were not gender neutral.
    c. constitutional because rape is a serious crime and it doesn't matter that only men could commit the crime under the statute.
    d. unconstitutional because only women could be the victims of rape as the law was written.

11. The *Smith v. State* capital murder case is important because:
    a. All capital murder cases are important.
    b. The court's decision contributed to a move to change the law.
    c. Juries do not need to know about the 40-year life sentence with no parole.
    d. Judges should be able to decide what a jury should be told.

12. The equal protection clause requires that:
    a. all persons in the state be treated exactly the same under all circumstances.
    b. Texans must be treated the same, but citizens from other states can be treated differently.
    c. persons in similarly situated circumstances must be treated similarly.
    d. every citizen is protected equally from arbitrary criminal prosecution.

13. The Texas Constitution, as interpreted by the Texas courts, cannot give the citizens of Texas greater protections than those afforded by the U.S. Constitution.
    a. True
    b. False

14. The Texas and U.S. Constitutions have very different equal protection provisions.
    a. True
    b. False

Section 4: FREE SPEECH

OVERVIEW

Article 1, section 8 of the Texas Constitution
Every person shall be at liberty to speak, write or publish his opinions on any subject, being responsible for the abuse of that privilege; and no law shall ever be passed curtailing the liberty of speech or of the press. In prosecutions for the publications of papers, investigating the conduct of officers, or men in public capacity, or when the matter published is proper for public information, the truth thereof may be given in evidence. And in all indictments for libels, the jury shall have the right to determine the law and the facts, under the direction of the court, as in other cases.

Article 8 parallels the part of the First Amendment of the U.S. Constitution that addresses freedom of speech. Texas has explicitly guaranteed the freedom of Texans to write, publish and speak ever since the Constitution of the Republic of Texas, dating back to 1836.

Criminal laws must be sufficiently clear to give a person of ordinary intelligence a reasonable opportunity to know what is prohibited and to establish guidelines for law enforcement. When issues of freedom of speech are involved, criminal laws must also be sufficiently definite to avoid chilling protected expression. When a criminal statute is capable of affecting freedom of speech and expression, the courts examine extra carefully the degree of specificity found in the statute. The U.S. Supreme Court held in *Gooding v. Wilson*, 405 U.S. 518, 92 S.Ct. 1103 (1972) that when a void-for-vagueness challenge involves First Amendment considerations, a criminal law may be held invalid even though it may *not* be unconstitutional as applied to the defendant's particular conduct.

CASES

1. *Long v. State*, 931 S.W.2d 285 (Tex. Crim. App. 1996)
Article 1, section 8 of the Texas Constitution

In this case, the Texas Court of Criminal Appeals reviewed the stalking provisions of the 1993 Texas harassment statute, Texas Penal Code, section 42.07 (a)(7), for possible void-for-vagueness problems. The stalking portion of the law provided:

> (a) A person commits an offense if, with intent to harass, annoy, alarm, abuse, torment, or embarrass another, he:
> (7)(A) on more than one occasion engages in conduct directed specifically toward the other person, including following that person, that is reasonably likely to harass, annoy, alarm, abuse, torment, or embarrass that person;
> (B) on at least one of those occasions by acts or words threatens to inflict bodily injury on that person or to commit an offense against that person, a member of that person's family, or that person's property; and
> (C) on at least one of those occasions engages in conduct after the person toward whom the conduct is specifically directed has reported to a law enforcement agency the conduct described by this subdivision.
> (e) It is an affirmative defense to prosecution under Subsection (a)(7) of this section that the actor was engaged in conduct that consisted of activity in support of constitutionally or statutorily protected rights.

Long was convicted under the stalking statute. He argued that section (a)(7)(A) was vague and rendered the entire statute unconstitutional. The Texas court began by noting,

> It is well-established that criminal laws must be sufficiently clear in at least three respects. First, a person of ordinary intelligence must be given a reasonable opportunity to know what is prohibited. Second, the law must establish determinate guidelines for law enforcement. Finally, where First Amendment freedoms are implicated, the law must be sufficiently definite to avoid chilling protected expression.
> * * * * *
> An examination of decisions from other jurisdictions in which stalking and harassment statutes have been upheld illustrates the deficiencies of the statute before us. Illinois supplies a nexus requirement not contained in the Texas statute: the Illinois statute requires a threat and relevant conduct in *furtherance of the threat*. Some other states require that the conduct evidence a "continuity of purpose." Ohio requires that the incidents be closely related in time. Indiana defines "harassment" as conduct which would cause a reasonable person to suffer emotional distress but defines the offense of "stalking" as harassment that would cause a reasonable person to feel "terrorized, frightened, intimidated, or threatened." *Johnson v. State*, 648 N.E.2d 666 (Ind. App. 1 Dist. 1995). This language appears to punish as stalking a series of acts where each of the predicate acts in isolation may cause only minor emotional distress such as annoyance but where the series of acts taken together causes more serious emotional distress, i.e. being terrorized, frightened, intimidated, or threatened.
>
> Some jurisdictions have supplied a general mental state provision and/or a reasonable person provision that specifies a more serious state of emotional distress than mere annoyance.

> Other courts have upheld their statutes by construing them to punish conduct only when the actor's *sole* intent was to annoy or cause other emotional distress to the recipient.
>
> All of the statutes described above contain additional limiting elements not found in the Texas criminal statutes. Many limit the vagueness of the conduct described by linking it to more specific conduct through a continuity of purpose requirement. Others tie the conduct together with a more specific mental state than a mere intent to annoy, such as an intent to place in fear of bodily injury, or with a more intense mental state, such as intent to frighten. In addition to creating greater specificity, these kinds of limiting elements help avoid a vagueness problem by taking the First Amendment out of the picture.
> *****
> The threat requirement in the present statute, however, does not successfully remove the First Amendment from the purview of the offense. In the absence of any nexus between the threat requirement and the conduct requirement, there is a real likelihood that the statute will chill the exercise of protected First Amendment expression.

The court was concerned that words like "harass," "annoy" and "alarm" are susceptible to uncertainties of meaning. Requiring the conduct to be "specifically directed" toward a particular person failed to limit the broad expanse of conduct covered by the law. Requiring the conduct to be "reasonably likely to harass ..." also failed to limit its expansive reach. The reporting requirement in (a)(7)(C) and the threat requirement in (a)(7)(B) did not remove the First Amendment concerns. Interestingly, Texas' prior harassment statute was also held unconstitutional because of vagueness in the case *Kramer v. Price*, 712 F.2d 174 (5th Cir. 1983).

2. *Haddad v. State*, 9 S.W.3d 454 (Tex. App.-Houston [1st Dist.] 1999)
Article 1, section 8 of the Texas Constitution

A Houston city ordinance made it unlawful for any entertainer to touch a customer or the customer's clothing while entertaining or exposing any specified anatomical areas or engaging in specified sexual activities. The ordinance defined "specified anatomical areas" and "specified sexual activities." Haddad was a topless dancer who was charged with intentionally touching a customer while she was dancing. She alleged that the ordinance was void-for-vagueness. The court disagreed. Neither did the court agree that the ordinance reached into constitutionally protected conduct. Topless dancing is protected by freedom of speech under the Texas constitution; however, the state is free to place time, place, and manner restrictions that help protect the welfare of customers and dancers.

REVIEW

15. The *Long* case was the first time the Texas stalking statute was challenged on void-for-vagueness grounds.
    a. True
    b. False

16. The Texas Court held that the First Amendment was threatened by the stalking statute because:
    a. without a connection or nexus between the threat requirement and the conduct, it is likely the law will chill the exercise of protected First Amendment speech.
    b. the First Amendment protects all of our speech from constitutional challenge.
    c. the statute did not specifically state that First Amendment speech is protected.
    d. stalking is not a serious offense and shouldn't be taken too seriously.

17. In *Haddad v. State*, the Texas Appeals court decided that:
    a. topless dancers are never protected by the First Amendment.
    b. the statute was unconstitutionally vague because it prohibits dancers from touching customers.
    c. the statute is constitutional because topless dancing needs to be regulated.
    d. topless dancing is protected by the Texas Constitution, however, the state is free to impose time, place, and manner restrictions that contribute to the welfare of customers and dancers.

18. Free speech protection:
    a. gives the ordinary intelligent person sufficient notice about what is against the law and establish guidelines for law enforcement personnel.
    b. imposes unnecessary restrictions on legislators who write and pass the laws.
    c. makes it difficult to prosecute certain crimes.
    d. is only provided by the U.S. Constitution and not the Texas Constitution.

19. When a criminal statute is so vague that it affects peoples' ability to exercise their rights under Article 1, section 8 of the Texas Constitution, it can be held invalid even though it may not be unconstitutional as applied to a defendant in a particular case.
    a. True
    b. False

FINAL COMMENTS ON THE CONSTITUTIONAL LIMITS ON THE CRIMINAL LAW

Constitutional issues are important issues in many criminal cases; however, they are not present in the majority of cases. Nonetheless, it is essential you understand the constitutional provisions, state and federal, which impact the drafting and interpretation of criminal law.The failure of a law to past constitutional muster often results in very serious consequences for the State. Courts obligated to uphold the constitution can strike down well-intentioned legislation. Legislatures must be aware of the constitutional ramifications of the laws they adopt. By understanding the state and federal constitutional provisions, you can better appreciate the decisions courts are sometimes forced to make.

Chapter Three

The General Principles of Criminal Liability: Actus Reus

INTRODUCTION

This chapter looks at cases decided by Texas courts that have interpreted Section 6.01 of the Texas Penal Code, which deals with the voluntary act requirement. It might seem as if it would be easy to prove that a criminal act was voluntary. Except for those few, unusual cases involving defendants who claim they acted while sleepwalking or were possessed by demons, what is there to voluntariness? Surprisingly, the issue can arise in cases that involve fairly direct and typical fact situations.

> **Section 6.01(a) of the Texas Penal Code**
> A person commits an offense only if he voluntarily engages in conduct, including an act, an omission, or possession.

Section 1: REQUIREMENT OF A VOLUNTARY ACT

OVERVIEW

The Code does not define "voluntary." Courts and juries have to struggle with deciding what is a voluntary act based on actual fact situations. The appellant often raises the issue by contending that the trial judge failed to give instructions to the jury about voluntariness. The Texas Code of Criminal Procedure requires the judge to deliver a set of written instructions to the jury that outline the law applicable to the case to be decided, without expressing an opinion about the weight of the evidence. Before these instructions, called a jury charge, are read to the jury, defendant's counsel and the prosecutor have the opportunity to review them and present objections. The objections can include protests about what is and what is not in the jury charge.

If there are no instructions specifically addressing voluntariness, jurors are required by law to assume the defendant's actions were voluntary. If the defendant is convicted, on appeal the voluntariness issue often gets tangled up with other issues involving the defendant's, now the appellant's, culpability - was the act performed intentionally, knowingly, recklessly, or negligently. In examining the facts for purposes of determining voluntariness, appellate courts frequently address the whole issue of blameworthiness. Whenever courts and judges delve into the human psyche, it is an imperfect, sometimes frustrating exercise. Remember that reasonable minds may differ.

CASES

1. *George v. State*, 681 S.W.2d 43, 44 (Tex. Crim. App. 1984)

Section 6.01(a) of the Texas Penal Code

Bobby George was convicted of aggravated assault. The court described the facts leading up to his offense,

> On the late afternoon of a March day, thirteen-year-old Leonard Martin was visiting younger brothers of appellant in the home of appellant and other members of his family. Appellant was then seventeen. All present were friends. Standing in front of a seated Martin, appellant demanded a dollar from him; when the latter verbally refused to produce it appellant drew a .22 caliber revolver from a pocket, thumbed its hammer partially back and, pointing it at Martin's face, told Martin to "give me the dollar," the gun discharged, its bullet striking Martin in the left maxilla of his face ...... Appellant threw the gun aside, striking a brother in the chest; he went with Martin to the home of a neighbor to seek aid, but they were denied. At another house, however, an ambulance was summoned.
>
> In his confession and testimony at trial appellant described in greater detail that after he asked Martin a second time for a dollar he cocked the hammer back short of its locked position; that he "struck [the gun] up in [Martin's] face;" that Martin "turned his face away," that the "the hammer slipped off my thumb" and the gun "went off." Appellant further told the jury that he did not know the gun would nor did he mean for it to go off "when he cocked the hammer back;" he denied ever pulling the trigger and stated that he did not intend to shoot Martin or harm him in any way - it was an accident.

Bobby George asked the trial judge to instruct the jury in his case about the voluntariness requirement under Section 6.01(a). The judge, however, only instructed the jury about the need to find that George had intentionally, knowingly, or recklessly caused bodily injury to the victim under the aggravated assault statute.

The intermediate court of appeals reversed George's conviction and concluded the judge should have given a voluntariness instruction. The Texas Court of Criminal Appeals, however, disagreed with the appellate court. The judges on the Court of Criminal Appeals began their analysis by holding that if there is evidence an act was performed accidentally, the jury should be instructed to consider whether the act was voluntary. Without saying so specifically, the court concluded that the defense of accident is found in Section 6.01(a). The court went on to construe Section 6.01(a) to mean that a person voluntarily engages in conduct when the conduct includes a voluntary act and its accompanying mental state. But here is where the court's holding gets tricky. Just because a person's conduct also includes an involuntary act does not necessarily mean the person engaged in that conduct involuntarily. Nor is conduct involuntary merely because a person does not intend the result of his conduct.

Wrote the court:

> Here the evidence shows that appellant's actions were sufficiently voluntary until "the hammer [of the handgun he was holding] slipped off [his] thumb," but the court of appeals then turned its focus to the handgun, finding that *it* discharged "involuntarily or by accident." We cannot accept that a mechanical object is capable of volition, and if the court meant to say that appellant was not at that moment doing an "act," we do not agree. If the hammer "slipped off [his] thumb," it had to be that the thumb holding the hammer partially back released just enough pressure for the hammer to "slip" forward. However, slight, that is "bodily movement" within the meaning of section 1.07(a)(1), and there is no evidence that it was involuntary. Accordingly, the trial court was correct in refusing the requested charge on "defense of involuntary conduct."

The court decided that George acted voluntarily in handling the gun. He acted voluntarily up to the second when he claimed the hammer slipped off his thumb and the gun discharged. According to the Criminal Court of Appeals, the gun did not discharge by accident. If the hammer slipped off George's thumb, the thumb holding the hammer released just enough pressure for the hammer to slip forward.

2. *Garcia v. State*, 605 S.W.2d 565, 566 (Tex. Crim. App. 1980)
Section 6.01(a) of the Texas Penal Code

Contrast the *George* case to *Garcia*, in which the Court of Criminal Appeals decided that the jury should have been instructed about the voluntariness of the appellant's conduct because there was evidence of an accident. The case reads:

> Testifying in his own behalf, appellant related that the deceased gave him the gun as they were walking on the sidewalk and that the hammer was already pulled. When appellant told the deceased that he was going to throw the gun into the canal, the deceased suddenly grabbed appellant's right elbow with one hand and the gun with his other hand in an attempt to take the gun away from appellant. Appellant testified:
>
>> "Q. Okay. Now, at what point did the gun go off?
>> "A. When he pulled on the gun, tried to get it out of my hand.
>>
>> * * * * * *
>> "Q. Okay. Did you have any intention or knowledge or any state of mind at all of the sort that would make you desire to harm Hector Jaimes (the deceased) in any way?
>>
>> "A. No, sir."
>
> * * * * *
> The testimony summarized and quoted above was sufficient to raise an issue of fact as to the voluntariness of appellant's conduct. It is settled that an accused is entitled to an instruction on every defense matter raised by the evidence. *Esparza v. State*, 520 S.W.2d 27 (Tex.Cr.App.). The failure to grant the timely filed and properly requested special instruction on accident constituted reversible error.

3. *Cruz v. State*, 838 S.W.2d 682 (Tex. App. - Houston [14th Dist.] 1992)
Section 6.01(a) of the Texas Penal Code

Robert Cruz, a prisoner in the Texas Department of Corrections, argued he was not guilty of aggravated assault of a correctional officer because his actions were not voluntary. He was convicted of assaulting a correctional officer while fighting with several officers. The facts showed that during the altercation Cruz fell on top of an officer thereby dislocating the officer's shoulder. He maintained that he did not intend to harm the officer. The appeals court did not agree that the jury should have been instructed on the issue of voluntariness:

> Here, the evidence did not raise the issue of the voluntariness of appellant's conduct. According to the testimony of the officers involved, appellant set off the chain of events that caused the injury to Officer Galloway when he became "violent, agitated, or belligerent." That testimony was not disputed. Appellant's witnesses testified only that Officer Wardell knocked Officer Galloway to the floor. They did not state whether the officer's conduct was unprovoked. Where the evidence shows only a lack of intent to cause resulting injuries or only an involuntary act that is only part of the overall voluntary conduct, the trial court is correct in refusing a requested charge on voluntary conduct.

The appellant set off the chain of events that led to the officer's injuries. Cruz may not have intended to cause injuries, but he voluntarily engaged in behavior that led to harm.

REVIEW

1. In the *George v. State* case, the Texas Court of Criminal Appeals upheld the jury's decision because:
    a. George was not guilty since he never intended to harm the victim.
    b. George was guilty on the grounds that playing with a weapon is inherently reckless.
    c. George was not guilty and the gun went off accidentally.
    d. George is guilty even though he didn't intend harm and he voluntarily in handling thc gun.

2. The difference between the *George* case and the *Garcia* case:
    a. George was voluntarily handling the gun when it fired, while Garcia's gun shot when the victim tried to wrestle the gun from Garcia.
    b. George intended to scare the victim and Garcia did not.
    c. George had cocked the hammer of the gun; Garcia had not.
    d. There is no difference and the two different opinions cannot be reconciled.

3. Terry refused to cut his grass and his yard was in shambles. Angry neighbors called the police, alleging that Terry was failing to abide by the terms of a homeowners' agreement. Every homeowner signed the agreement in the neighborhood, including Terry. It stated specifically that the signers agreed to care for their lawns.
    a. The police can issue a criminal citation to Terry for failing to live up to the agreement.
    b. The police can issue a criminal citation to Terry because he omitted to abide by a legal obligation.
    c. Terry can be sued but there's no criminal matter here.
    d. Terry has a right not to cut his grass and live like nature intended.

4. As long as a defendant can produce some evidence that she did not intend to cause the harm that actually resulted from her actions, the trial court judge is obligated to give the jury an instruction on voluntariness.
    a. True
    b. False

5. Smithie was a diabetic who was supposed to take 3 shots of insulin a day. She was careless about her medication and would often forget it. Other times she'd decide she didn't want to take it. Smithie decided to ignore her insulin and went without it for a couple of days. She was driving an automobile when she hit and killed a pedestrian who was walking in a crosswalk zone. She argued she was not guilty because her vision was blurry, and she didn't even see the pedestrian. Doctors testified that her blurry vision was a result of not taking insulin.
    a. Smithie's right – her poor vision resulted from a medical condition.
    b. Smithie's crazy – this is a strict liability offense.
    c. Smithie voluntarily chose not to take her insulin and is responsible for what resulted from that decision.
    d. Smithie did not want to harm anyone and is not guilty.

Section 2: FAILURE TO ACT AS AN ACT

OVERVIEW

In order to understand crimes of omission, students first need to define key words.

Section 6.01(c) of the Texas Penal Code
A person who omits to perform an act does not commit an offense unless a law as defined by Section 1.07 provides that the omission is an offense or otherwise provides that he has a duty to perform the act.

Section 1.07(30) of the Texas Penal Code
"Law" means the constitution or a statute of this state or of the United States, a written opinion of a court of record, a municipal ordinance, an order of a county commissioners court, or a rule authorized by and lawfully adopted under a statute.

Section 1.07(34) of the Texas Penal Code
"Omission" means failure to act.

There are very few laws that require a person to perform an act. Crimes of omission are not everyday offenses. Listed below of some of the Texas statutes that create crimes of omission.

Section 22.04 of the Texas Penal Code

(a) A person commits an offense if he intentionally, knowingly, recklessly, or with criminal negligence, by act or intentionally, knowingly, or recklessly by omission, causes to a child, elderly individual, or disabled individual:

(1) serious bodily injury;

(2) serious mental deficiency, impairment, or injury; or

(3) bodily injury.

(b) An omission that causes a condition described by Subsections (a)(1) through (a)(3) is conduct constituting an offense under this section if:

(1) the actor has a legal or statutory duty to act; or

(2) the actor has assumed care, custody, or control of a child, elderly individual, or disabled individual.

Sections 22.041(c) and (g) of the Texas Penal Code

(c) A person commits an offense if he intentionally, knowingly, recklessly, or with criminal negligence, by act or omission, engages in conduct that places a child younger than 15 years in imminent danger of death, bodily injury, or physical or mental impairment.

* * * * *

(g) It is a defense to prosecution under Subsection(c) that the act or omission enables the child to practice for or participate in an organized athletic event and that appropriate safety equipment and procedures are employed in the event.

Section 25.05(a) of the Texas Penal Code

An individual commits an offense if the individual intentionally or knowingly fails to provide support for the individual's child younger than 18 years of age, or for the individual's child who is the subject of a court order requiring the individual to support the child.

Section 38.17 of the Texas Penal Code

(a) A person, other than a person who has a relationship with a child described by Section 22.04(b), commits an offense if:

(1) the actor observes the commission or attempted commission of an offense prohibited by Section 22.021(a)(2)(B) under circumstances in which a reasonable person would believe that an offense of a sexual or assaultive nature was being committed or was about to be committed against the child;

(2) the actor fails to assist the child or immediately report the commission of the offense to a peace officer or law enforcement agency; and

(3) the actor could assist the child or immediately report the commission of the offense without placing the actor in danger of suffering serious bodily injury or death.

Section 38.17 makes it a Class A misdemeanor to fail to stop or to report aggravated sexual assault of a child even if the person did not assume care, custody, or control of the child as defined in section 22.04.

The Texas Legislature recently passed a new law effective September 1, 2003 that adds another crime of omission.

> **Section 38.171 of the Texas Penal Code**
> (a) A person commits an offense if the person:
> (1) observes the commission of a felony under circumstances in which a reasonable person would believe that an offense had been committed in which serious bodily injury or death may have resulted; and
> (2) fails to report the commission of the offense to a peace officer or law enforcement agency under circumstances in which:
> (A) a reasonable person would believe that the commission of the offense had not been reported; and
> (B) the person could immediately report the commission of the offense without placing himself or herself in danger of suffering serious bodily injury or death.

CASE

Moore v. State, 2001 Tex. App. LEXIS 447 (Tex. App. – Texarkana 2001)
Article 62.02(a) of the Texas Code of Criminal Procedure

Laws that require certain acts be performed are not always located in the Penal Code. John Dennis Moore appealed from a jury conviction for failure to register as a sex offender under Chapter 62 of the Texas Code of Criminal Procedure. Moore had been convicted of Indecency With a Child in 1993 and was sentenced to prison. He was released on mandatory supervision in 1998. His parole officer advised him he had a duty to register as a convicted sex offender under a law that went into effect September 1, 1997. Moore argued that he should not have to register because failure to register is a crime of omission under section 6.01 and requires a statutory duty to register as an element of the offense. Since he was convicted in 1993, his conviction is an element of the crime of failure to register as a sex offender that occurred prior to September 1, 1997. The court ruled:

> [T]he State here was required to prove Moore's status as a person with a reportable conviction at the time he failed to register, not that the date on which he attained such status was later than September 1, 1997.

It was Moore's *status* as a convicted sex offender that was an element of the offense of failure to register. The State's burden was to prove Moore's status as a person with a reportable conviction at the time he failed to register, not that the date he was convicted was later than September 1, 1997.

REVIEW

6. In the case of *Moore v. State*, the court concluded that Moore was required to register as a sex offender because:
   a. he was convicted after 1990, and that's the cutoff date.
   b. it's his status as a sex offender that matters, not the date of conviction.
   c. his failure to register was a clear indication of his dangerousness.

7. Doris hated her sister Karen for stealing her husband. Karen was also a successful ballerina and Doris had two left feet. Doris hoped that something terrible would happen to Karen as pay back. During a family reunion, Karen and Doris found themselves alone together on the family boat in the middle of a large lake. They argued. Karen got so upset she stood up in the boat and threw her arms around in a crazy motion. Suddenly, she fell into the water. Doris, an accomplished swimmer, watched her drown, smiling as Karen's body went down.
   a. Doris was obligated to try to save a family member and is guilty of a criminal act of omission.
   b. Doris was obligated to try to save anyone who she voluntarily chose to be in a boat with because she had assumed that person's care.
   c. Doris was within her legal right not to assist her sister.
   d. Doris may or may not be guilty depending on whether she realized how serious Karen's situation was.

8. Sally decided to take an elderly man into her home because he was unable to care for himself. He was unable to prepare meals for himself and clean his clothes regularly. Sally agreed to provide him a bedroom, meals, and clean his clothes in exchange for a portion of his Social Security check. The elderly man didn't realize that Sally was only interested in his money, not in his care. She often failed to feed him, and he never received a good meal when she did prepare food. His health deteriorated significantly, to the point that neighbors called the police.
   a. Sally may be guilty under section 22.04 if her elderly tenant was over 65.
   b. Sally may be guilty under 22.04 no matter how old her tenant is because she assumed his care.
   c. Sally breached a contract, no more than that.
   d. Sally is not guilty because the elderly man was not seriously ill and had the ability to move out if things were that bad.

9. Don was coming home from happy hour tipsy when he noticed a person lying by the side of the road, obviously in pain. Don, a former medic in the armed services, decided to see if the person needed assistance. Even in his drunken state, he realized the person needed CPR, but he was tired and decided the heck with it. He didn't try to call out to other people who were passing by or make a 911 call on his cell phone. The person died. Doctors told police that if Don had performed CPR, the person probably would have lived.
   a. Don was cruel, but not guilty of a crime.
   b. The dead person's family can sue Don for being negligent, but that's all.
   c. Don assumed care of the person once he stopped to check on him and is guilty.
   d. Don had the legal obligation to call for help if he did not intend to give it himself.

Section 3: POSSESSION AS AN ACT

OVERVIEW

The actus reus of possession is defined in two different Code statutes.

Section 1.07(39) of the Texas Penal Code
"Possession" means actual care, custody, control, or management.

Section 6.01(b) of the Texas Penal Code
Possession is a voluntary act if the possessor knowingly obtains or receives the thing possessed or is aware of his control of the thing for a sufficient time to permit him to terminate his control.

Ownership is not required, nor is it required that the item actually be on your person, as long as you are exercising care, control, or management over it. Possession is a common issue raised in cases involving illegal possession of drugs or possession of drugs with intent to distribute.

CASE

1. *Linton v. State*, 15 S.W.3d 615 (Tex. App.- Houston [14th] 2000)
Section 6.01(b) of the Texas Penal Code

Houston police officers stopped Linton for failure to display an inspection sticker on his vehicle. The officers conducted a background check and discovered he had outstanding city warrants. He was arrested and his vehicle towed. During an inventory search, officers found a small glass pipe with burn marks and a chalky, white film inside it. When asked, Linton admitted the pipe was his. On appeal, Linton argued that there was insufficient evidence that he possessed cocaine long enough to allow him to terminate control over it.

The appeals court ruled against Linton and reviewed the status of the law in Texas. It held the State has to prove two things when it charges someone with unlawful possession. First, it must show that the defendant exercised actual care, custody, control, or management over the contraband. Second, the State must prove the defendant knew the object he possessed was contraband. Without an admission of guilt, the knowledge element of the crime can be inferred and possession can be proved by circumstantial evidence. When contraband is not found on the defendant's person, or it is not in his or her exclusive possession, additional facts must affirmatively link the defendant to it. Those links can include: 1) evidence about whether the contraband was in plain view; 2) whether it was in close proximity to the defendant; 3) whether the amount of the substance was large enough to indicate the defendant knew of its presence; 4) whether the defendant owned or was closely related to the owner of the vehicle or residence where the substance was found and; 5) whether the defendant made furtive gestures. All the facts do not necessarily need to point directly or indirectly to the defendant's guilt. The evidence is sufficient if the combined and cumulative effect of all the incriminating circumstances point to the defendant's guilt.

In Linton's case, the court concluded there were sufficient affirmative links between him and the cocaine to indicate that he had a long enough time to terminate his control over it. He was the sole occupant and driver of the car where it was found. It was located in the center console, in close proximity to him. The cocaine was in a glass pipe that was in plain view next to Linton's wallet in the console and could be observed from the passenger seat. Linton admitted that it was his pipe. There was evidence he controlled the pipe and knew of its presence.

2. *Luke v. State*, 2001 Tex. App. LEXIS 652 (Tex. App.- Houston [14th] 2001)
Section 6.01(b) of the Texas Penal Code

The court reached a similar conclusion in this case. Luke had been under surveillance by undercover narcotics officers who had information he was selling cocaine. They followed him to a school where he picked up his girlfriend after work. He was driving his girlfriend's car. When she came out to meet him, he got out of the car from the driver's seat and moved to the passenger side. His girlfriend sat in the driver's seat and drove off. At that point, police pulled him over. As an officer approached the vehicle, he saw Luke look left and right and move something with his left hand. After the officer removed Luke from the car and handcuffed him, the officer found a baggy with rock cocaine where Luke's hand had been. Luke argued on appeal that there was insufficient evidence linking him to possession of cocaine. The court did not agree. Not only was he in close proximity to the cocaine, he exercised sole control over the automobile until just a few minutes before he was stopped, and he was closely related to the owner. Police observed him making furtive gestures as they approached him.

REVIEW

10. Mr. Linton was guilty of possession because:
    a. the contraband was illegal drugs and everyone knows drug possession is criminal.
    b. the drugs were in his car, which automatically makes him guilty of possession.
    c. the circumstantial evidence was that the drugs were in his car console in plain view and he admitted the pipe was his.
    d. He wasn't found guilty because the drugs were not on his person.

11. Mr. Luke:
    a. was found not guilty of possession because it the drugs were in his girlfriend's car.
    b. was guilty of possession because there was enough circumstantial evidence that he controlled the drugs.
    c. was found not guilty because circumstantial evidence is insufficient to support a drug possession conviction.
    d. was found guilty because his girlfriend snitched on him.

12. Possession can be an act under the Penal Code:
    a. even if the possessor is not aware of what he or she possesses.
    b. only if the possessor knowingly receives the thing possessed.
    c. only if the possessor refuses to rid himself or herself of the item.
    d. if the possessor actually has the contraband on his person or among his possessions.

13. Jerry kept his marijuana in his briefcase. When the police entered the apartment he shared with a friend with a search warrant to look for illegal drugs, his briefcase was in the living room. They asked if they could open it and Jerry consented. The police discovered the marijuana and arrested Jerry who acknowledged the pot was his. Jerry alleged that even though he admitted to owning the marijuana he did not possess it and, therefore, was not guilty.
    a. Jerry is correct. He is not guilty because the pot was not on his person.
    b. Jerry would have been ok if he just hadn't admitted that the pot belonged to him.
    c. Jerry has an uphill battle because the pot was found in his briefcase in his apartment.
    d. Jerry isn't guilty because the pot was for his personal use.

14. Ken, an experienced drug dealer, decided it was safer to have someone carry the drugs for him. If the police busted the other person, he could keep a distance. Ken arranged for Stevie to carry cocaine to a purchaser. He shadowed Stevie along the way. The police stopped Stevie who was nervous and confused. During a legal stop, they asked a few questions that raised their suspicions. They asked Stevie for permission to search him, and he agreed. They found the cocaine. As he was arrested, Stevie pointed to Ken who was lurking nearby.
    a. Ken did not have possession of illegal drugs and the State has no case.
    b. Ken could argue that even if he owned the cocaine, he didn't possess it at the time Stevie was searched.
    c. If the State gathers enough evidence to show a connection between Ken and Stevie, Ken may be in trouble because he had control of the cocaine even while it was in Stevie's possession.
    d. Ken can argue that once he gave the coke to Stevie to transport, he lost control of it because Stevie could have dashed into a waiting car and fled with the drugs if he wanted.

Section 4: DURESS AS A DEFENSE

OVERVIEW

Section 8.05 of the Texas Penal Code recognizes duress as a defense to a criminal act. It will be discussed further in Chapter 8 of this Supplement. More than one defendant, however, has also tried to use duress as grounds for proving his or her actions were not voluntary, and, therefore, did not meet the requirements of Section 6.01. Why would someone use duress to argue his acts were involuntary? When you study the duress defense, notice it has a fairly stringent and narrow definition. If a defendant is unable to prove up the facts needed to establish the defense, voluntariness may be a weak fall back case. Defense attorneys may also use the defense realizing it may not spare their client entirely, but hoping it might be influential during sentencing.

CASES

1. *Alford v. State*, 866 S.W.2d 619 (Tex. Crim. App. 1993)
Section 6.01(a)(1) of the Texas Penal Code

Alford was convicted of aggravated robbery and sentenced to fifty years confinement. He argued that his friends had threatened serious bodily injury if he failed to participate in the crimes. He maintained he was acting under duress. Duress is an affirmative defense in Section 8.05 of the T.P.C., but the appellant argued that an act performed under duress is also an involuntary act under Section 6.01(a). After an extensive review of the Penal Code, the court decided,

> If voluntariness embraces only a physical element, in the sense of one's bodily movements, then the issue of duress would have no bearing on the issue of voluntariness unless the coerced actor claims his bodily movements in committing the crime were not controlled through his own efforts, which appellant does not contend. However, if voluntariness includes a mental element, in the nature of free will, then the issue of duress may bear upon the issue of voluntariness. Appellant's arguments assume that voluntariness incorporates such a mental element. However, the traditional view of criminal responsibility as comprised of an act and a mental state, the embodiment of that concept within the scheme of Chapter 6, and our view of the role of section 6.01(a)(1) to date, support the conclusion that the term "voluntary", as used in section 6.01(a)(1), does not include the concept of a free will.
>
> [W]e hold that the term "voluntarily" as utilized in section 6.01(a)(1) means the absence of an accidental act, omission, or possession.
>
> Voluntariness, within the meaning of section 6.01(a)(1), refers only to one's physical bodily movements.

2. *Ardis v. State*, 2001 LEXIS 22 (Tex. App.- Dallas 2001)
Section 6.01(a)(1) of the Texas Penal Code

Shelly Ardis was convicted of possession of cocaine. The Dallas Court of Appeals wrote in its opinion:

> The evidence showed that at about three o'clock in the morning on February 1, 1997, Officer Shawn L. Byrum stopped a car on Elm Street in the "Deep Ellum" for driving the wrong way down a one-way street. Byrum arrested the driver for driving while intoxicated. Appellant was a passenger in the vehicle. Byrum asked appellant whether she wanted to drive the car home. When appellant indicated she would, Byrum told her he would first have to determine whether or not she was intoxicated. Therefore, he told appellant to get out of the car, and appellant complied.
>
> After appellant got out of the car, Byrum concluded that appellant was intoxicated. Byrum based his opinion on the fact that she had a strong odor of alcohol on her breath, bloodshot eyes, slurred speech and had failed the horizontal gaze nystagmus test. Byrum further concluded appellant would have been a danger to herself or others if she had driven the car. Furthermore, she may have been in danger if he had left her alone

> because she was in a high crime area and would have been a prime target because of her intoxicated condition. Consequently, Byrum arrested appellant for public intoxication. In a subsequent search incident to arrest, cocaine was found on appellant's person.
>
> The evidence showed appellant was in a vehicle that was being driven on a public road in "Deep Ellum," the "entertainment district" of downtown Dallas. When the vehicle was stopped, it pulled into a parking lot that was accessible to the public. The officer could reasonably conclude appellant was in a public place.
>
> In any event, after the officer stopped the vehicle, appellant got out of the car and was, at that time, in a public place. Appellant nevertheless asserts that Byrum could not arrest her for public intoxication at that time because her action in getting out of the car was not voluntary. The only authority appellant cites for this proposition is article 6.01 of the penal code, which requires a person to engage in voluntary conduct to be guilty of an offense. *See* TEX. PEN. CODE ANN. Section 6.01 (Vernon 1994). However, "voluntariness" within the meaning of section 6.01 only refers to one's physical movements. ... Appellant got out of her car so that Byrum could determine whether he could safely release her car to her, as she had requested. Appellant's physical action in getting out of the car was voluntary bodily movement. Therefore, for purposes of section 6.01, appellant did voluntarily exit the car. We conclude that Byrum had probable cause to conclude appellant was in a public place.

A police officer's order "to get out of the car" did not transform Byrum's conduct into an involuntary act.

REVIEW

15. Alford argued that participation includes a mental element and a physical element. The Texas court:
    a. agreed but decided Alford didn't prove he did not want to participate in the crimes.
    b. agreed and decided Alford's friends forced him to commit crimes.
    c. disagreed, deciding that voluntariness doesn't include a mental element.
    d. disagreed and decided Alford's friends kidnapped him and took him to the crime scenes.

16. The Texas court concluded that Ardis got out of her car:
    a. voluntarily.
    b. voluntarily, but it was an illegal request.
    c. involuntarily because she wouldn't have gotten out if the officer had not so requested.
    d. It doesn't matter if it was voluntary or not, she was drunk and a danger on the road.

17. After reviewing the voluntary act requirement, it is clear that:
    a. it is difficult to prove that an act is not voluntary.
    b. the law is open to many definitions of what is voluntary.
    c. all acts are considered voluntary.
    d. only sleepwalking works as a defense.

FINAL COMMENTS ON THE ACTUS REUS REQUIREMENT

The actus reus of a crime must be proved beyond a reasonable doubt. In cases where voluntariness, possession, or omission is the issue, the State's burden can be difficult. The law allows the jury to make reasonable inferences based on circumstantial evidence in those instances where direct evidence is missing or in dispute. Without the ability to reach reasonable conclusions using circumstantial evidence many cases would never go to trial and many offenders would never be punished. On the other hand, the reasonable doubt standard protects individuals from unreasonable inferences based on evidence that is too speculative or tangential. It is a delicate balance sometimes that requires sound judgment and a genuine concern that justice is done.

Chapter Four

The General Principles of Criminal Liability: Mens Rea, Concurrence, and Causation

INTRODUCTION

This Chapter begins with the principle of mens rea, moves to a discussion about strict liability, and ends with a look at issues surrounding the causation requirement. With the important exceptions noted in Chapter Three, it is generally easy for a prosecutor to prove the actus reus of a crime. The greater challenge is to convince a judge or jury beyond a reasonable doubt that the defendant had the mens rea required by the statute. How do we reach into the hearts and minds of people to determine the whys and wherefores of their behavior? There is often no confession that clearly explains the defendant's mental state at the time the crime was committed. The defendant may choose not to testify. We rely on circumstantial evidence to help reveal criminal intent, including such things as the type of crime, surrounding circumstances, how the crime was executed, and what victims and witnesses observed about the defendant's behavior and demeanor.

Criminal intent is one of the most complex areas of criminal law. The definitions of intent are necessarily vague and open-ended. The law recognizes there are variations of intent because criminals are not equally blameworthy. Do we punish someone whose reckless driving caused a vehicular homicide the same way we punish someone who has committed a deliberate, cold-blooded murder? Is a bar room brawl that results in serious bodily harm the same crime as a carefully planned and executed assault that causes serious injury?

Section 1: PROVING MENS REA AND THE FOUR KINDS OF MENS REA

OVERVIEW

The State must prove the defendant's culpable mental state at the time of the offense beyond a reasonable doubt. The Code lists and defines four culpable mental states.

> **Section 6.02(d) of the Texas Penal Code**
> (d) Culpable mental states are classified according to relative degrees, from highest to lowest, as follows:
> (1) intentional;
> (2) knowing;
> (3) reckless;
> (4) criminal negligence.

Section 6.03 of the Texas Penal Code

(a) A person acts intentionally, or with intent, with respect to the nature of his conduct or to a result of his conduct when it is his conscious objective or desire to engage in the conduct or cause the result.

(b) A person acts knowingly, or with knowledge, with respect to the nature of his conduct or to the circumstances surrounding his conduct when he is aware of the nature of his conduct or that the circumstances exist. A person acts knowingly, or with knowledge, with respect to the result of his conduct when is he is aware that his conduct is reasonably certain to cause the result.

(c) A person acts recklessly, or is reckless, with respect to circumstances surrounding his conduct or the result of his conduct when he is aware of but consciously disregards a substantial and unjustifiable risk that the circumstances exist or the result will occur. The risk must be of such a nature and degree that its disregard constitutes a gross deviation from the standard of care that an ordinary person would exercise under all the circumstances as viewed from the actor's standpoint.

(d) A person acts with criminal negligence, or is criminally negligent, with respect to circumstances surrounding his conduct or the result of his conduct when he ought to be aware of a substantial and unjustifiable risk that the circumstances exist or the result will occur. The risk must be of such a nature and degree that the failure to perceive it constitutes a gross deviation from the standard of care that an ordinary person would exercise under all the circumstances as viewed from the actor's standpoint.

An accused's mental state can be inferred from his or her acts, words, and conduct. In determining culpability, the jury is entitled to consider events that occurred before, during, and after the commission of a crime.

When appellate courts review the sufficiency of the evidence, they are required to view the evidence in the light most favorable to the jury's verdict. Appellate courts are not in the business of setting aside jury verdicts. Their inquiry is whether any rational trier of fact would have found that the essential elements of the offense existed beyond a reasonable doubt. It is the jury's job to reconcile conflicting evidence and to judge the credibility of the witnesses.

CASES

1. *Norris v. State*, 902 S.W.2d 428 (Tex. Crim. App. 1995)
Sections 6.03 and 6.04 of the Texas Penal Code

Appellant was convicted of capital murder for killing his girlfriend and her two-year old child. Norris was angry with his girlfriend, went to her home with a high-powered deer rifle, and shot the baby and the mother at close range. He testified that he only intended to kill his girlfriend, but his girlfriend was holding the child when he aimed at her. In two statements made to the police after the crime, appellant never claimed he accidentally killed the child. The jury was instructed that they could convict Norris of capital murder if they found he intentionally caused the death of the baby and the baby's mother and the deaths occurred during the same criminal transaction. Under the Texas Penal Code at that time, Norris committed capital murder if he murdered more than one person during the same criminal transaction.

The jury was also instructed that if Norris meant to cause the mother's death but accidentally caused the baby's death, the intent to kill the mother could be transferred to the baby.

> **Section 6.04(b) of the Texas Penal Code**
> A person is nevertheless criminally responsible for causing a result if the only difference between what actually occurred and what he desired, contemplated, or risked is that:
> (1) a different offense was committed; or
> (2) a different person or property was injured, harmed, or otherwise affected.

Norris argued there was insufficient evidence that he intended to kill the baby. The Criminal Court of Appeals disagreed and wrote:

> The evidence shows appellant inflicted the fatal wounds to the baby from a short distance with a high powered rifle that had to be recocked and reaimed between each shot. The baby was in full view of appellant, and appellant admitted seeing him. Four of the five shots appellant fired initially struck the baby, and most of the mother's wounds were caused by fragments of bullets that first hit the baby. We agree with the following statements made in the State's brief:
>
> "A rational jury could certainly have concluded, from the conduct of appellant in shooting a high-powered hunting rifle at the baby (whom he admitted he saw) and [the mother] with every wound to the baby being an initial penetration and only some of the wounds to [the mother] being possible initial penetration wounds, from the admissions of the appellant that he shot both victims and from the only mention of lack of intent to shoot the baby being brought up for the first time at trial in a most credible manner, that the appellant intentionally caused the death of [the baby]."

The appellant also argued that the transfer doctrine should not be applied to capital murder prosecutions. By applying that doctrine, his homicides could be prosecuted as capital murders. The Court again disagreed, and Norris's murders were elevated to capital offenses.

2. *Hull v. State*, 871 S.W.2d 786, 787-789 (Tex. App. - Houston [14th Dist.] 1994)
Sections 6.03(a) and (b) of the Texas Penal Code

The definitions of intentionally and knowingly performing an act were the focus of the Court of Appeals in this case. Hull was found guilty of murder. Read some of the court's opinion:

> The record reveals that on October 17, 1990, Tarra Smotherman and Terri Cross went to Pac's Ice House, located on Corpus Christi and Freeport Streets in Harris County, Texas. They visited with their friend Shorty, who introduced them to David Nash.
>
> Around 6:30 p.m., Jennifer Cater and her mother arrived at Pac's and invited the other two girls to go with them to Taco Bell. After leaving Taco Bell, Cater's mother drove back to Pac's and dropped off Cater, Smotherman, and Cross. Then Nash, Shorty, and the three girls got into Nash's car to go for a ride.

They drove around for about an hour, and then Smotherman asked Nash to drop her off at a trailer house on Hershey Street. Nash drove to the trailer, and Smotherman got out of the car in front of appellant's house. When Nash drove down the dead end street to turn around, he saw Smotherman running down the street and appellant walking behind her.

Cater yelled, "Watch out. He's starting to pop caps." Nash thought this meant that appellant was about to start shooting. Nash saw appellant raise his arm and aim a gun at them. Then, Nash ducked down over his car's console and accelerated past appellant.

Nash heard a gunshot, and Shorty yelled that Cater had been hit.
Nash stopped his car at the first intersection. Nash and Cross got out of the car and looked at Cater in the back seat. Cross left to call 911, and Nash and Shorty took Cater to the hospital, where she was later pronounced dead.
* * * * *
Here, appellant took the stand during the guilt-innocence phase of the trial. He testified that he intentionally shot at the car that Cater was riding in. He stated that he was not aiming the gun at any particular person, but he was trying to hit the car. He stated further that he did not know where the bullet went when he shot the gun. However, appellant admitted that he was aware when he shot the gun of the possibility that someone could have been killed.

Appellant argued there was insufficient evidence for the jury to conclude that he intentionally or knowingly caused the death of Cater. The appeals court upheld the jury's guilty verdict by ruling the jury could convict of murder if it believed the appellant *knowingly* caused Cater's death. The evidence supported such a conclusion because it established the appellant was aware his act could result in someone's death. A murder conviction can rest on facts that show a dangerous act was performed with knowledge of its possible consequences.

3. *Ormsby v. State*, 600 S.W.2d 782 (Tex. Crim. App. 1980)
Sections 19.05(a) and 19.07(a) of the Texas Penal Code

Robert Ormsby appealed his involuntary manslaughter conviction involving an accident that occurred when he fell asleep at the wheel of his automobile. His car crossed over the centerline and struck an oncoming car, killing the driver. There was also evidence that the appellant was intoxicated. Ormsby wanted the jury to be instructed on the law of criminal negligence, a less serious offense than involuntary manslaughter. The Court of Criminal Appeals compared the definitions of the two offenses, as they were defined in 1980:

Section 19.05(a) of the Texas Penal Code
(a) A person commits an offense if he:
(1) recklessly causes the death of an individual; or
(2) by accident or mistake when operating a motor vehicle while intoxicated and, by reason of such intoxication, causes the death of an individual.

Section 19.07(a) of the Texas Penal Code
A person commits an offense if he causes the death of an individual by criminal negligence.

The court also noted the difference between how "reckless" and "negligent" were defined in T.P.C. Sections 6.03(c) and (d) and concluded there was evidence of criminal negligence. The facts showed the appellant was driving while in a state of exhaustion and had driven this particular road many times. Coupled with his admission that he had drank about three beers on an empty stomach prior to driving the car, the Court of Criminal Appeals decided there was sufficient evidence of criminal negligence to warrant a jury instruction about negligence.

The current Texas Penal Code excludes vehicular homicide from Section 19.05. Intoxication manslaughter is now found in Section 49.08 of the Penal Code.

Section 2: LIABILITY WITHOUT MENS REA: STRICT LIABILITY

OVERVIEW

Strict liability offenses are acknowledged in the Penal Code:

Section 6.02(b) and (c) of the Texas Penal Code

(b) If the definition of an offense does not prescribe a culpable mental state, a culpable mental state is nevertheless required unless the definition plainly dispenses with any mental element.

(c) If the definition of an offense does not prescribe a culpable mental state, but one is nevertheless required under Subsection (b), intent, knowledge, or recklessness suffices to establish criminal responsibility.

Several cases have established the strict liability nature of offenses related to driving an automobile. In *Owen v. State*, 525 S.W.2d 165 (Tex. Crim. App. 1975), the court concluded the crime of driving while intoxicated is a strict liability offense. In *Clayton v. State*, 652 S.W.2d 810 (Tex. App. - Amarillo 1983), the court decided driving a car with a suspended driver's license is a strict liability offense. Exceeding the speed limit does not require mens rea, as decided in *Zulauf v. State*, 591 S.W.2d 869 (Tex. Crim. App. 1979).

CASE

***Pollard v. State*, 687 S.W.2d 373 (Tex. App. - Dallas 1985)**
Section 6.02(b) of the Texas Penal Code

The strict liability issue was not so clear in the case of Garland Pollard, who was found guilty of sleeping and dozing in a public place in violation of a Dallas city ordinance. He argued the complaint against him should be dismissed because it failed to allege a culpable mental state. The appellate court agreed. The Texas Constitution article XI, section 5 provides that no city ordinance shall contain a provision that is inconsistent with the state constitution or the laws enacted by the state legislature. The Dallas ordinance provided that a person commits an offense if he sleeps or dozes in a street, alley, park, or other public place. There was no mention in the ordinance of a required mental state. Looking at Sections 6.02 (a) and (b), the court ruled that when the city ordinance was enforced against Pollard without a culpable mental state, it was inconsistent with Section 6.02. Section 6.02 (b) provides that unless the definition of the offense plainly dispenses with any mental element, a culpable mental state is required. In a decision that emphasizes that it is important to draft statutes and ordinances carefully, the court felt bound to conclude:

The definition of sleeping in public does not plainly dispense with any culpable mental state because it fails to mention mental state at all. Consequently, section 6.02(b) applies and adds the requirement of a culpable mental state to the definition of the offense. Since, as a result, a culpable mental state was an element of the offense of sleeping in public, the failure to allege that element renders the complaint fundamentally defective.

REVIEW

1. A negligent criminal act is committed if the actor:
   a. ignored a substantial and unjustifiable risk of which he ought to have been aware.
   b. ignored a substantial and unjustifiable risk of which he was aware.
   c. knew he was negligent.
   d. intended to be negligent.

2. An intentional act is committed if the actor:
   a. deliberately committed the act.
   b. planned the act in advance.
   c. consciously engaged in the act.
   d. is aware that his conduct is reasonably certain to cause a particular result.

3. As provided in the Texas Penal Code, proof of a higher degree of culpability than that charged constitutes proof of the culpability charged.
   a. True
   b. False

4. Culpable mental states are ranked from the highest to the lowest in the Texas Penal Code.
   a. True
   b. False

5. Bob shot his gun in Mandy's direction, not to do bodily harm but to scare her. He did not intend for the bullet to strike. The wind, however, carried the bullet toward Gary, who was hit by the bullet and killed. Bob is deeply grieved.
   a. Bob can argue his bullet was never directed at Gary, so he's not guilty of a crime.
   b. Bob can argue he never intended for anyone to be harmed and he is not guilty.
   c. Bob's in trouble. His actions were arguably criminally negligent.
   d. Bob killed someone and it doesn't matter what his mens rea was at the time.

6. Strict liability crimes are not permitted according to the Texas Constitution.
   a. True
   b. False

Section 3: THE CAUSATION REQUIREMENT

OVERVIEW

In the majority of cases, it's not difficult for the state to prove the defendant caused the harm that resulted from his or her criminal activities. If the state can prove the defendant committed the act, it's clear that "but for" the defendant's conduct, the harm would not have occurred. There are circumstances, however, when the "but for" test is not so simple and some interesting questions must be resolved in court.

Section 6.04(a) of the Texas Penal Code
A person is criminally responsible if the result would not have occurred but for his conduct, operating either alone or concurrently with another cause, unless the concurrent cause was clearly sufficient to produce the result and the conduct of the actor is clearly insufficient.

CASES

1. *Nugent v. State*, 749 S.W.2d 595, 597 (Tex. App. - Corpus Christi 1988)
Section 6.04(a) of the Texas Penal Code

Paul Nugent was convicted of involuntary manslaughter as a result of an automobile collision he had with Marcus Meza. Three passengers in the Meza auto were killed. The evidence showed Nugent was speeding greatly in excess of the speed limit and was intoxicated at the time of the accident. There was also evidence, however, that Meza's driving contributed to the accident. The jury charge read in

> Now if you believe from the evidence beyond a reasonable doubt that on or about the 16th day of February 1986, in Nueces County, Texas, the defendant, Paul Nugent, did then and there by accident and mistake, and by reason of such intoxication, *cause* the death of Marcus Anthony Meza, Jr., you will find the defendant guilty of involuntary manslaughter. Unless you so find beyond a reasonable doubt, or if you have a reasonable doubt thereof, you will acquit the defendant.

Nugent argued on appeal that the charge did not instruct the jury sufficiently on the issue of causation. The appellate court agreed with Nugent by first noting that a defendant is entitled to an instruction on every issue raised by the evidence. The instruction cannot just be an abstract explanation of what the Penal Code requires. It must be applied to the facts of the particular case. In this case, the jury should have been instructed that if they found Meza's driving was clearly sufficient to cause the accident and Nugent's conduct clearly insufficient to cause the accident, they should acquit Nugent.

2. *Mendoza v. State*, 840 S.W.2d 697 (Tex. App. - Corpus Christi 1992)
Section 6.04(a) of the Texas Penal Code

Concurrent causation was not an issue, decided the appellate court in the case of Adriana Mendoza, who was convicted of stabbing her victim to death. The court explained:

> Appellant claims that the State failed to prove that appellant's conduct caused the victim's death because the evidence showed a concurrent cause sufficient to cause death. Dr. Marguerite DeWitt, a pathologist, testified that she performed an autopsy on the deceased. DeWitt stated that she found blood coming from the stab wound to the victim's left upper chest. She further testified that the wound damaged two large vessels in the body. When asked whether the deceased would have survived if he had received treatment within fifteen to twenty minutes, DeWitt related that his chances would probably have been pretty good if he had been timely treated by a competent vascular surgeon. Appellant now contends that the deceased's failure to receive immediate medical treatment, perhaps due to his own intoxication, renders the evidence insufficient to sustain a conviction. We disagree.

> Under Tex. Penal Code Ann. Section 6.04 (Vernon 1974), a person is criminally liable if his conduct, regardless of a concurrent cause, caused the harm or if his conduct, together with another cause, caused the harm. ... Only when the person's conduct, by itself, is clearly insufficient to cause the harm may he not be convicted. When the evidence shows a causal connection between the conduct of the defendant and the death of the deceased, no issue concerning causation arises. ... The evidence in this case shows a causal connection between appellant's conduct (stabbing victim in the chest and cutting arteries) and the victim's death. The evidence is sufficient to support a verdict.

A pathologist testified in *Hutcheson v. State*, 899 S.W.2d 39 (Tex. App. - Amarillo 1995), that either the gunshot wound inflicted on the victim by his estranged wife or the gun shot wound inflicted on the victim by the police would have sufficed to cause death. The victim and the appellant had been arguing. The appellant shot the victim just as the police arrived on the scene. In the confusion, a police officer thought his fellow officer was under fire and shot the victim accidentally. Both the appellant's and the officer's shots inflicted extensive damage. The Amarillo Court of Appeals ruled the appellant should be considered the cause of the victim's death because the evidence indicated that her gunshot was sufficient to have caused it.

REVIEW

7. In the case *Nugent v. State*, Nugent:
    a. convinced the appellate court the jury instruction at his trial was incorrect.
    b. convinced the appellate court that he shouldn't be held criminally responsible.
    c. didn't convince the appellate court he wasn't responsible for Meza's death.
    d. decided to challenge the constitutionality of the statute.

8. In the *Mendoza* case, causation:
    a. was impossible for the state to prove because the victim didn't get good medical help.
    b. was not an important issue.
    c. was clear and there was no reason to question it.
    d. was established because a causal connection was proved between Mendoza's conduct and the victim's death.

9. The defense that a concurrent cause eliminated criminal responsibility for harm or damage is only successful if the concurrent cause:
    a. was serious enough to have contributed to at least ½ of the harm done.
    b. was clearly sufficient to have produced the harm.
    c. was clearly sufficient to have produced the harm even if the actor's conduct was also clearly sufficient.
    d. was clearly sufficient to have produced the harm and the actor's conduct was clearly insufficient.

10. In cases involving issues of concurrent causation, the court is willing to split the criminal responsibility in such a way that each cause shares the criminal blame.
    a. True
    b. False

11. Sara refused to testify at her murder trial. She never confessed to the murder. The only evidence the State has is an eyewitness who saw Sara take a loaded gun into a room and close the door. The witness then heard a loud bang and saw Sara rush out of the room and proceed out the building. The witness went into the room and found Skippy's dead body with a bullet in his chest. The gun that shot Skippy was never found. Sara had no gun residue on her hands when she was arrested.
    a. There is no direct evidence against Sara and the State cannot not prove her guilt beyond a reasonable doubt.
    b. If the witness is credible, the State has a case.
    c. There is no way for the State to prove up Sara's mens rea even if they could prove up her actus reus.
    d. The jury will be instructed to assume that Sara intentionally shot the victim.

FINAL COMMENTS ON THE MENS REA, CONCURRENCE, AND CAUSATION

The principles of criminal liability discussed in this chapter are among the most difficult principles of criminal law. How do you determine what a defendant was thinking and feeling at the time he or she committed a crime? Different jurors can listen to the same testimony and reach vastly different conclusions about a defendant's mens rea. Proof is generally circumstantial. Perhaps the strength of the criminal law is that we attempt to determine culpability at all.

Chapter Five

Parties to Crime and Vicarious Liability

INTRODUCTION

Seven male prisoners escaped from a Texas maximum-security prison facility in December 2000. While burglarizing a sporting goods store in Irving, Texas on Christmas Eve, where they stole guns and ammunition, George Rivas shot and killed an Irving police officer. After evading law enforcement for over a month, five of the seven escapees were apprehended in Colorado on January 22, 2001. One of the five committed suicide rather than be arrested. Two days later the other two escapees were taken into custody, also apprehended in Colorado. All six prisoners were eventually convicted of capital murder for killing a police officer. Several of the escapees fought the murder charge on the grounds they did not shoot the gun and never intended to commit the crime of murder. George Rivas admitted he shot and killed the officer. , We must understand the law of parties in order to understand how offenders who did not intend to commit murder and did not shoot the murder weapon were nevertheless convicted of the offense and sentenced to death.

This chapter looks at the law of parties in Texas, Sections 7.01 and 7.02 of the Penal Code. Like most states, Texas has abolished the common law distinctions between accomplices and principals. According to the T.P.C., each party to an offense may be charged and convicted of that offense.

Section 1: PARTICIPATION *BEFORE* AND *DURING* THE COMMISSION OF A CRIME

OVERVIEW

Section 7.01 of the Texas Penal Code
(a) A person is criminally responsible as a party to an offense if the offense is committed by his own conduct, by the conduct of another for which he is criminally responsible, or by both.
(b) Each party to an offense may be charged with commission of the offense.

Section 7.02 of the Texas Penal Code
(a) A person is criminally responsible for an offense committed by the conduct of another if:
(1) acting with the kind of culpability required for the offense, he causes or aids an innocent or nonresponsible person to engage in conduct prohibited by the definition of the offense;
(2) acting with intent to promote or assist the commission of the offense, he solicits, encourages, directs, aids, or attempts to aid the other person to commit the offense; or

(3) having a legal duty to prevent commission of the offense and acting with intent to promote or assist its commission, he fails to make a reasonable effort to prevent commission of the offense.
(b) If, in the attempt to carry out a conspiracy to commit one felony, another felony is committed by one of the conspirators, all conspirators are guilty of the felony actually committed, though having no intent to commit it, if the offense was committed in the furtherance of the unlawful purpose and was one that should have been anticipated as a result of the carrying out of the conspiracy.

According to the Penal Code, allegations that an accused was a party to an offense must be supported by sufficient evidence the accused acted with the intent (mens rea) to promote or assist in the commission of the offense and solicited, encouraged, directed, aided, or attempted to aid (actus reus) a person to commit a crime.

By now you recognize how reluctant appellate courts are to overturn the decisions of trial courts. They are especially reluctant to overturn jury verdicts when a convicted offender alleges on appeal that there was insufficient evidence to convict him. It's one thing to overturn a case because there was a violation of an accused's Fourth Amendment search and seizure right or Sixth Amendment right to counsel. It's another thing altogether for an appellate court to sit in judgment on the facts of a case. In Texas, as in every jurisdiction, courts of appeal have held that evidence will be considered sufficient to support a conviction if after the court evaluates the evidence *in the light most favorable to the verdict*, it concludes a rational jury would have found the elements of the offense beyond a reasonable doubt. The jury members are the fact finders. It is their exclusive right to decide the credibility, weight, and balance of the evidence. An appellate court steps in only when a jury's decision is so against the great weight and preponderance of the evidence as to be manifestly unjust.

Cases involving the law of parties are often based on circumstantial evidence as opposed to direct evidence. Direct evidence would include a confession or eyewitness testimony about what actually occurred. It is evidence that directly demonstrates the ultimate fact to be proved. Circumstantial evidence is direct proof of a secondary fact that logically demonstrates the ultimate fact to be proved. In a circumstantial evidence case, proof amounting to a strong suspicion is not enough to support a conviction. However, every fact in a case need not point directly and independently to the defendant's guilt. A guilty verdict can rest on the combined and cumulative force of all the incriminating circumstances.

As you read about the Texas cases in this chapter and throughout the Supplement, notice how difficult it is for an appellant to convince an appeals court to reverse his or her case based on the theory there was insufficient evidence proving they were parties to criminal activity.

CASES

1. *Gilchrist v. State*, 904 S.W.2d 935 (Tex. App. – Amarillo 1995)

Sections 7.01 and 7.02 of the Texas Penal Code

The appellant, Shawn Gilchrist, and his friend Mark Hanson parked a borrowed pickup truck in a grocery parking lot in Lubbock, Texas. According to the court that decided Gilchrist's appeal:

> Noting that they "were totally broke," Hanson began "talking about stealing someones (sic) purse." The two originally planned for appellant to drop his companion off, for appellant "didn't want to do it [him]self." Once a victim was found and her purse taken, appellant would then "drive by and pick [Hanson] up in the truck." Soon they spied Ms. Louester Marshall, a 76 year old widow and grandmother, briskly walking across the lot.
>
> As the proposed victim drew near, Hanson, who sat in the passenger seat, asked her for directions to Slide Avenue. Ms. Marshall answered, turned and attempted to walk away. As she did, Hanson reached out and grabbed her wrist, thereby pulling her arm and purse into the cab of the truck. Appellant immediately started the vehicle and "took off like a bat out of hell." The acceleration jerked Ms. Marshall off her feet. ... Hanson eventually "peeled" her arm and removed the purse.
>
> * * * * *
>
> Summary of the evidence at bar revealed two individuals without monies. To rectify their situation one proposed stealing a purse. Though the other one did not want to take the item himself, he nevertheless, agreed to help. His assistance would come in the form of operating the getaway vehicle. ... Once Hanson had grabbed her purse, which she could not release, appellant completed his part of the plan by driving away.

Even though Gilchrist did not snatch the victim's purse, under the law of parties he can be prosecuted for the same offense as Hanson.

2. *Hill v. State*, 883 S.W.2d 765, 767-768 (Tex. App. – Amarillo 1994)
Sections 7.01 and 7.02 of the Texas Penal Code

Sometimes the facts of a case get quite complex. Read excerpts from the *Hill* case and determine whether there was sufficient evidence of both mens rea and actus reus to convict Anita Mae Hill of injury to a child.

> Jason Hill, the nine year old son of appellant and her husband, Marvin Hill, was admitted to Northwest Texas Hospital on 17 May 1990 with severe and infected bruises and injuries, admittedly inflicted by his father in "spanking" him with a metal rod. Carolyn Jordan, a registered nurse, noticed Jason had various bruises and injuries obviously inflicted at different times, some of which were emitting a greenish pus with blackened, dead skin over or around them. The injuries were the worst she had ever seen, and were of a type causing permanent disfigurement.
>
> * * * * *
>
> Marvin confessed to Corporal Michael Allen, an Amarillo police officer, that several days before, he had taken a metal rod from a screen door, located at his home, and spanked Jason. Although he spanked Jason repeatedly, Marvin said he did not realize he had injured him badly.
>
> * * * * *
>
> Jason testified that for several years before the event leading to the prosecution, Marvin, and sometimes appellant herself, would beat him with a metal rod or stick. Jennifer and Heidi [Jason's sisters], who had been beaten by Marvin in their parents' bedroom, confirmed Jason's beatings by his father, and Jennifer said that when appellant asked Marvin not to do those things, he would become abusive toward her. Usually, Jason said, appellant would report to Marvin that he had been bad, and Marvin would beat him.
>
> * * * * *

The testimony of Karlene Conner, the Hill's former next door neighbor, was that Jason acted scared all the time, and he would recoil from her anytime she made a movement toward him. On six or seven occasions when Marvin was not home, she would hear the children screaming, "no, Mommy, no," for periods of at least one hour. Her daughter, Leslie Conner, said the family stopped using their backyard swimming pool because they got tired of hearing the Hill children crying all day and screaming, "No, mommie. Please mommie, stop."

* * * * *

Kim Wrazidlo, the Texas Department of Protective and Regulatory Services caseworker who accompanied the officers to the Hill residence, said appellant was concerned with what was happening to Marvin, and did not inquire about Jason.

* * * * *

After the emergency hearing requested by the Department to remove the Hill children to a foster home, Rick Keffler, an attorney who represented appellant at the hearing, drove Marvin to the hospital. He recalled that Marvin said he alone had caused the injuries to Jason and that appellant did not have anything to do with it.

* * * * *

Appellant's friend, Nadine Boyd, who knew the Hills since 1985 and often visited in their home, testified that when she was with appellant and the children in the absence of Marvin, there was no violence and the children acted normal, but when Marvin was present, the children were very subdued and quiet. She never saw injuries on the children.

Jan Markham, who lived with the Hills for two months in 1988 and saw appellant daily until she moved away, stated it was a very pleasant atmosphere, the children were not afraid of appellant, and showed her great affection. Marvin was extremely strict, the children appeared to be fearful of him, and he was cruel to them.

Pat Walsh generally confirmed the testimony of his wife, Betty Walsh, Boyd and Markham. He stated the children were quiet, that appellant was a very solicitous mother, and that he saw no signs of physical abuse on the children.

Given this evidence, appellant presents two challenges to its sufficiency to support her conviction. Initially, she points out that to convict her under the law of parties, the State had to prove conduct by Marvin that constituted an offense, plus conduct by her with the intent to promote or assist Marvin's conduct.

* * * * *

Appellant contends that the evidence does not show any act on her part which promoted or assisted Marvin in the commission of the offense, but if there is, then there is absolutely no evidence of her intent to promote or assist the commission of the offense of causing serious bodily injury to Jason.

* * * * *

Appellant acknowledges that in determining whether an individual is a party to an offense and bears criminal responsibility, the court may look to events before, during, and after the commission of the offense. Circumstantial evidence may be sufficient to show that an individual is a party to the offense, and it is not necessary that the individual be present at the scene of the crime. *Morrison v. State*, 608 S.W.2d 233, 234 (Tex. Crim. App. 1980).

> From the evidence, the jury could discern a pattern, existing during a number of years, that on the occasions when Marvin arrived home from work and appellant told him one of the children had been bad, Marvin would take the child into his bedroom and "spank" the child with a metal rod or a stick. There was evidence that these "spankings" had resulted in physical injuries to the children, including knots on the heads of Jennifer and Heidi, and the fracture of eight of Jason's ribs. On some of these occasions, appellant would be present; at other times she would leave the house at Marvin's direction. The jury could reasonably infer from the evidential pattern that on the last occasion when Marvin arrived at home and engaged in a conversation with appellant, followed by Marvin's immediate beating of Jason, appellant had told Marvin Jason had been bad, knowing that Marvin would "spank" him. Thus, the evidence is sufficient for the jury to find that appellant, albeit not present during the "spanking" acted to promote or assist in the "spanking" of Jason.

After examining the actus reus element of the charge against the appellant, the court examined the mens rea element.

> Nevertheless, appellant proposes, without disagreement by the State, that to be criminally responsible, the evidence must show not only that she acted to promote or assist in Jason's "spanking," but that she intended to promote or assist the commission of the offense of causing serious bodily injury to a child. ... It follows that appellant is criminally responsible for the offense committed by Marvin only if the evidence shows that she *knew Marvin's unlawful intent* when she acted to promote or assist in his conduct.
>
> The evidence heard by the jury included testimony bearing on appellant's knowledge of Marvin's unlawful intent. ... Consequently, the evidence, viewed in the light most favorable to the verdict, is sufficient for any rational trier of fact to have found appellant criminally responsible for the offense committed by Marvin beyond a reasonable doubt. Her point of error is overruled.
>
> The judgment is affirmed.

Anita Mae Hill was found guilty of the same offense as Marvin Hill even though there was no evidence she administered the "spanking" in question or that she was even present when it occurred. The jury could infer from her actions that she promoted or assisted in the "spankings" (her actus reus) and intended to promote the causing of serious bodily harm to a child (her mens rea).

3. *Urtado v. State*, 605 S.W.2d 907 (Tex. Crim. App. 1980)
Sections 7.01 and 7.02 of the Texas Penal Code

Mere physical presence at a crime scene is not enough evidence of complicity. Alfonso Urtado was convicted of attempted burglary of a habitation. Like Anita Mae Hill, he alleged in his appeal there was insufficient evidence that he aided and abetted the commission of a crime. Tom DeLoach testified that he observed a strange man and two women in a neighbor's back yard. He saw the man making a cutting-type motion across the top of the neighbor's kitchen window while the two women stood and watched. That man was later identified as Urtado. DeLoach did not observe a tool or object in the Urtado's hand. DeLoach approached the man and the women and asked if they were trying to break in the house. The three left quickly, got into the same car and sped away. The evidence showed there was a ten to twelve inch cut across the top rim of the window screen.

Urtado's testimony was that he drove the two young women to apply for jobs as housekeepers for a home advertised in the newspaper. He and the young women testified they had difficulty locating the right house. The girls told Urtado to wait in the car for them while they walked down the street. They knocked on the door of the almost burglarized home. When no one answered, the girls walked around to the back door, took out a knife and started to cut the window screen. Urtado appeared, scolded the young women, examined the damage to the screen, and told them they were leaving. As they were exiting the yard, they met up with DeLoach. Concerned and afraid, all three walked quickly to the car and left the scene as fast as they could. The women testified that their decision to burglarize the house was made on the spur of the moment and Urtado was not aware of their actions until he caught them in the act.

The Court of Appeals emphasized that to be guilty of a crime requires more than physical presence. Appellant's "flight" from the scene and his assistance in helping the young women leave did not amount to an agreement to commit a burglary. In this case, the appellate court concluded the evidence was insufficient for a conviction. Aiding and abetting a crime requires more than Urtado's actions.

4. *Lacy v. State*, 782 S.W.2d 556 (Tex. App. - Houston [14th Dist.] 1989)
Sections 7.01 and 7.02 of the Texas Penal Code

Lacy was convicted of the delivery of a controlled substance, crack cocaine. He argued on appeal that there was insufficient evidence of his guilt under the law of parties. Undercover narcotics officers approached the Lacy at a strip shopping center in Houston, Texas. After a short conversation, an unsuspecting Lacy led the officers to an apartment complex where the officers completed a drug transaction with an unknown third person. The unknown person delivered the cocaine to the officers and took their money. Lacy requested a sample of the cocaine from the officers, but he did not deliver the drugs to them nor did he receive money from them. Lacy was arrested and convicted of delivery of a controlled substance. The State argued that because of the law of parties, Lacy had actually transferred the drugs to the officers. Lacy claimed the state could not make a case of actual delivery. The court concluded:

> [T]he trial court in the instant case could convict Lacy of actual delivery of the controlled substance if sufficient evidence existed to show that the unknown participant committed the offense and appellant encouraged, directed, or aided him in the commission of that offense. We conclude that sufficient evidence does exist.

Lacy was convicted of the same offense as someone who carried illegal drugs on their person, physically handed them over to the undercover officers, and received payment for them. What Lacy may have considered to be a minor role in a drug transaction was not recognized as such by the law.

REVIEW

1. In the *Hill v. State* case, in order to convict her under the law of parties of the same offense for which Marvin was convicted, the jury had to find that Anita:
   a. knew about Marvin's conduct.
   b. knew, approved, and intended to promote or assist his conduct.
   c. The law of parties didn't apply to Anita.
   d. knew about, even though she didn't approve of his conduct.

2. The differences between the *Hill* and *Utardo* decisions are
   a. Anita knew about Marvin's conduct, and Utardo didn't know what the girls were doing until he discovered them.
   b. Circumstantial evidence showed Anita intended to promote Marvin's actions, and there was no such evidence in the *Utardo* case.
   c. There was evidence Anita's conduct promoted Marvin's conduct, and the only evidence implicating Utardo was his physical presence.
   d. All of the above.

3. In the eyes of the law, Lacy's role in the distribution of drugs was:
   a. relatively minor – all he did was direct prospective purchasers
   b. relatively minor – he didn't get any money from the purchasers.
   c. As serious as the role of the actual distributors.
   d. A serious participant but not on the same level as the actual distributors.

4. The phrase "law of parties" refers to:
   a. laws that define what types of parties involve criminal nuisance.
   b. laws that relate to complicity and participation in criminal offenses.
   c. the manner in which the government decides the amount of punishment that should be administered to various convicted defendants involved in the same crime.
   d. how responsibility is assigned to the individuals involved in a crime depending on whether they were at the scene of the crime or not.

5. Ben decided to rob a convenience store. The only problem was his younger brother Teddy was with him, and Teddy was studying for the priesthood. Ben robbed the store clerk while Teddy was a few feet away looking longingly at the candy bars. Teddy was shocked by what he saw and heard but was caught up in the moment. As Ben ran out the door, Teddy ran after him. The police caught them both a few blocks from the store.
   a. Teddy can be convicted as a party to a robbery because he was at the scene.
   b. Teddy can be convicted as a party to the robbery because he fled with Ben.
   c. Teddy cannot be convicted of robbery unless the evidence shows he gave assistance to the crime.
   d. Teddy cannot be convicted of robbery because there is no evidence he demanded money from the clerk.

6. The surrounding circumstances and events before and after the commission of a crime can be introduced into evidence to support a finding that a defendant was a party to a crime.
   a. True
   b. False

7. The law of parties only requires a finding that the defendant assisted or aided in the commission of the crime. It does not require separate proof that the defendant intended to aid in the commission of a crime.
   a. True
   b. False

8. Helen studied Section 7.02 of the T.P.C. and noticed that if she encouraged her husband to bribe a public official, she could face charges of being a party to his crime. Helen decided she would not voice encouragement, but neither would she advise him not to engage in bribery when he discussed it with her (they discuss all their business with each other):
   a. Helen could still face charges under the law of parties for her failure to advise her husband that bribery is against the law.
   b. Helen could still face charges because she knew what her husband was contemplating and failed to inform the authorities.
   c. Helen probably will not face charges because there will be no evidence she encouraged her husband to break the law.
   d. Helen could still face charges because by her silence she gave tacit encouragement.

9. The *best* lesson a person can learn after reading about the law of parties:
   a. Beware who your friends are.
   b. Beware of who your enemies are.
   c. Don't agree to pick up a friend from a bank or convenience store.
   d. Be careful not to put agreements in writing.

10. According to the Texas Penal Code, if the person who committed an offense is acquitted, the person who is being prosecuted as a party to that same offense cannot be convicted.
    a. True
    b. False

11. According to the Texas Penal Code, if the person who committed an offense is found guilty of a certain type or class of crime, the person who has been charged as a party to that same offense can only be convicted of that same crime.
    a. True
    b. False

Section 2: PARTICIPATION *AFTER* THE COMMISSION OF A CRIME

OVERVIEW

Participation after the commission of a crime becomes a criminal act in Texas if it meets the requirements of Section 38.05.

Section 38.05 of the Texas Penal Code

(a) A person commits an offense if, with intent to hinder the arrest, prosecution, conviction, or punishment of another for an offense or, with intent to hinder the arrest, detention, adjudication, or disposition of a child for engaging in delinquent conduct that violates a penal law of the grade of felony, he:

(1) harbors or conceals the other;
(2) provides or aids in providing the other with any means of avoiding arrest or effecting
(3) the escape; or
warns the other of impeding discovery or apprehension.
(b) It is a defense to prosecution under Subsection (a)(3) that the warning was given in connection with an effort to bring another into compliance with the law.

CASES

1. *Guillory v. State*, 877 S.W.2d 71 (Tex. App. - Houston [1st Dist.] 1994)
Sections 7.01, 7.03 and 38.05 of the Texas Penal Code

Sometimes the line is fuzzy between being guilty of a crime under the law of parties versus being guilty of providing a criminal with a means of effecting escape. Guillory was convicted of being a party to a robbery. He admitted he was more than just present at the scene of the crime but alleged that he was only guilty of helping the robber avoid capture. Betty Howard was in a Kroger parking lot when Jamie McBride grabbed her arm, threw her against the car, took her purse, and ran off. Guillory drove a late model pick-up truck by McBride and opened the passenger door. McBride jumped in, and the truck drove away. Onlookers tried to stop the truck. Several hours later, McBride and Guillory returned to the store in a different vehicle. The security guard recognized them and called the police. Several people identified them as the robbers, and they were arrested.

Guillory argued that the facts showed he assisted McBride in avoiding capture. It was certainly in Guillory's best interest to argue that he assisted in McBride's escape. Section 38.05 of the Texas Penal Code addresses Hindering Apprehension or Prosecution. Robbery is a second-degree felony. Hindering apprehension is a third-degree felony. The appeals court, however, upheld the jury's verdict. Although there were no facts in evidence as to what the truck was doing before the robbery or whether McBride and Guillory were seen together at the parking lot before the crime, there was evidence that Guillory drove the truck very quickly, picked up McBride after the robbery, and opened the passenger door for her to get in. There was evidence that when the two were finally arrested, they possessed items they had also shoplifted from the store and that they were romantically involved. This was clearly a case of circumstantial evidence, which the appellate court considered persuasive enough for a jury to infer that Guillory was a party to robbery.

2. *In the Matter of D.L.N.*, 930 S.W.2d 253, 256 (Tex. App. - Houston [14th Dist.] 1996)
Sections 7.01 and 7.02 of the Texas Penal Code

A very serious issue involving the law of parties was raised D.L.N., a juvenile charged with capital murder. He was transferred from the juvenile system to the adult system for trial as an adult. His appeal came up in the context of his certification proceeding. He alleged there was insufficient evidence to support a probable cause finding that he was a party to a murder and should be transferred to the adult justice system.

The facts showed that D.L.N. and his friend Gartrell had been discussing the possibility of committing a car-jacking. D.L.N. followed Gartrell's instructions to take a gun from the bedroom of a father of one of their friends. At Gartrell's house, the two of them took turns firing the pistol into the air. They also drank several bottles of beer and became "pretty drunk." A friend took them to a store parking lot. They switched off carrying the gun in their pants. Gartrell told D.L.N., "let's just carjack that fool right there," as a Mustang drove by, and D.L.N. said, "shut up, don't be stupid." They walked over to the store and bought cigarettes. The court opinion reads:

> Gartrell saw a truck he wanted to carjack, and appellant said, "alright dude, whatever." Appellant heard a gunshot, which killed Joe Darin Campbell, and then saw Gartrell drive around some apartments and pull up to where he was. Gartrell told appellant, "get in." Appellant ran around to the passenger's side, got into the truck, and they drove off.
>
> Later, appellant helped dispose of the truck by putting it into neutral to roll into a creek. Appellant took off his socks so he could wipe down the truck and the gun clip. In addition, appellant discarded the gun Gartrell used to kill Campbell.
>
> [Police Officer Shirley Brown] testified that there was no evidence that appellant shot Joe Darin Campbell.

The appeals court ruled there was enough evidence that D.L.N. was not merely present at the crime scene and to find there was probable cause that he was a party to the commission of a capital murder, the same offense charged against Gartrel. The law of parties opened the door to an adult criminal conviction for capital murder even though D.L.N. was not the shooter, and there was some evidence that he was not present at the murder itself.

Texas courts recognize the "independent impulse" defense to a charge under the law of parties, *Fincher v. State*, 980 S.W.2d 886 (Tex. App.- Fort Worth 1998). Under this theory, the accused admits that although he intended to break the law, he did not contemplate the extent of wrongdoing that his fellow conspirators actually engaged in. For this reason he should not be held criminally responsible for their conduct. The courts are careful, however, to apply this defense very narrowly. The defense is not available if the crime was committed to further the unlawful purpose in which all the conspirators were involved, *and* it was a crime the accused should have anticipated might happen as a result of committing the offense they had agreed to. How could this defense be argued when D.L.N. faces his capital murder trial?

FINAL COMMENTS ON THE LAW OF PARTIES

The law of parties aims to enlarge the criminal justice net to include individuals who should be held criminally liable for actions they may not have caused directly but in which they exercised some significant level of participation. The difficult issue becomes at what point do we want to wield the power of the State against a person who aided, encouraged or abetted the commission of a crime. At what point should moral culpability be considered legal culpability? When did Anita Mae Hill's failure to act become criminal? At what point did D.L.N.'s admittedly culpable behavior become serious enough to result in a charge of capital murder? Why is it good public policy to hold someone liable for an offense he should have anticipated that his criminal co-conspirator would commit? The complicity statutes are important because they allow the prosecution of persons who could otherwise hide behind the fact that they themselves were not the shooter or the abuser. On the other hand, the law of parties should not be permitted to reach too far. At some point, the criminal justice system is not the appropriate vehicle of social control.

Chapter Six

Inchoate Crimes: Attempt, Conspiracy, and Solicitation

INTRODUCTION

This chapter looks at the law of attempt, conspiracy and solicitation in Texas. As you read the cases, ask yourself how you would argue as a prosecutor to sustain a conviction on appeal and then as a defense attorney attempting to overturn your client's conviction. Many cases on appeal involve very close judgment calls. The facts are often subject to interpretation and manipulation. Criminal attempt and conspiracy statutes are especially subject to debate. Being able to argue both sides of a legal issue may seem awkward at first. You may have a sense about what you think is a correct result and be reluctant to champion the opposite position. The more you take time to understand the other side, however, to the point where you can be its advocate, your understanding of the law will increase considerably. You will better understand the statute, what criminal behavior it is intended to prohibit or deter, and what type of offender should be brought into the criminal justice system with all of its awesome power. The best advocates know and appreciate their opponents' arguments.

Section 1: ATTEMPT

OVERVIEW

Section 15.01 of the Texas Penal Code

(a) A person commits an offense if, with specific intent to commit an offense, he does an act amounting to more than mere preparation that tends but fails to effect the commission of the offense intended.

(b) If a person attempts to commit an offense that may be aggravated, his conduct constitutes an attempt to commit the aggravated offense if an element that aggravates the offense accompanies the attempt.

(c) It is no defense to prosecution for criminal attempt that the offense attempted was actually committed.

The two elements of criminal attempt law that generate most appeals are the mens rea requirement of "specific intent to commit an offense" and the actus reus requirement of performing an act that amounts to "more than mere preparation." In the Texas cases discussed in this chapter, the appellants often challenge their conviction on the grounds there was insufficient evidence to prove both the actus reus and mens rea of attempt beyond a reasonable doubt. Most appeals are a combination of several different legal challenges. From an appellant's perspective, every reasonable legal argument should be made. In addition, defense attorneys are obligated by their professional code of ethics to represent their clients zealously.

As you read the cases presented in this chapter, notice how the appellants' lawyers weave the stories about the crimes their clients were convicted of around the legal requirements of the statutes. Stories about greed, hate, love, obsession, and fear are reinterpreted in the light of legal doctrines that, in the case of criminal attempt law, impose concepts like "specific intent" and beyond "mere preparation" in a way that sometimes strain the actual events. The ability to weave facts creatively and persuasively around legal definitions is the skill of lawyering.

CASES

The first two cases in this section discuss the crime of attempted burglary. After reading about the cases, you can see why a defense attorney would challenge allegations of attempted burglary on the grounds there was insufficient evidence of an act amounting to more than mere preparation.

1. *Bledsoe v. State*, 578 S.W.2d 123 (Tex. Crim. App. 1979)

Sections 15.01 and 30.04 of the Texas Penal Code

Authorities charged attempted burglary against Bledsoe. A Dallas police officer was called to the scene of an attempted burglary and found Bledsoe near the passenger side door of a 1979 Ford L.T.D. He observed Bledsoe ducked between the cars as if he was trying to conceal himself. The officer searched the immediate area and found a screwdriver and a clothes hanger on the ground approximately three feet from Bledsoe. The officer arrested him. The officer testified at Bledsoe's trial that he could not see the appellant's hands because he was facing away from him and could only guess that Bledsoe was trying to unlock the car door. There was no evidence of scratches or marks on the L.T.D. Review the definition of the crime of burglary of a vehicle.

Section 30.04 of the Texas Penal Code

(a) A person commits an offense if, without the effective consent of the owner, he breaks into or enters a vehicle or any part of a vehicle with intent to commit a felony or theft.
(b) For purposes of this section, 'enter' means to intrude:
(1) any part of the body; or
(2) any physical object connected with the body.
(c) For purposes of this section, a container or trailer on a rail car is a part of the rail car.

Assuming for the moment that the appellant was burglarizing a car, did his activity amount to more than mere preparation? He was not seen touching the car. He was not on the parking lot premises unlawfully. And how important is the screwdriver and clothes hanger? The Texas Court of Criminal Appeals concluded:

> Nor, under the circumstances, do we attach significance to the fact that a screwdriver and clothes hanger were found within the appellant's immediate control. A person should not be held criminally responsible simply because a vigilant police officer intervenes before he begins to implement his criminal designs.

The court set aside Bledsoe's conviction. Notice the court does not suggest the appellant was innocent. The opinion noted that if the police officer had arrived on the scene a few minutes (seconds?) later, Bledsoe may have gone beyond mere preparation and entered the realm of criminal attempt. There was a vigorous dissenting opinion that said the facts supported an attempted criminal act.

2. *Flournoy v. State*, 668 S.W.2d 380 (Tex. Crim. App. 1984)
Sections 15.01 and 30.02 of the Texas Penal Code

In this case, the Texas Court of Criminal Appeals addressed an attempted burglary of a habitation. Lyndia Conley was in her mobile home at approximately 9:00 a.m. when she observed Mr. Flournoy accompanied by a passenger, park a car, get out, and approach her house. The passenger remained in the car. Conley did not recognize Flournoy or the passenger. She checked her front and back doors and placed herself in a position to watch what was going on outside. Flournoy knocked on the front door. When no one responded, the passenger got out of the car and went to the rear of the mobile home where he tried to look in the windows, but they were too high for him to see in so he returned to the car. Conley testified at trial that Flournoy tried to unlock the front door with a screwdriver or some other tool. He tried to get through the screen door to the main door. At this point, Conley got her rifle, opened the front door and told Flournoy to leave. He ran to the car and sped away. Conley made a note of the license plate number and called the police who arrested Flournoy for attempted burglary.

Section 30.02 of the Texas Penal Code

(a) A person commits an offense if, without the effective consent of the owner, the person:
(1) enters a habitation, or a building (or any portion of a building) not open to the public, with intent to commit a felony, theft, or an assault; or
(2) remains concealed, with intent to commit a felony, theft, or an assault, in a building or habitation; or
(3) enters a building or habitation and commits or attempts to commit a felony, theft, or an assault.
(b) For purposes of this section, "enter" means to intrude:
(1) any part of the body; or
(2) any physical object connected with the body.

The intermediate court of appeals ruled there was insufficient evidence of attempted burglary because Flournoy's acts did not go beyond mere preparation. They were concerned that the only evidence was Conley's interpretation of what she thought the appellant was trying to do. The Texas Court of Criminal Appeals disagreed and found that when Flournoy reached his hand through Conley's screen door, his act amounted to more than mere preparation. Appellate courts are obligated to review the evidence in the light most favorable to the jury's verdict. In this case, the Court of Criminal Appeals concluded that Conley's observations of the appellant's behavior provided sufficient evidence to support the jury's finding that Flournoy was attempting a burglary.

Proving beyond a reasonable doubt that a defendant performed acts beyond mere preparation makes attempt law a very tricky endeavor. By its very nature, burglary involves sneaky, undercover activities that can be interpreted in different ways. It is not an easy task for the prosecutor to take those actions and weave the story that they cross the line separating preparation from actually engaging in the crime. In the *Bledsoe* and *Flourno* cases, the courts relied on shades of differences in the circumstances surrounding the charges even though the facts strongly suggested that both appellants were up to no good.

3. *Santellan v. State*, 939 S.W.2d 155 (Tex. Crim. App. 1997)
Sections 15.01, 19.03(a)(2), and 20.01(2) of the Texas Penal Code

Section 19.03 of the Texas Penal Code, discussed in Chapter 8, outlines the offense of capital murder. In Texas a felony capital murder is defined as:

> **Section 19.03(a)(2) of the Texas Penal Code**
> the person intentionally commits the murder in the course of committing or attempting to commit kidnapping, burglary, robbery, aggravated sexual assault, arson, obstruction or retaliation, or terroristic threat under Section 22.07(a)(1), (3), (4), (5), or (6).

The State had to prove that Santellan committed the crime of attempted kidnapping beyond a reasonable doubt in order to convict him of capital murder. Santellan and his girlfriend were having relationship problems. After writing a letter addressed to his family apologizing for the murder he said he was about to commit, Santellan went to his girlfriend's place of employment. As she was walking to her car in the parking lot, he approached her, veered her away from the direction of her car, engaged her in a conversation, and finally shot her. He lifted her body into the passenger seat of his car and drove away. In his confession he stated he thought his victim might still be alive, and he wanted to spend some time with her. He took her to a motel where they spent the night, and he made love to her. When the police found Santellan two days later his girlfriend was deceased. The medical examiner testified at trial that she had probably died within minutes of the shooting.

Did the State prove that Santellan murdered his girlfriend during the commission of an attempted kidnapping? He argued that his actions did not amount to more than mere preparation for kidnapping prior to killing his girlfriend. During the trial, the State agreed that a dead body could not be kidnapped, however, the acts amounting to more than mere preparation occurred when Santellan diverted the victim from her path to her automobile *before* her death. The crime of kidnapping occurs under the Penal Code when a person intentionally or knowingly abducts another person.

> **Section 20.01(2) of the Texas Penal Code**
> "Abduct" means to restrain a person with intent to prevent his liberty by:
> (A) secreting or holding him in a place where he is not likely to be found; or
> (B) using or threatening to use deadly force.

The Texas Court of Criminal Appeals concluded there was some evidence, despite the medical examiner's testimony, that the victim was alive for a little while after the shooting. The court rejected the State's argument that the acts that went beyond preparation occurred when Santellan diverted his girlfriend in the parking lot. Instead, the court noted that Texas case law has established that a kidnapper need not restrain a victim for any certain period of time. In addition, the Texas law of attempt does not require an offender to accomplish every act short of actual commission of the offense to be guilty of attempt. The Court of Criminal Appeals ruled that Santellan's act of loading the victim into his car and driving away with her was a sufficient act of restraint to amount to more than mere preparation.

Texas courts have not clearly announced in their opinions which one of the four tests is applicable in Texas for distinguishing mere preparation from criminal attempt: the physical proximity doctrine, the probable desistance doctrine, the equivocality approach, or the substantial steps/Model Penal Code standard. The courts have held that every act short of commission does not have to be performed for an attempted crime to have been committed, suggesting they reject the physical proximity test which requires the actor to have performed all but the last act to be guilty of an attempted offense. This chapter reviews some cases that indicate Texas judges have also rejected the probable desistance approach which asks whether an act ordinarily would lead to the commission of a crime but for timely interference. It would be helpful if judges would clearly define the legal doctrine on which they are relying. That is often not the case. Although never acknowledged directly, most of the cases reviewed in this chapter support the substantial steps standard.

4. *Flanagan v. State*, 675 S.W.2d 734,741 (Tex. Crim. App. 1984)
Sections 15.01 and 19.02 of the Texas Penal Code

Flanagan was convicted of attempted murder for shooting a gun while driving his car on the freeway at an off-duty police officer in his automobile. The officer was not injured. The court had to decide whether the shooting of a gun by a person in one automobile at another automobile, with both vehicles traveling at between 50 and 60 miles per hour, with the shot striking approximately the center of the front grill of the other vehicle, doing only slight damage, was sufficient evidence that the shooter had specific intent to kill the driver. Without specific intent to commit a murder, the appellant could not be convicted of attempted murder.

This case proved troublesome to the Texas Court of Criminal Appeals. They reviewed prior case law that held the intent to murder may be inferred from the use of a deadly weapon. Prior case law, however, also held that simply because a person shoots at another with a gun does not necessarily make it an assault with intent to murder. How the weapon was used, the type of shot fired, and the surrounding circumstances all have to be considered. The court decided that in this case there was insufficient evidence of intent to murder: the gun was fired from a significant distance at a speeding car, only slight damage was done to the car, and the driver was not injured. Although appellant's acts were reprehensible, the offense committed was not attempted murder.

The State asked the court to reconsider its finding. The State argued that the offense of murder does not require specific intent to kill, therefore, the court was incorrect in engrafting such intent onto the offense of attempted murder. All that is required is specific intent to cause serious bodily injury.

Section 19.02(b)(1) and (2) of the Texas Penal Code
(b) A person commits an offense if he:
(1) intentionally or knowingly causes the death of an individual;
(2) intends to cause serious bodily injury and commits an act clearly dangerous to human life that causes the death of an individual.

The court reconsidered its original finding but rejected the State's argument. It wrote about criminal attempt law:

> The element "with specific intent to commit an offense" has traditionally been interpreted to mean that the actor must have the intent to bring about the desired result, which in the case of attempted murder is the death of the individual. Thus, a specific intent to kill is a necessary element of attempted murder. The authorities in support of this interpretation are numerous and convincing.

Although the State's argument did not persuade the Court of Criminal Appeals, it decided to reconsider its first opinion for other reasons. The court concluded their first opinion failed to look at the totality of circumstances. The facts established at trial that the driver of the car under attack saw the appellant pick up a gun and aim it directly at him before pulling the trigger. The court's second opinion found there was sufficient evidence that Flanagan had specific intent to kill. Flanagan's conviction was upheld.

The *Flanagan* case is a good example of how reasonable and intelligent minds can differ, even among judges serving on the same court. Take a look at the aggravated assault statute in Texas and see how attempted murder and aggravated assault could overlap if the court had accepted the State's position.

REVIEW

1. Suppose in the *Bledsoe* case that the officer had found the screwdriver and clothes hanger in one of Bledsoe's hands while he stood next to the car door, while his other hand was on the car door handle:
    a. Unless the officer sees Bledsoe trying to break in the car, there is no crime of attempt.
    b. The evidence for attempted burglary is getting much, much stronger.
    c. Unless the State could prove Bledsoe had a past history of burglary, there is no case of attempt.
    d. The evidence must include a witness in addition to the officer to prove attempted burglary.

2. The facts in the *Flournoy* case were:
    a. absolutely obvious and the Court of Appeals and Court of Criminal Appeals easily agreed it was an attempted burglary.
    b. so confusing that it as unfair to charge attempted burglary.
    c. subject to different interpretation by two different courts.
    d. all a lie created by Lydia Conley.

3. The *Santellan* case is:
    a. so tragic, why care if Santellan kidnapped his girlfriend.
    b. an excellent example of how in a case involving a murder, the State will sometimes argue that a felony was attempted so the State can pursue a capital murder charge also.
    c. an example of how not to commit a murder.
    d. Both b and c.

4. The Court of Criminal Appeals decided that in order to convict Flanagan of attempted murder, the State had to prove he:
    a. had specific intent to kill when he fired his gun.
    b. wanted to seriously injure another person when he fired his gun.
    c. decided he didn't care if his conduct was dangerous or reckless.
    d. was grossly negligent with his weapon.

5. A person cannot be convicted of criminal attempt if the crime was actually committed.
    a. True
    b. False

Section 2: CONSPIRACY

OVERVIEW

In Texas, criminal conspiracies involve agreements to commit only felonies and the agreement must be accompanied by an overt act in pursuance of the agreement. The overt act need not be of a criminal nature.

Section 15.02 of the Texas Penal Code

(a) A person commits criminal conspiracy if, with intent that a felony be committed:

(1) he agrees with one or more persons that they or one or more of them engage in conduct that would constitute the offense; and

(2) he or one or more of them performs an overt act in pursuance of the agreement.

(b) An agreement constituting a conspiracy may be inferred from acts of the parties.

CASES

1. *Williams v. State*, 646 S.W.2d 221 (Tex. Crim. App. 1984)
Section 15.01 of the Texas Penal Code

This is an important case defining the law of conspiracy in Texas. The Dallas police asked Steve Jennings, Williams' alleged coconspirator, to cultivate a friendship with the Williams and report any suspicious activity to them. Williams asked Jennings if he wanted to make some money by setting up a kidnapping of the son of the Williams' former employer. The ransom money would be split between them. Jennings agreed and details of the kidnapping were discussed further. Two days before the crime was to occur, Jennings contacted the police. The police wired Jennings for sound, and he met with the Williams. Williams was arrested after several conversations that he had with Jennings were recorded. At the trial, Jennings testified he never intended to go along with the kidnapping and was only acting as an agent for the police.

The Texas Court of Criminal Appeals examined whether there really was an agreement between the appellant Williams and Jennings to commit a crime. An agreement involves a union between two or more minds in a thing to be done. In this case, the court concluded there was no meeting of the minds because there was no criminal intent in the minds of both individuals. The court rejected the State's argument that section 15.02 was meant to adopt an entirely unilateral approach with each person's culpability determined without regard to the culpability of the alleged coconspirators. The Court of Criminal Appeals noted that the reason conspiring to commit a felony is defined by statute as a separate crime is to attack the special danger that criminal combinations pose to society. Without such a combination based on a mutual agreement, there is no conspiracy.

The unilateral approach the State was referring to in *Williams* involved was based on:

Section 15.02(c) of the Texas Penal Code

(c) It is no defense to prosecution for criminal conspiracy that:

(1) one or more of the coconspirators is not criminally responsible for the object offense;

(2) one or more of the coconspirators has been acquitted, so long as two or more coconspirators have not been acquitted;

(3) one or more of the coconspirators has not been prosecuted or convicted, has been convicted of a different offense, or is immune from prosecution;

(4) the actor belongs to a class of persons that by definition of the object offense is legally incapable of committing the object offense in an individual capacity; or

(5) the object offense was actually committed.

The court refused to waive what it thought was the most essential requirement of conspiracy: a mutual and actual agreement to commit a felony. The Texas position is contrary to most states where conspiracy can be a unilateral crime.

2. *Butler v. State*, 758 S.W.2d 856 (Tex. App. - Houston [14th Dist.] 1988)

Section 15.02 of the Texas Penal Code and Article 38.14 of the Texas Code of Criminal Procedure

A common issue in many conspiracy, solicitation, and engaging in organized crime cases is raised when one of the coconspirators testifies against his or her "colleagues" in crime.

Article 38.14 of the Texas Code of Criminal Procedure

A conviction cannot be had upon the testimony of an accomplice unless corroborated by other evidence tending to connect the defendant with the offense committed; and the corroboration is not sufficient if it merely shows the commission of the offense.

Texas courts have interpreted article 38.14 to mean that the testimony of an accomplice witness is sufficiently corroborated if, after eliminating that testimony from consideration, there is evidence that *tends to connect* the defendant with the crime. The corroborating evidence, however, does not need to link the defendant directly to the crime or be sufficient itself to establish guilt.

In *Butler v. State*, the issue before the appeals court was the testimony of Dale Cureton against his coconspirator Jimmie Butler. While driving his car, Cureton was stopped by police who found guns, ammunition, gloves and masks in his vehicle. He and his companion told police Butler hired them to kill his ex-wife's husband, and the equipment in the car was for that purpose. Cureton agreed to be wired and cooperated with the police. On tape he discussed the murder plans with Butler. Cureton testified at the trial when the taped conversations were introduced. Butler argued on appeal that Cureton's testimony had not been sufficiently corroborated under article 38.14. The court disagreed and found that Cureton's testimony was amply corroborated by the discovery of the guns and equipment, the testimony of four other persons to whom Butler had mentioned his plans, and his own comments on tape.

Section 3: SOLICITATION

OVERVIEW

Section 15.03 of the Texas Penal Code

(a) A person commits an offense if, with intent that a capital felony or felony of the first degree be committed, he requests, commands, or attempts to induce another to engage in specific conduct that, under the circumstances surrounding his conduct as the actor believes them to be, would constitute the felony or make the other a party to its commission.

Unlike conspiracy and attempt law, there is no requirement that an overt act be committed. The criminal mens rea requires the intent to commit a capital felony or a felony of the first degree. Section 15.03(b) provides that a person cannot be convicted of solicitation on the uncorroborated testimony of the person solicited. There must be evidence strongly corroborative of the solicitation and the solicitor's intent that the person he solicited actually commit the crime. By setting high standards of proof, the State hopes to weed out cases involving set-ups and to tap only genuine criminal activity, not just wishful, half-hearted thinking. The offense of solicitation is complete once a request or inducement is *unilaterally* presented. Unlike conspiracy crimes, there is no requirement of a meeting of the minds.

Section 15.031 makes it a separate offense to solicit a minor to commit a crime listed in Section 3g(a)(1) of Article 42.12 of the Texas Code of Criminal Procedure. For the purposes of Section 15.031, a minor is under 17 years old. "Section 3(g)" offenses include: capital murder, murder, indecency with a child, aggravated kidnapping, aggravated sexual assault, aggravated robbery, sexual assault, and certain drug offenses under the Texas Health and Safety Code. As a group, these offenses have been labeled "3(g) offenses" and appear as a group throughout the Code of Criminal Procedure. Offenders convicted of a crime included in this group earn reduced good time in prison and have limited opportunities available for receiving probated sentences. The 76th Texas legislature further amended Section 15.031 to make it a crime to solicit a minor to commit a sexual performance with another child. The statute's goal is to provide severe and certain punishment for adults who use minors to commit crimes on their behalf or for their enjoyment.

A very recent addition to the arsenal of solicitation crimes in Texas is Section 71.022. The new law makes it a crime to knowingly cause, enable, encourage, recruit, or solicit a person to become a member of a criminal street gang if a condition of initiation, admission or membership requires that person to commit any crime that is a Class A misdemeanor or felony. The term "criminal street gang" is defined as three or more persons that have a common identifying sign, symbol, or leadership and who continuously engage in committing crime. Section 71.022 is located in the chapter of the penal code reserved for organized crime and addresses many of the same concerns that caused the legislature to adopt the organized crime statute.

Section 4: ENGAGING IN ORGANIZED CRIMINAL ACTIVITY

OVERVIEW

The Texas statute that addresses engaging in organized criminal activities is an important companion statute to criminal conspiracy under section 15.02. In many ways it is far more comprehensive and sweeping than Section 15.02.

Section 71.02 of the Texas Penal Code
(a) A person commits an offense if, with intent to establish, maintain, or participate in a combination or in the profits of a combination or as a member of a criminal street gang, he commits or conspires to commit one or more of the following:
(1) murder, capital murder, arson, aggravated robbery, robbery, burglary, theft, aggravated kidnapping, kidnapping, aggravated assault, aggravated sexual assault, sexual assault, forgery, deadly conduct, assault punishable as a Class A misdemeanor, burglary of a motor vehicle, or unauthorized use of a motor vehicle;
(2) any gambling offenses punishable as a Class A misdemeanor;
(3) promotion of prostitution, aggravated promotion of prostitution, or compelling prostitution;
(4) unlawful manufacture, transportation, repair, or sale of firearms or prohibited weapons;
(5) unlawful manufacture, delivery, dispensation, or distribution of a controlled substance or dangerous drug, or unlawful possession of a controlled substance or dangerous drug through forgery, fraud, misrepresentation, or deception;
(6) any unlawful wholesale promotion or possession of any obscene material or obscene device with the intent to wholesale promote the same;
(7) any offense under Subchapter B, Chapter 43, depicting or involving conduct by or directed toward a child younger than 18 years of age;
(8) any felony offense under Chapter 32, Penal Code;
(9) any offense under Chapter 36, Penal Code;
(10) any offense under Chapter 34, Penal Code; or
(11) any offense under Section 37.11(a), Penal Code
(12) any offense under Chapter 20A.

Section 71.01 of the Texas Penal Code provides key definitions:
(a) "Combination" means three or more persons who collaborate in carrying on criminal activities, although:
(1) participants may not know each other's identity;
(2) membership in the combination may change from time to time; and
(3) participants may stand in a wholesaler-retailer or other arm's length relationship in illicit distribution operations.
(4) "Conspire to commit" means that a person agrees with one or more persons that they or one or more of them engage in conduct that would constitute the offense and that person and one or more of them perform an overt act in pursuance of the agreement. An agreement constituting conspiring to commit may be inferred from the acts of the parties.

(a) "Profits" means property constituting or derived from any proceeds obtained, directly or indirectly, from an offense listed in Section 71.02.
(b) "Criminal street gang" means three or more persons having a common identifying sign or symbol or an identifiable leadership who continuously or regularly associate in the commission of criminal activities.

Section 71.03 states that it is no defense to prosecution under section 71.02 that:
(1) one or more members of the combination are not criminally responsible for the object offense;
(2) one or more members of the combination have been acquitted, have not been prosecuted or convicted, have been convicted of a different offense, or are immune from prosecution;
(3) a person has been charged with, acquitted, or convicted of any offense listed in Subsection (a) of Section 71.02; or
(4) once the initial combination of three or more persons is formed there is a change in the number or identity of persons in the combination as long as two or more persons remain in the combination and are involved in a continuing course of conduct constituting an offense under this chapter.

The Legislature carefully worded the statute to withstand challenges to its constitutionality, in particular void-for-vagueness or overbreath. The Legislature has amended it several times to clarify certain terms and concepts and to strengthen its provisions. The original statute required a combination of five persons. That number has been reduced to three.

CASES

1. *Lucario v. State*, 677 S.W.2d 693, 700 (Tex. App. - Houston [1 Dist.] 1984)
Section 71.02 of the Texas Penal Code

Texas' courts have also been instrumental in clarifying the various provisions of Section 71.02. The statute's constitutionality was upheld in the *Lucario* case. Lucario was convicted of engaging in organized criminal activity as a result of his participation in an aggravated robbery ring. He complained that the mens rea element of Section 71.02 fails to give sufficient notice of what conduct is criminal and fails to require that a person be aware that his activities are aiding an illegal combination. This allows people to be prosecuted who do not realize they are involved in illegal conduct. The court rejected his arguments and wrote:

> The provisions concerning "collaboration in carrying on" would only apply if the requisite intent under the statute was established and would not include the lawful activity of a fiduciary or employee of a combination where the requisite intent is absent. Furthermore, the definition of a combination requires that the group of persons involved "collaborate" in carrying on a criminal activity. The scienter element of the offense requires that a person intend to establish, maintain, or participate in a group which collaborates in carrying on a criminal activity. ... The scienter element of the statute requires that the actor know of the criminal activity of the group.

2. *Nguyen v. State*, 1 S.W.3d 694 (Tex. Crim. App. 1999)
Section 71.02 of the Texas Penal Code

The actus reus of engaging in organized crime is collaborating to carry on criminal activity. The Court of Criminal Appeals decided a recent case that refined the meaning of the actus reus requirement. A tragic set of circumstances led to Nguyen's conviction for murder and engaging in organized criminal activity under Section 71.02 of the Penal Code. Nguyen and a group of friends attended a party sponsored by the Asian Cultural Committee on the University of Texas campus. After the party they went to an Austin restaurant where a group four young men, including Jose de la Morena, were eating after attending a gathering of the UT Latin American Student Association. A woman from Nguyen's group walked past Morena's table when Morena allegedly asked her to show her nipples. She reported the remark to her friends. Before departing the restaurant, Nguyen and several of his group confronted Morena and demanded he step outside to fight. The police arrived and asked Nguyen and his friends to leave and Morena and his friends to leave as soon as their meal was finished. Nguyen left and with three other males and retrieved a semi-automatic rifle from his apartment. They returned to the restaurant to scare Morena. As Morena and his friends were leaving, Nguyen fired his rifle, shot and killed Morena and injured another man.

Nguyen argued that the State inappropriately charged him under Section 71.02 because he and his friends only collaborated to commit a single crime. He maintained that the language "collaborating in carrying on criminal activities" was meant to address activities that continue over time and involve more than a single act. The Court of Criminal Appeals agreed with Nguyen and his conviction under Section 71.02 was overturned. The court was careful to note that a conviction under Section 71.02 can rest on only one criminal offense as long as there is proof of intent to carry on additional criminal activities. A conviction can also result if none of the enumerated offenses were committed as long as offender participated in committing an overt act.

3. *Shears v. State*, 895 S.W.2d 456 (Tex. App.- Tyler 1995)
Section 71.02 of the Texas Penal Code

Section 71.02 has been used extensively in prosecuting drug-related offenses involving organized distribution networks. It has also been used in connection with loosely knit networks of sellers and wholesalers. In the *Shears* case, appellant was convicted of engaging in organized criminal activity by conspiring to commit the offense of unlawful delivery of a controlled substance. Police suspected Shears and others of selling crack cocaine from an apartment. They began a covert operation, videotaped the apartment complex, noting the cars coming and going, dates, and times. Finally, three officers went under cover and purchased cocaine from of the various sellers operating out of the same apartment, including Shears. Appellant argued there was insufficient evidence to show that he and the others agreed to work within a combination to sell drugs. The activities at the apartment were too loosely knit to comprise a combination. In fact, the dealers were competing against each other for profits.

The court was not persuaded. The taped video showed an extensive and busy drug distribution operation at the apartment. Shear actively participated in that operation, approaching cars, make exchanges, and going back and forth from the apartment delivering the drugs. Informants testified at trial that Shears sold drugs to make his living. Based on circumstantial evidence, the court ruled there were sufficient facts to establish a combination under the law.

4. *Caddell v. State*, 902 S.W.2d 554 (Tex. App. - Tyler 1995)
Section 71.02 of the Texas Penal Code

A similar set of circumstances occurred in the *Caddell* case. Caddell was convicted of engaging in organized activity to distribute drugs. He sold drugs in an open field in Tyler, Texas called the "Graveyard." Police videotapes documented large numbers of drug transactions occurring there on a daily basis. Caddell sold drugs to several undercover police officers. He argued there was no criminal combination. The court pointed to the existence of a loosely organized drug market that evidenced a tacit agreement among the sellers. The sales took place in a common area, at a common time, using a common method, from the practice of selling for others and giving warnings when the police entered the area. There was a common "burn barrel," where contraband would be thrown and destroyed in the event of a raid. The court concluded that the jury could rationally decide these were not discreet, unrelated drug transactions, but constituted a criminal collaboration with a common purpose.

REVIEW

6. Dick decided to rob the Megabucks Bank and approached Hank and Oscar for their participation. They agreed and the planning began. Hank purchased the ski masks, tape, and rope. Oscar bought the weapons. Before Dick could reconnoiter the bank (his assignment) and scope out the right time of day and escape route, the police found out about their plans. Oscar told his wife who went to the police. The three had never been involved together in criminal activity. This was their first group effort. The D.A. has to decide on the charges. He starts with Dick, the acknowledged leader and inspiration for the group.
    a. Dick can be charged with engaging in organized criminal activity under Section 71.02.
    b. Dick cannot be charged with a crime under Section 71.02 and the D.A. should consider Section 15.02.
    c. Dick can be charged under Sections 15.02 and 71.02.
    d. Dick is not guilty of a crime since none was attempted.

7. After discovering that his wife had reported him to the authorities for his role in the Megabucks Bank scheme, Oscar decided to bump off his wife. Before going to prison, he contacted a friend and together they planned. Oscar wrote up a map with detailed directions and instructions about how the crime should be committed. Unfortunately, the friend turned out to be an undercover police officer. Can the D.A. charge Oscar with conspiracy?
    a. Yes, he reached an agreement with the officer.
    b. Yes, he reached an agreement and performed an overt act in furtherance of it.
    c. No, he cannot conspire with a police officer.
    d. No, because the officer also has to commit an overt act.

8. Hank also decided to bump off Oscar's wife, who he never particularly liked. He contacted a "real" friend and requested he commit the job. The friend refused because Hank could only pay $1000. The friend wanted at least $5000. Hank figured he wouldn't find a decent murderer for $1000, so he dropped the idea. Hank's friend was a blabbermouth and told about Hank's offer. Word filtered back to the police who arrested Hank for criminal solicitation. There was no other evidence but the friend's testimony. Can he be charged with the crime?
    a. Yes, it does not matter that the person he solicited refused.
    b. No, no overt acts were committed.
    c. No, there is no evidence to corroborate the friend's testimony.
    d. Yes, because the friend had no ax to grind against Hank, otherwise he would have gone directly to the police.

9. Dick decided to take matters into his own hands and wipe out Oscar's wife once and for all. He decided to do the job himself. He watched Oscar's house and noted the wife's coming and goings. He procured a weapon. He followed her around town and got to know her schedule. He was ready to jump her one morning as she walked to her car in the parking lot of the apartment complex. It was 5 a.m. and no one was watching, or so he thought. Just as he was about to dash at her, he noticed she had a large German shepherd dog by her side. Dick stopped in his tracks. He was dressed in army fatigues and had his gun pulled. A neighbor watched the entire scene from her balcony and called the police who got there before Dick could make a getaway. Oscar's wife never saw Dick coming.
    a. Dick is guilty of attempted murder.
    b. Dick is just short of being guilty of attempted murder because he is still in the mere preparation stage.
    c. Dick abandoned the attack. He's not guilty of anything, just lucky.
    d. Dick is guilty of harassing Oscar's wife.

10. A person cannot be convicted of criminal solicitation if the felony was actually committed.
    a. True
    b. False

11. If Dick and Oscar are acquitted of criminal conspiracy in the scenario above, Hank cannot be convicted of criminal conspiracy.
    a. True
    b. False

12. It is necessary that the participants to a combination engaging in organized crime know each other's identity.
    a. True
    b. False

13. In a case under Section 71.02 of the Texas Penal Code, a participant in the combination does not have to commit an overt act themselves in order to be found guilty under that statute.
    a. True
    b. False

14. In a case under Section 71.02, at least how many people must commit overt acts for a participant to be found guilty?
    a. at least 4
    b. at least 1 - the participant who has been charged
    c. at least 2 - one of whom must be the participant being charged
    d. at least 1- any one, not necessarily the participant charged

FINAL COMMENTS ON INCHOATE CRIMES

Section 15.04 of the Texas Penal Code allows an accused to plead a renunciation defense to prosecution for any of the crimes charged under Section 15.01. The accused must show that he or she voluntarily and completely renounced their criminal objective, thereby avoiding the commission of the crime or, if that was not possible, took affirmative action to prevent its commission. Renunciation is not voluntary if it was motivated by circumstances that were not present or apparent at the beginning of the criminal project that would have increased the probability of detection or apprehension or would make it more difficult to accomplish the objective. Renunciation also does not cover those instances when the perpetrator decides to postpone the crime until another time or with another victim. As an affirmative defense, the Penal Code Section 2.04 requires that the defendant prove renunciation by a preponderance of the evidence.

Chapter Seven

Defenses to Criminal Liability: Justifications

INTRODUCTION

Defenses to criminal charges raise some of the most controversial questions of law and often implicate broader public policy concerns. Chapter Seven examines defenses to criminal charges in the form of justifications, concentrating on two major justification defenses:

1) self-defense, including all the variations of defense of third parties and defenses of property, and
2) the necessity or choice of evils defense.

In the case of self-defense, how do we vigorously protect a citizen's right to self-defense without encouraging a spirit of vigilante justice? To what extent do we want citizens to defend their property? Is it always better to kill the intruder? Is it safe for property owners to use force to defend their property? Texas has a reputation for liberally applying the right to defend oneself and one's property. Is that reputation deserved?

In certain fact situations, the necessity of evils defense is related to a defense of coercion discussed in Chapter Eight. This chapter will look at the narrow interpretation the courts have placed on the necessity defense. A necessity defense can also involve a court in a tough decision that has ramifications beyond the facts of an individual case.

Section 1: SELF-DEFENSE

OVERVIEW

Because self-defense raises many issues, this section of Chapter Seven is divided into several distinct subject matter areas. Self-defense statutes are lengthy and convoluted, so they have been rearranged from the Penal Code format to make for easier reading. Many cases present more than one issue for a court to consider and those issues may be difficult to separate and often overlap. Using deadly force to defend yourself sometimes also involves the right to defend property or a third person.

Section 9.31(a) of the Texas Penal Code

(a) Except as provided in Subsection (b), a person is justified in using force against another when and to the degree he reasonably believes the force is immediately necessary to protect himself against the other's use or attempted use of unlawful force.

The Penal Code places specific limits on the use of self-defense that apply to both non-deadly and deadly uses of force.

Section 9.31(b) of the Texas Penal Code

(b) The use of force against another is not justified:

(1) in response to verbal provocation alone;

(2) to resist an arrest or search that the actor knows is being made by a peace officer, or by a person acting in the officer's presence and at his direction, even though the arrest or search is unlawful, unless the resistance is justified under Subsection (c);

(3) if the actor consented to the exact force used or attempted by the other;

(4) if the actor provoked the other's use or attempted use of unlawful force, unless:

(A) the actor abandons the encounter, or clearly communicates to the other his intent to do so reasonably believing he cannot safely abandon the encounter; and

(B) the other nevertheless continues or attempts to use unlawful force against the actor; or

(5) if the actor sought an explanation from or discussion with the other person concerning the actor's differences with the other person while the actor was:

(A) carrying a weapon in violation of Section 46.02; or

(B) possessing or transporting a weapon in violation of Section 46.05.

The circumstances under which deadly force is permissible in defense of a person are defined in a separate section of the Penal Code.

Section 9.32 of the Texas Penal Code

(a) A person is justified in using deadly force against another:

(1) if he would be justified in using force against the other under Section 9.31;

(2) if a reasonable person in the actor's situation would not have retreated; and

(3) when and to the degree he reasonably believes the deadly force is immediately necessary:

(A) to protect himself against the other's use or attempted use of unlawful deadly force; or

(B) to prevent the other's imminent commission of aggravated kidnapping, murder, sexual assault, aggravated sexual assault, robbery, or aggravated robbery.

(b) The requirements imposed by Subsection (a)(2) does not apply to an actor who uses force against a person who is at the time of the use of force committing an offense of unlawful entry in the habitation of the actor.

Section 2.03 of the Penal Code places the burden of proof on the self-defense issue on the State. Once a defendant argues self-defense, defense of a third person or defense of property, the State's job is to disprove that claim beyond a reasonable doubt. This means the court must charge the jury that if the State has not shown beyond a reasonable doubt that the defendant was not acting in self-defense, they should decide for acquittal.

If a defendant raises any proof during trial that supports his claim of self-defense, he is entitled to a jury instruction on the issue. A jury instruction explains to the jury what the law is in Texas about a specific matter and instructs the members of the jury to apply the law to the particular facts of the case they are considering. It does not matter whether the evidence supporting the claim is strong or weak. The credibility of the evidence or whether it conflicted with other evidence also does not matter. Those are issues for a jury to weigh. The defendant does not even have to testify during the trial in order for there to be enough evidence that he or she acted in self-defense.

CASES

1. *Ogas v. State*, 655 S.W.2d 322 (Tex. App. - Amarillo 1983)
Sections 1.07(42) and 9.31 of the Texas Penal Code

Using deadly force is only justified if a defendant reasonably believed deadly force was immediately necessary to protect himself against the actual or attempted use of unlawful deadly force or to prevent the commission of certain violent crimes. Section 1.07(42) of the Texas Penal Code defines "reasonable belief" as a belief that would be held by an ordinary and prudent person in the same circumstances as the defendant.

In *Ogas v. State*, the Amarillo court of appeals ruled that a blow to the face with an open or closed hand does not give rise to the use of deadly force. In that case, a pregnant woman shot a man after he slapped her. The court decided that non-deadly force might have been justified, but not deadly force. A slap to the face that did not threaten the fetus failed to support the claim Ogas reasonably feared death or serious bodily injury. In a similar case, *Molitor v. State*, 827 S.W.2d 512 (Tex. App. - Austin 1992), without other threats, a blow to the head struck by a hand did not convince the Austin appeals court that Molitor reasonably believed deadly force was necessary.

2. *Werner v. State,* 711 S.W.2d 639 (Tex Crim. App. 1986)
Sections 1.07(42) and 9.31 of the Texas Penal Code

Texas case law suggests that courts should use an objective standard to determine whether a person was reasonable in using deadly force in self-defense. Under an objective standard, the defendant is judged by what a reasonable person in the same or similar circumstances would have believed was necessary. In contrast to the objective standard is the subjective standard, which focuses on what the defendant honestly believed at the time was necessary for protection.

In recent years, the Texas Court of Criminal Appeals has been somewhat inconsistent in explaining the reasonableness standard. Several cases decided in the 1970s set forth a subjective standard. They held that reasonableness should be judged from the accused person's standpoint at the instant he responds to an attack. In *Valentine v. State*, 587 S.W.2d 399 (Tex Crim. App. 1979), however, the court moved to an objective standard to affirm a wife's manslaughter conviction against a claim of self-defense. In that case, Valentine shot and killed her husband through the locked door of their trailer home. He had been pounding on the door, shouting obscenities, and threatening to kill her. He also had a history of violence toward her. The court ruled the subjective standard was not applicable. *Valentine*, however, was followed by several cases that seemed to return to the subjective approach.

It now appears the Court of Criminal Appeals has moved to a blend of the two standards. In *Werner*, the court held that determining whether deadly force was justifiable requires evaluating 1) whether the defendant acted on appearances from his own standpoint in deciding whether force was immediately necessary, and 2) whether an ordinary prudent person in the defendant's situation would have retreated. In *Werner*, the defendant witnessed the victim run into a parked car. When the victim did not stop, Werner pursued him. He could not see the victim's hands and could not tell if he was carrying a weapon. Werner said he feared for his life and shot the victim. Other recent self-defense cases also evaluate reasonableness by viewing the circumstances from the defendant's standpoint at the time while also applying a prudent/reasonable person approach.

Texas case law is clear that a person has the right to defend herself against apparent danger to the same extent as actual danger. It does not matter that the defendant's evaluation of the danger was incorrect, as long as the perception of danger was reasonable.

3. *Aguilar v. State*, 914 S.W.2d 649 (Tex. App. - Texarkana 1996)
Section 9.31(c) of the Texas Penal Code

An important limitation on self-defense involves searches and arrests conducted by law enforcement officers or their agents. There is no right to self-defense during an arrest or search even if the officer is acting unlawfully. The only exception is if the officer is using excessive force before the defendant offers any resistance. Of course, as in all self-defense situations, the defendant must have reasonably believed that self-defense was immediately necessary. This limitation also requires the defendant know that the person attempting to arrest or search him is a peace officer or an agent of an officer.

Section 9.31(c) of the Texas Penal Code
(c) The use of force to resist arrest or search is justified:
(1) if, before the actor offers any resistance, the peace officer (or person acting at his direction) uses or attempts to use greater force than necessary to make the arrest or search; and
(2) when and to the degree the actor reasonably believes the force is immediately necessary to protect himself against the peace officer's (or other person's) use or attempted use of greater force than necessary.

The *Aguilar* case raised the issue of self-defense against an officer's excessive use of force. Aguilar was arguing with his girlfriend. Officers saw him hanging from the front door of her car as she was driving out of a restaurant parking lot. They stopped the car to question the couple. The officers testified that Aguilar appeared intoxicated, became loud and belligerent, pulled away to avoid being handcuffed and struck one of the officers. They shot pepper spray in his face to subdue him. At his trial for resisting arrest, Aguilar's girlfriend testified he was not belligerent and was thrown to the ground and sprayed for no reason. The trial court refused to instruct the jury on the right of self-defense against a police officer who uses excessive force. The Court of Appeals reversed Aguilar's conviction. Evidence was introduced at trial suggesting the officers had used excessive force. The credibility of the evidence was for the jury to decide, ruled the appeals court, and an instruction on self-defense was warranted.

4. *Evans v. State*, 876 S.W.2d 459 (Tex. App. - Texarkana 1994)
Section 9.31(c) of the Texas Penal Code

In contrast to *Aguilar* is the Evans case. Evans was convicted of aggravated assault of a police officer. Like *Aguilar,* the trial court refused to instruct the jury on self-defense. Evans claimed that an officer stopped him for an expired inspection sticker as he pulled up to his residence. He refused to produce proof of insurance, arguing he was on private property and did not have to cooperate with the police. The officer wrote several tickets, which Evans refused to accept. When the officer attempted to arrest him, he walked toward his front door. The officer grabbed Evans' arm to try to pin it against his back. Evans broke free and struck the officer with his elbow. The two fell to the ground and broke into a fistfight. In this case, the appellate court did not reverse and order jury instructions on self-defense because the evidence did not raise self-defense as a real issue. The officer's attempt to pin Evans' arm behind his back was justified because Evans refused arrest. There was no evidence the officer used or attempted to use excessive force.

In both *Aguilar* and *Evans*, the appellants challenged the force used by police. In the *Aguilar* case, there was eyewitness testimony that the police were excessive. It was for the jury to decide the credibility of this testimony. In *Evans*, the evidence was the defendant's version of events versus the officer's version. Evans admitted trying to avoid arrest and refusing the tickets. The officer had a lawful right to use some force to arrest him. The facts were not strong enough for the court to reverse his conviction.

5. *Matthews v. State*, 708 S.W.2d 835 (Tex Crim. App. 1986)
Section 9.31(b)(4) of the Texas Penal Code

Probably the most important limitation on self-defense is found in Section 9.31(b)(4), which provides that self-defense is not available to a defendant who provoked the victim into using or attempting to use unlawful force. Known as the "provoking the difficulty" defense, a trial judge will charge the jury on provoking the difficulty if:

(1) self-defense is an issue in the case;
(2) there are facts in evidence showing the victim made the first attack against the defendant; and
(3) there are facts in evidence showing the defendant did some act or used words intended to and calculated to bring on the difficulty in order to have a pretext for injuring the victim.

A defendant can provoke the difficulty through words alone. It is not necessary to show the defendant used force or a threat of force in order to decide the defendant provoked the victim into a first attack. Before a judge can inform the jury about the provoking the difficulty limitation, however, there must be some evidence the defendant intended to provoke. If he or she did not intend to provoke the victim into attacking, their right to defend themselves is not limited.

Matthews was a 29-year old man convicted of murdering a 75-year old man. The victim was a realtor who was negotiating a land sale to Matthews. Matthews testified that he was arguing with the victim about the sale price when the victim pulled out a gun, pointed it at him, and ordered him to leave his office. Matthews lost his head and grabbed the gun away from the realtor. He then pulled out his knife and stabbed the realtor to death. Matthews argued he acted in self-defense, that he had never intended to provoke an altercation although his words may have angered the realtor into displaying a weapon. After examining all the evidence, the court found there was reason to believe that Matthews intended to provoke the victim into attacking him first. Matthews stole $500 from the victim after he killed him, and there was evidence he was having financial problems. There was also reason to doubt whether Matthews was serious about purchasing the land the victim showed him. The court concluded that the jury should be advised about the provoking the difficult limitation and permitted to evaluate the facts.

6. *Thomas V. State*, 750 S.W.2d 324, 325 (Tex. App. – Dallas 1988)
Section 9.31(b)(4) of the Texas Penal Code

Sometimes it is difficult to know who provoked whom. According to Thomas's testimony, every family member was armed with a gun and more than willing to waive them about. John Thomas was not getting along well with his wife Shirley and his mother-in-law. Shirley Thomas decided to leave John and was packing up her belongings with the help of her mother and her daughter from a previous marriage. John testified at his trial for involuntary manslaughter that his mother-in-law cursed him and told him they were taking as much as they could from the house. At one point his stepdaughter pulled a gun on him and said she had wanted to kill him for a long time and shot at him. He also testified that his mother-in-law had shot at him with a shotgun on a previous occasion. The court's opinion goes on:

> He [appellant] ran, got his gun from under the mattress of the bed and looked around to shoot at the stepdaughter, but she had left the room. He then stated he was going to put his gun back but saw his mother-in-law sitting in a chair in another part of the same room. He testified that he knew she always carried a gun. She cursed at him again and accused him of desiring to shoot the stepdaughter, and he then observed her reaching down to pick up a foil package. He said he knew that the package contained a gun so he fired a shot at Mrs. Johnson's hands, although he did not see a gun in her hand. At this point, his wife Shirley came to the middle of the room and exclaimed "you shot my mama and I'll kill you" and reached into her bra where he believed she had a gun. Appellant testified that he leaped toward her to get the gun from her and during the struggle she was shot and killed. Although he was "almost positive" she had a gun, he never saw one nor was one found.

Thomas argued self-defense and contested the judge's decision to issue a jury charge on provoking the difficulty. The appeals court decided there was enough evidence to issue a charge that limited Thomas's right of self-defense because there was reason to believe he had provoked the encounter with his wife by first shooting his mother-in-law. The jury could reach the conclusion that shooting his wife's mother was a pretext for attacking his wife.

In the *Thomas* case, you can see how confusing and convoluted some of these fact situations can get. With angry people yelling and cursing at each other, issues of provoking the difficulty can be hard to untangle. Judges may feel most comfortable issuing the provoking jury instruction and letting the jury decide.

The Common Law Right to Arm Oneself

If the trial judge limits a defendant's right to self-defense by giving the jury an instruction on provoking the difficulty, Texas case law requires the jury should also be instructed about the right to arm oneself. Under Texas common law, a person has the right to carry arms to the scene of a difficulty. In other words, a person's right to self-defense is not limited by the fact that he or she carried a weapon when they sought an explanation or attempted to resolve a problem with another person. The jury is advised of the "right to arm and seek an explanation" only if:

(1) there are facts in evidence that the defendant was armed when he sought a resolution; and
(2) the judge has instructed the jury that they must evaluate whether the defendant provoked the victim into attacking him first.

An instruction on the right to arm oneself is intended to make certain that a jury not conclude the defendant provoked the difficulty because he was armed when he went to meet with the victim. The common law in Texas protects the right of citizens to carry arms when they reasonably anticipate the potential need to defend themselves. In 1994, the legislature added a new provision to Section 9.31(b)(5) of the Penal Code that abolished the common law right to arm oneself if the defendant was carrying a weapon in violation of Section 46.02 of the Penal Code or possessing or transporting a weapon in violation of Section 46.05.

Duty to Retreat

One of the most drastic changes in the 1974 Texas Penal Code was the adoption of the duty to retreat in Section 9.32(2) which requires that before deadly force can be used in self-defense, the defendant must retreat if a reasonable person in his or her situation would have retreated. Retreat was not necessary to the right of self-defense in the old penal code. In fact, the old statute specifically provided that there was no duty to retreat.

The duty to retreat is triggered by Section 9.31 if a reasonable person in the defendant's situation would have retreated. The word "situation" means a combination of circumstances at a given moment. Whether the defendant had the ability and opportunity to retreat is considered a part of the circumstances. In 1995, the Legislature added new language to the duty to retreat provision. The new language removes the duty to retreat when the victim was unlawfully entering a habitation at the time the defendant used deadly force in self-defense. The change reflects the Legislature's concern that persons who use deadly force against house burglars not be subjected to a court inquiry as to whether they should have retreated from their homes. The new provision, however, does not eliminate the duty to retreat from one's own home under circumstances other than a burglary.

Family Violence

In 1991, the Texas Legislature enacted a new law to address domestic violence cases involving battered spouses who kill their spouse-abusers, amending. Up until that time, in murder and voluntary manslaughter cases where the defendant raised self-defense, the Penal Code allowed evidence to be introduced concerning the previous relationship between the accused and the deceased along with all the relevant circumstances surrounding the killing. The new amendment expanded Section 19.06 to allow evidence to be introduced that the accused had been the victim of family violence at the hands of the deceased, as defined by Section 71.01 of the Family Code. The amendment also allowed relevant expert testimony to be introduced concerning the condition of the accused's mind at the time of the offense, including facts and circumstances relating to family violence that were the basis of the expert's opinion. Since that time, the added protections have been removed from the Penal Code and placed in Article 38.36 of the Texas Code of Criminal Procedure.

CASE

***Fielding v. State*, 756 S.W.2d 309 (Tex Crim. App. 1988)**
Section 19.06 of the Texas Penal Code (now Article 38.36 of the Texas Code of Criminal Procedure

The 1991 legislation came on the heels of an important domestic violence case. The jury convicted Fielding of voluntary manslaughter for killing her husband. There were facts that showed Fielding had suffered severe physical and sexual sadomasochistic abuse at the hands of her gynecologist husband. On several occasions, he threatened to kill her if she disclosed his sexual practices and abuse. On the day of the killing, Fielding told her husband she had contacted a divorce attorney. He became furious and abusive. He pulled her inside when she tried to leave their home. He got a pistol and slammed it on the table. She grabbed the gun and started to walk away from him. When he came toward her, she killed him. The State argued that Fielding was in a jealous rage because she had learned her husband was having an affair.

The defense wanted to introduce testimony from a psychologist as to why Fielding remained in a physically and sexually abusive relationship. The trial court refused. The appeals court reversed Fielding's conviction and ruled it was error to refuse evidence that addressed why Fielding was afraid and how fear and impacted her behavior. The issue of her fear was important because it addressed the statute's requirement that a person reasonably believe it was immediately necessary to defend themselves. The Criminal Court of Appeals decision in the *Fielding* case played a major role in convincing the state legislature to change the law introducing evidence concerning family violence in murder prosecutions.

Self-Defense in the Punishment Phase

Criminal trials in Texas are bifurcated. The first part of a trial determines the guilt or innocence of the accused. If the accused is found guilty, the second part of the trial determines punishment. During the penalty phase, both the defendant and the State can offer evidence relevant to matters of sentencing, including evidence about the defendant's prior criminal history, general reputation in the community, character, and the circumstances surrounding the offense. If a trial judge decides during the guilt or innocence phase that a defendant's evidence on self-defense is not sufficient for a charge to the jury, evidence about self-defense can be brought up during the punishment phase to mitigate the severity of punishment.

Section 2: DEFENSE OF OTHERS

Much of the law defining the right to self-defense is applicable to defending a third person. There must be an actual or apparent attack on the other person, and the defendant must reasonably believe his intervention is immediately necessary. At issue, then, are the circumstances of the third person and the defendant's state of mind. It is not necessary that the defendant and the third person be related for the defense to be successful. There is no duty to retreat before using deadly force to defend another person. To require otherwise would mean leaving the other person to the assailant's attack.

Non-deadly and deadly force can be used by a defendant to protect a third person under section 9.33 if the defendant would have been justified in using force under sections 9.31 or 9.32 to protect himself against the force being used against the third person, and he believes that his intervention is immediately necessary to protect the third person.

Section 3: DEFENSE OF HOME AND PROPERTY

OVERVIEW

The right to use *non-deadly force* to protect your property is discussed in Section 9.41 of the Texas Penal Code.

Section 9.41 of the Texas Penal Code

(a) A person in lawful possession of land or tangible, moveable property is justified in using force against another when and to the degree the actor reasonably believes the force is immediately necessary to prevent or terminate the other's trespass on the land or unlawful interference with the property.

(b) A person unlawfully disposed of land or tangible, moveable property by another is justified in using force against the other when and to the degree the actor reasonably believes the force is immediately necessary to reenter the land or recover the property if the actor uses the force immediately or in fresh pursuit after the dispossession; and
(1) the actor reasonably believes the other had no claim of right when he dispossessed the actor; or
(2) the other accomplished the dispossession by using force, threat, or fraud against the actor.

To be justified in using *deadly force* to protect your real or personal property, you must first be justified in using non-deadly force under Section 9.41. Additional requirements include:

Sections 9.42(2) and (3) of the Texas Penal Code
(2) when and to the degree he reasonably believes the deadly force is immediately necessary:
(A) to prevent the other's imminent commission of arson, burglary, robbery, aggravated robbery, theft during the nighttime, or criminal mischief during the nighttime; or
(B) to prevent the other who is fleeing immediately after committing burglary, robbery, aggravated robbery, or theft during the nighttime from escaping with the property; and
(3) he reasonably believes that:
(A) the land or property cannot be protected or recovered by any other means; or
(B) the use of force other than deadly force to protect or recover the land or property would expose the actor or another to a substantial risk of death or serious bodily injury.

Notice the important differences between Subsections 9.42(2) and 9.42(3). Deadly force can be used to prevent arson or criminal mischief happening to your property during the nighttime, as long as the other provisions of Section 9.42 are also met. Deadly force, however, is not lawful to prevent someone who is fleeing *after* having committed arson or criminal mischief during the nighttime on your property.

Section 9.43 of the Penal Code also allows a person to use non-deadly or deadly force to protect the real or personal property of a third person if, under the circumstances as he believes them to be, he would be justified in using force to protect his own property; and he reasonably believes: 1) the third person requested him to protect the property, or 2) he has a legal duty to protect the property, or 3) the third person is the actor's spouse, parent, or child, resides with him or is under his care.

CASES

1. *Hernandez v. State*, 914 S.W.2d 218 (Tex. App.- El Paso 1996)

Section 9.42 of the Texas Penal Code

Danny Hernandez's home was the target of a drive-by shooting. Hernandez was a couple blocks away when it occurred, but he heard the shots and saw a white Monte Carlo speed away. Members of his family were in the home at the time of the shooting but no one was injured. Hernandez and six friends jumped into a car and went looking for the Monte Carlo. A high-speed chase ensued once they found it, and shots were exchanged. One of the occupants of the Monte Carlo died as a result of a gunshot wound to the head. Hernandez argued that he should have received a jury instruction on the issue of defense of property because his home had been shot at and he testified he was concerned that the perpetrators might return to harm his family. The appeals court, however, found there was no evidence that the Monte Carlo perpetrators were going to engage in additional criminal mischief, much less that it was imminent. Besides the drive-by shooting occurred prior to Hernandez's use of deadly force.

2. The Gerald Zeigler Case
Section 9.42 of the Texas Penal Code

In an article appearing on March 8, 1994, the *Houston Chronicle* reported a tragic story about a case of defense of property. A 13-year old boy was fatally shot by Gerald Zeigler, a frightened homeowner. Zeigler decided to plead guilty to murder and received ten years deferred adjudication with the further requirement that he attend two meetings with victims' groups. The story reported:

> The case against Zeigler, 45, began in the early morning hours of October 1990, when the disabled Air Force veteran said he heard someone in his truck around 3:30 a.m. and went out to investigate. He confronted Silby, who then threw a brick at Zeigler's head and fled on his 10-speed bicycle. Silby was shot in the back as he pedaled away.
>
> Prosecutor Connie Spence said evidence about what Silby was actually doing around Zeigler's truck is conflicting. They surmise that Silby ventured out early that morning to sneak out on a camping trip with a friend, she said. He passed by Zeigler's house on the way for a soft drink, then returned, stopping by Zeigler's truck for some unknown reason. The lit dome light inside suggested Silby may have tampered with the vehicle, she said. "But I don't know why he was there."
>
> Zeigler's attorney, Randy McDonald, said his client was already in a heightened state of fear when Silby rode up his drive. His Spring neighborhood was on edge because of repeated reports of prowlers and a Peeping Tom. Zeigler had climbed onto his roof on several nights to keep watch.
>
> Pointing out that the brick thrown by Silby could have been deadly, McDonald said Zeigler was protecting both his property and himself when he fired at the teen. Although Zeigler felt justified in his actions, McDonald said his client has been distraught ever since. "He has been unable to talk about it without breaking up," McDonald said. His client never realized he was shooting at a young boy, and even tried to resuscitate the boy.
>
> Zeigler entered the guilty plea to help "put it behind him, for his family and the boy's," McDonald said.

In addition to defining the right of self-defense and defense of property, Chapter 9 of the Penal Code defines situations in which the use of force is lawful as long as the person using force reasonably believes it is necessary and uses no more than is necessary:

- **Section 9.51** sanctions the use of force by a peace officer when it is reasonably necessary to make an arrest or conduct a search. Deadly force is justified when the officer reasonably believes the conduct for which an arrest is authorized involved the use or attempted use of deadly force or the officer reasonably believes there is a substantial risk that the arrestee will cause death or serious bodily injury to the officer or another person if the arrest is delayed.
- **Section 9.52** provides that the use of force including deadly force is justified to prevent the escape of an arrested person from custody.

- **Section 9.61** provides that the use of non-deadly force against a child less than 18 years old is justified by the child's parent or someone acting in loco parentis in order to discipline the child or promote his welfare.
- **Section 9.62** allows for the use of non-deadly force by persons having the care and supervision of a child for a special purpose or to maintain discipline, most notably teachers.
- **Section 9.63** permits persons who care for the mentally incompetent to use non-deadly force if it is necessary to promote the incompetent person's welfare, or if he is in an institution, to maintain discipline.

REVIEW

1. Barbara was sitting home reading a book and watching T.V. She heard someone at her backdoor and grabbed her revolver. She went to the door and ascertained that someone was trying to break in. She shot and killed the perpetrator. Barbara argues she was justified:
    a. Her defense will not be successful because the perpetrator was not yet in her home.
    b. She can argue self-defense and defense of property.
    c. She has a good self-defense claim, but no claim of defense of property.
    d. She can claim defense of property if she can show that she reasonably believed the perpetrator was armed.

2. Deadly force can be used in defense of property:
    a. only when the property is very valuable and can never be replaced.
    b. to prevent a person from the immediate commission of arson, burglary, robbery, aggravated robbery, theft or criminal mischief during the nighttime.
    c. there is never an occasion when deadly force can be used, only non-deadly force can be used to protect property.
    d. only if a sign is posted warning that deadly force will be used.

3. Jimmy was angry with Sid because of his arrest while at Sid's house and decided to get even. Since he did not want to destroy his chances of being a successful lawyer, Jimmy decided against physical violence. Instead, upon Sid's release on bail, Jimmy went to Sid's house one evening and slit the tires on Sid's classic Mustang convertible, which was parked in the driveway out front. Sid heard someone outside and retrieved his revolver. He opened the door just as Jimmy was running away from the scene and saw the damage to his car. Sid shot and killed Jimmy.
    a. Sid can claim defense of his property because Jimmy was committing criminal mischief at nighttime.
    b. Sid can claim self-defense because Jimmy was committing burglary.
    c. Sid cannot claim self-defense because the criminal mischief had already been completed and Jimmy was fleeing the scene.
    d. Sid cannot claim self-defense because he provoked Jimmy to get even with him.

4. Barbara decided to put up an electric fence around her home that would cause serious bodily injury to anyone who crossed it. Such a device is:
    a. legal in Texas.
    b. illegal in Texas because it is designed to cause serious harm.
    c. legal if Barbara posts a warning sign.
    d. illegal because such devices are never allowed, no matter how much harm they cause.

5. Your mother requested you watch her house and yard while she tours the world. You visit her home daily and do a check to make sure things are going well. During one of your daytime visits, you notice a person in the backyard, which was not fenced in, taking the patio furniture. You run after him with a baseball bat and knock him in the head. He lives:
    a. You can argue you were permitted to use force because your mother requested your help.
    b. You can argue you were defending yourself.
    c. You cannot use force to defend someone else's property.
    d. You cannot use what might have been deadly force to protect your mother's property.

6. While watching your mother's home, the prowler died as a result of your powerful blow:
    a. You were justified because you could have used the same deadly force to protect your own property. The prowler was committing theft.
    b. You were justified because there was no other way to recover the property.
    c. You were not justified because the crime was being committed during the daytime.
    d. You were not justified because deadly force to protect a third party's property is never allowed. Call the police!!

7. Jimmy was at the wrong place at the wrong time. As he was leaving the apartment of his fellow law school buddy, the police knocked down the door and ordered everyone to lie on the floor. Jimmy's buddy, unbeknownst to him, turned out to be a drug dealer. The police were asking few questions. Without search warrants or arrest warrants, they hauled Jimmy and his friend down to the station. Jimmy figured it was an illegal arrest and reviewed his options:
    a. Jimmy had the right to resist the officers with force because it was an unlawful arrest.
    b. Jimmy had the right to resist the officers because he was innocent.
    c. Both a and b
    d. Jimmy had no right to use force to resist the officers unless they used more force than was necessary to arrest him and Jimmy needed to protect himself.

8. Sid decided to pick a fight with Lloyd. Unfortunately for Sid, Lloyd was a black belt in karate. Sid was losing and held up a white handkerchief in surrender, yelling, "I quit, you win." Lloyd kept chopping away, ignoring the signs of surrender. Sid was forced to keep fighting. Lloyd testified at Sid's trial that Sid provoked the fight:
    a. Sid cannot argue self-defense because he started it.
    b. Sid cannot argue self-defense because he should have tried to leave the scene in an obvious retreat.
    c. Sid can argue that he tried to abandon the encounter and continued the fight in self-defense.
    d. Sid can argue self-defense if he first tried to talk through his disagreement with Lloyd.

9. In Texas, a person can carry a weapon when they visit their rival about their various disagreements, without jeopardizing their claim of self-defense in the event things did not go well:
    a. True
    b. False

Section 4: THE CHOICE - OF - EVILS DEFENSE

OVERVIEW

When the Texas Legislature revised the Penal Code in 1974, it included a specific provision recognizing the general necessity defense. Prior to 1974, Texas recognized the principle of the necessity defense in special, limited statutes: allowing abortion to save a mother's life, destruction of a house to save another house from fire and speeding for police, fire and emergency vehicles.

The 1974 statute and is largely based on the Model Penal Code statute.

Section 9.22 of the Texas Penal Code
Conduct is justified if:

(1) the actor reasonably believes the conduct is immediately necessary to avoid imminent harm;
(2) the desirability and urgency of avoiding the harm clearly outweigh, according to ordinary standards of reasonableness, the harm sought to be prevented by the law prohibiting the conduct; and
(3) A legislative purpose to exclude the justification claimed for the conduct does not otherwise plainly appear.

"Harm" is defined:

Section 1.07(25) of the Texas Penal Code
"Harm" means anything reasonably regarded as loss, disadvantage, or injury, including harm to another person in whose welfare the person affected is interested.

There is generally no limit on the type of harm to be avoided. The harm does not have to involve a personal threat to the individual claiming the necessity defense. The statute does not place a limit on the magnitude of the harm to be avoided. The law anticipates a balancing between the harm caused by the offense and the harm an actor was trying to escape. Texas courts have refused to recognize the defense in situations involving political protest, such as abortion clinic demonstrations that have led to disorderly conduct charges or campus demonstrations against university policies.

The necessity defense in Texas is very broad. The law does not require the actor be guilt-free of contributing to the emergency causing him to face a choice in order to claim the defense. It also does not deny the defense to people whose choices were based on reasonable and honest mistakes. Unlike some states, Texas does not limit the defense to only certain crimes. Even the offense of murder can be justified under the necessity defense.

CASES

1. *Bush v. State*, 624 S.W.2d 377 (Tex. App. - Dallas 1981)
Section 9.22 of the Texas Penal Code

The appellate court refused to allow the necessity defense to a woman who was convicted of driving while intoxicated. She claimed she feared her husband would physically harm her, and she had to leave the scene. Unfortunately, after she stopped for 15 minutes at her place of employment, she got on the road again. The court concluded that Bush failed to show that her conduct was reasonably necessary to avoid imminent harm.

2. *Johnson v. State*, 650 S.W.2d 414 (Tex Crim. App. 1983)
Section 9.22 of the Texas Penal Code

The Court of Criminal Appeals was faced with the claim that Johnson was justified in unlawfully carrying a weapon because he was in a high crime area. The court refused the necessity defense, finding that merely being in a high crime area does not constitute a reasonable belief that carrying a weapon is necessary to avoid imminent harm. On the other hand, in *Vasquez v. State*, 830 S.W.2d 948 (Tex Crim. App. 1992), the Court of Criminal Appeals ruled that unlawfully carrying a weapon may be justified under the necessity defense because the appellant was a former state prisoner who was in danger from other ex-inmates in the free world. There was evidence he had been attacked by former prisoners in a prison gang-related vendetta. In *Armstrong v. State*, 653 S.W.2d 810 (Tex Crim. App. 1983), Armstrong had been raped two weeks before being arrested for illegally carrying a handgun. The rapist had threatened her with death if she reported the crime and had been harassing her. The court ruled the jury should have been permitted to evaluate her necessity defense.

FINAL THOUGHTS ON JUSTIFICATION DEFENSES

The law makes it difficult to justify the commission of a crime for a good reason. Violence should be discouraged. Individuals should seek peaceful, non-violent resolutions to their conflicts. They should seek legal ways of resolving difficult situations. Nonetheless, self-defense and defense of property are often raised in criminal cases. A lot of violent crimes involve people who know each other. The facts get complicated. It is a close call as to who provoked whom, who attacked first, was more force used than was necessary to protect oneself, was the danger immediate. Juries are asked to ferret through conflicting evidence and make judgments that deeply affect the lives of defendants and victims. Juries reflect evolving social standards. We have come a long way from the Wild West and vigilante justice. Progress has been slow, however, because the decisions are not easy, and we can imagine the need to defend our loved ones or ourselves. Justification defenses strike us at a gut level.

Chapter Eight

Defenses to Liability:
Excuses

INTRODUCTION

Unlike justification defenses to criminal liability, excuse defenses do not claim the defendant had the right to engage in behavior that under other circumstances would be considered criminal. Excuse defenses claim that for certain clearly established legal reasons, the defendant's actions should be excused. Just as with the justification defenses discussed in Chapter Seven, the defendant must introduce sufficient evidence at trial to establish that the jury should be instructed to consider the excuse defense during its deliberations. This chapter will focus on several excuse defenses as defined by Texas law:

(1) the insanity defense;
(2) age;
(3) duress;
(4) intoxication;
(5) entrapment;
(6) mistake of fact;
(7) mistake of law

There are significant differences among state and federal penal codes in the area of excuse defenses. Like justification defenses, excuse defenses are controversial and have been the subject of significant public debate. In recent years state legislatures have been active in revamping insanity and entrapment defenses. There is considerable disagreement concerning the age at which individuals should be held responsible for their crimes in the adult criminal justice system. As you read the Texas statutes and case law, anticipate the future direction this area of law might go.

Section 1: THE INSANITY DEFENSE

OVERVIEW

According to Section 2.04 of the Texas Penal Code, insanity is an affirmative defense, which means the burden of persuasion is on the defendant to convince the jury of his or her claim by a preponderance of the evidence. As an affirmative defense, the defendant has both the burden of initially raising the defense and the burden of proving it by a preponderance of the evidence. Texas has adopted a strict M'Naghton insanity defense.

Section 8.01(a) of the Texas Penal Code

(a) It is an affirmative defense to prosecution that, at the time of the conduct charged, the actor, as a result of severe mental disease or defect, did not know that his conduct was wrong.

Prior to 1983, Section 8.01 also included an "irresistible impulse" test. It provided that if because of mental disease or defect, the accused did not know his conduct was wrong *or was unable to conform his behavior to the law*, he was entitled to be acquitted on the basis of insanity. In 1983, the Texas Legislature considered abolishing the defense entirely but decided against it after similar efforts failed for constitutional reasons in Florida, Wyoming, and Arizona. Instead, the legislature abolished the irresistible impulse test.

The issue of insanity is not strictly medical. It also generates both legal and ethical considerations. Texas courts have said that in deciding the ultimate issue of sanity, only the jury can bring together the non-medical components that must be considered to reach a final outcome. Otherwise, insanity would be decided in the hospitals and not in the courtrooms. A person may suffer from a mental disease or defect and not be legally exonerated for criminal acts. Stated the Texas Court of Criminal Appeals in *Graham v. State*, 566 S.W.2d 941, 952 (Tex. Crim. App. 1978):

> Ultimately the issue of insanity at the time of the offense excusing criminal responsibility lies in the province of the jury, not only as to the credibility of the witnesses and the weight of the evidence, but also as to the limits of the defense itself.

If an insanity defense is submitted to the jury, there are three possible verdicts: guilty, not guilty, or not guilty by reason of insanity. A defendant found not guilty by reason of insanity is acquitted of the offense. Under the Texas Code of Criminal Procedure, article 46.03, section 1(e), jurors are not permitted to have information about the legal meaning of the not guilty by reason of insanity verdict. They are not told what happens after such a verdict is rendered. The underlying notion of this restriction is once a jury decides to find a person not guilty by reason of insanity, its responsibility ends. The consequences of the verdict are not the jurors' concern. This provision of the Code of Criminal Procedure is different from provisions in several other jurisdictions where the defendant can request that the jury be informed about what happens after an insanity verdict is rendered. In those jurisdictions, jurors are advised about the civil commitment proceedings that follow such a verdict.

Even though the jury has the final say on the issue of insanity, mental health experts play a pivotal role in the adversarial system. Both the defendant and the State can call experts to testify about the defendant's mental health and his or her ability to know right from wrong. Psychiatrists not only present testimony, they help to determine before trial whether the insanity defense is viable and assist in preparing cross-examination of the other side's psychiatric expert. Because psychiatry is not an exact science, equally competent practitioners confronted with the same information often disagree in their diagnoses in an area that is complex and strange to lawyers and jurors alike.

An indigent defendant needs a psychiatrist as much as someone who can afford to retain one. The Texas Court of Criminal Appeals ruled in *De Freece v. State*, 848 S.W.2d 150 (Tex. Crim. App. 1993) that under the Texas Code of Criminal Procedure due process requires that indigent defendants are appointed a competent psychiatrist to provide technical assistance, help evaluate the strength of the defense, identify the weakness in the State's case, and testify and/or prepare counsel to cross-examine the opposing experts. The defendant is not entitled to a psychiatrist of his choice, or even one who believes he was insane at the time of the crime. Under the Texas Code of Criminal Procedure, the trial judge can also appoint a disinterested expert to examine the defendant. The appointment of a neutral expert, however, does not negate the defendant's right to have an expert appointed on his behalf.

Although experts are generally involved in insanity cases, the law is clear that lay witnesses can recount germane observations of a defendant and give an opinion on the defendant's sanity. In fact, lay opinion testimony alone can support a finding of insanity. In the same vein, if a defendant presents expert testimony on the insanity issue, the State does not have to counter with an expert. The State can counter with lay testimony, and the jury can reject the psychiatric testimony based on the lay testimony.

1. *Morris v. State*, 744 S.W.2d 290 (Tex. App. - Corpus Christi 1987)
Section 8.01of the Texas Penal Code

Morris was convicted of murdering Ramirez with a pistol in Corpus Christi outside of a bar around 1:00 a.m. Police found Morris hiding in a park nearby. He did not resist arrest and gave no signs he did not understand what was happening. Seven hours after the shooting, on June 7, Morris appeared before the magistrate. The magistrate later testified at Morris's trial that Morris was not incoherent when he was before him, but was alert and responded to questions. On July 3, Morris was placed in the jail's mental health ward. A jail rehabilitation counselor testified at Morris's trial that the other inmates were complaining they were afraid to be around Morris. In November, Morris was found incompetent to stand trial and spent seven months at Rusk State Mental Hospital. He was eventually released to stand trial for the murder.

The defense offered the testimony of several mental health experts about Morris's ability to know right from wrong as a result of a mental disease. They diagnosed him as suffering from schizophrenia at the time of the shooting and in their opinions did not know right from wrong. The State offered the testimony of several police officers and several witnesses who observed Morris before and after the murder. They all testified that in their opinion Morris was sane. The prosecution vigorously cross-examined Morris's expert witnesses, but did not offer any medical expert testimony of its own. The jury found Morris guilty. Morris argued on appeal that the verdict was against the weight of the evidence. Wrote the court:

> Insanity is not strictly a medical issue; it involves ethical and legal issues as well. One may be medically insane by reason of a mental disease or defect, yet not legally exonerated for criminal acts unless the condition causes an inability to distinguish right from wrong.... Expert witnesses may aid the jury in its determination, but it is not necessary for the State to present expert medical testimony that the accused was sane in order to counter the testimony provided by defense experts. Implicit jury findings that the accused was not legally insane at the time of the offense can be upheld even though no medical expert testified to that effect. ... A jury may accept or reject in whole or in part the opinion testimony of physicians, and can accept lay testimony over the testimony of experts.

*****

> Having reviewed the evidence in the light most favorable to the implicit finding of the jury that appellant was sane at the time of the commission of his offense, and after reviewing all the evidence concerning the insanity defense, we find that a rational trier of fact could have found that the appellant failed to prove his insanity defense by a preponderance of the evidence.

2. *Sanders v. State*, 604 S.W.2d 108 (Tex. Crim. App. 1980)
Section 8.01(b) of the Texas Penal Code

> **Section 8.01(b) of the Texas Penal Code**
> (b) The term "mental disease or defect" does not include an abnormality manifested only by repeated criminal or otherwise antisocial conduct.

In other words, a defendant cannot prove insanity by presenting evidence of nothing other than repeated criminal acts and other antisocial behavior.

An argument introducing a variation of the 8.01(b) provision occurred in the *Sanders* case. Sanders pled insanity to a charge of murder. Four psychiatrists and a psychologist testified that he had been seriously mentally ill since 1970 and did not know right from wrong. The State tried to introduce evidence about a murder Sanders committed in 1970 for which he had been found not guilty by reason of insanity. The State's theory was that based on his prior experience, the appellant knew that he could plead insanity and be acquitted. The court refused to allow evidence of his prior insanity acquittal to be introduced because it was not relevant to his current offense.

3. *Bigby v. State*, 892 S.W.2d 864 (Tex. Crim. App. 1994)
Section 8.01 of the Texas Penal Code

The question of whose moral code should be used to determine whether a defendant knew right from wrong was at issue when Bigby murdered his friend and co-worker and his friend's son. There was conflicting expert evidence about Bigby's mental state and the seriousness of his mental disorder at the time of the offense. When the police arrested him, Bigby admitted he was guilty of the murders. Several experts testified that in their opinion, Bigby knew his conduct was illegal, but he did not know it was morally wrong. Others testified that in their opinion, Bigby did know his conduct was wrong.

Bigby had been injured while working for the Frito Lay Company. He became convinced that the company was conspiring against him to prevent him from collecting worker's compensation. He got to the point where he believed the conspirators were trying to "take him out." He even rammed his car into the automobile of one of the insurance investigators. He was eventually hospitalized for psychiatric treatment but left the hospital before his treatment was complete. A few weeks after leaving, he killed his former co-worker and the worker's son.

The court decided Bigby's moral beliefs were not relevant and upheld his conviction. According to the court's opinion:

> Several expert witnesses testified appellant knew his conduct was illegal, however, these experts contended that appellant did not know the act was "morally" wrong. In other words, appellant believed that regardless of society's views about this illegal act and his understanding it was illegal, under his "moral" code it was permissible. This focus upon appellant's morality is misplaced. The question of insanity should focus on whether a defendant understood the nature and quality of his action and whether it was an act he ought to do. ... By accepting and acknowledging his action was "illegal" by society's standards, he understood that others believed his conduct was "wrong."

4. *Olivier v. State*, 850 S.W.2d 742 (Tex. App. - Houston [14th Dist.] 1993)
Section 8.01 of the Texas Penal Code

Marie Olivier was convicted of murder. The evidence showed she had been institutionalized numerous times for mental illness, had been in psychotherapy since high school, received electric shock treatments, and was in a psychiatric hospital a few days before the offense. Before the murder, she was taking Elavil and Vicodin but stopped taking them after a religious group influenced her. Olivier left the hospital a few days before the murder and met with the religious group to pray for healing and to cast out Satan. For several days she wandered throughout the city of Houston preaching to street people. She killed her 14-month old child because, as she testified, she thought her daughter was Satan. Three psychiatrists testified at trial that Marie was insane at the time of the murder and did not know right from wrong. The State argued that the appellant was faking her mental illness. The State presented no expert testimony. The Court of Appeals reversed the jury's decision that Olivier was guilty, writing:

> After reviewing all the evidence in the record relevant to the issue of appellant's insanity, we must conclude that the verdict of the jury, which implicitly rejected the affirmative defense of insanity, is so against the great weight and preponderance of the evidence as to be manifestly unjust.

A different result was reached in *Taylor v. State,* 856 S.W.2d 459 (Tex. App. -Houston [1st Dist.] 1993). Taylor was convicted of murdering her four-year old daughter. The evidence showed that Valerie Taylor had significant mental problems that led to paranoid delusions, including the delusion that her daughter was trying to kill her infant brother. Taylor stabbed the little girl over 20 times. The two psychiatrists who testified at trial reached different conclusions as to Taylor's sanity. One of the experts concluded Taylor was a paranoid schizophrenic who did not know right from wrong when she killed her daughter. The other expert concluded Taylor suffered from paranoid personality disorder and decompenasated at times into a psychosis of paranoid schizophrenia. Nonetheless, in his opinion, Taylor knew her actions were wrong. Several laypersons who knew Taylor testified both before and after the murder testified that she appeared sane. The appeals court refused to overturn the jury's guilty verdict, deciding that the finding was not against the great weight of the preponderance of evidence.

Competency to Stand Trial

The insanity defense is different from a decision that a defendant is incompetent to stand trial. Competency addresses the defendant's ability to consult with his lawyer with a reasonable degree of rational understanding concerning the proceedings against him. The law of competency to stand trial is found in the Texas Code of Criminal Procedure, article 46.02. The issue of competency is resolved in advance of a guilt/innocence trial on a motion from the defendant. In Texas, a jury decides whether there is sufficient evidence that a defendant is incompetent. The jury that decides competency cannot determine guilt or innocence. The burden of production and persuasion is on the defendant, and proof must be established by a preponderance of the evidence. A finding of incompetency to stand trial does not mean the defendant was legally insane at the time of the offense. The insanity defense focuses on the defendant's ability to know his behavior was wrong. The competency question focuses on his ability to assist in his criminal defense.

REVIEW

1. In the *Morris* case, the State did not offer any expert testimony:
    a. as a result, the defense convinced the jury that Morris was legally insane
    b. the State violated the requirements of the statute which requires expert testimony from both the defense and prosecution
    c. the State was not required to offer an expert and convinced the jurors with lay testimony
    d. Morris was incompetent to stand trial and, therefore, was automatically considered insane under the statute.

2. Not knowing that your conduct is illegal is not all that is required to prove insanity, you must also:
    a. not know your conduct is immoral.
    b. think you are doing God's will.
    c. be schizophrenic
    d. the correct test is that you don't know right from wrong or the nature of your act

3. Insanity in Texas must be proved by the defendant beyond a reasonable doubt.
    a. True
    b. False

4. Texas courts have ruled the prosecution must counter evidence of a defendant's insanity with expert testimony from a mental health practitioner that the defendant was sane because lay testimony is not sufficient.
    a. True
    b. False

5. Marie Olivier was able to convince the appellate court that the jury's conviction was unjust; Taylor was not able to do so. Both had experts testify about their mental health. These two cases illustrate:
    a. how difficult it is to prove not guilty by reason of insanity
    b. that murdering a younger child is more likely to help you prove you are insane.
    c. that the insanity defense should be eliminated
    d. that mental health experts are bad witnesses.

Section 2: AGE

OVERVIEW

Can there be a more controversial topic than the age at which perpetrators of crime should be prosecuted as adults? As rates of violent juvenile crime rise, so does the intensity of the discussion. State legislatures throughout the country are revisiting their laws about adult responsibility for certain types of offenses. Although most people agree we still need a juvenile justice system, there are many voices arguing the adult system is more appropriate for young offenders who commit violent crimes.

Section 8.07(a) of the Texas Penal Code

(a) A person may not be prosecuted for or convicted of any offense that the person committed when younger than 15 years of age, except:

(1) perjury and aggravated perjury when it is appears by proof that the person had sufficient discretion to understand the nature and obligation of an oath;

(2) a violation of a penal code statute cognizable under Chapter 729, Transportation Code, except for:

(A) an offense under Section 521.457, Transportation Code;

(B) an offense under Section 550.021, Transportation Code;

(C) an offense punishable as a Class B misdemeanor under Section 55.022, Transportation Code;

(D) an offense punishable as a Class B misdemeanor under Section 550.024, Transportation Code; or

(E) an offense punishable as a Class B misdemeanor under Section 550.025, Transportation Code;

(3) a violation of a motor vehicle traffic ordinance of an incorporated city or town in this state;

(4) a misdemeanor punishable by fine only other than public intoxication;

(5) a violation of a penal ordinance of a political subdivision;

(6) a violation of a penal statute that is, or is a lesser included offense of, a capital felony, an aggravated controlled substance felony, or a felony of the first degree for which the person is transferred to the court under Section 54.02 Family Code, for prosecution if the person committed the offense when 14 years of age or older; or

(7) a capital felony or an offense under Section 19.02 for which the person is transferred to the court under Section 54.02(j)(2)(A), Family Code.

For a clear reading of Section 8.07, it must be read in conjunction with Section 54.02 of the Texas Family Code. A juvenile younger than 17 cannot be prosecuted in an adult criminal court for any offenses except those listed in the Penal Code 8.07(a)(1)-(5). The juvenile court can waive jurisdiction and certify a 14 to 17 year old for prosecution in the adult courts pursuant to Section 54.02 of the Texas Family Code in the event the child committed a capital felony, an aggravated controlled substance felony, or a felony of the first degree.

The procedures for waiving jurisdiction to an adult court are found in Chapter 54 of the Family Code. In addition to making certain the child is of the correct age to be transferred and that he or she has committed a transferable offense, the Family Court is mandated by section 54.01 to look at:

- whether the offense was committed against a person or property;
- whether the offense was committed in an aggressive and premeditated manner;
- whether there is evidence on which a grand jury could indict;
- the child's sophistication and maturity;
- the record and previous history of the child; and
- prospects for protecting the public and the likelihood of the child's rehabilitation in the juvenile justice system.

Although the United States Supreme Court ruled the death penalty could not be enforced against any person found guilty of a crime committed under the age of 16, Section 8.07(c) of the Texas Penal Code provides that no person can be executed in Texas for a crime committed under the age of 17.

Section 3: DURESS

OVERVIEW

Section 8.05 of the Texas Penal Code

(a) It is an affirmative defense to prosecution that the actor engaged in proscribed conduct because he was compelled to do so by threat of imminent death or serious bodily injury to himself or another.

(b) In a prosecution for an offense that does not constitute a felony, it is an affirmative defense to prosecution that the actor engaged in the proscribed conduct because he was compelled to do so by force or threat of force.

(c) Compulsion within the meaning of this section exists only if the force or threat of force would render a person of reasonable firmness incapable of resisting the pressure.

Texas makes a distinction between the amount of force that can be relied on to argue duress in a felony case and the amount of force that can be relied on for the duress defense to a misdemeanor. The duress defense can be used even against murder charges.

An objective or reasonable person test is used to determine whether the requisite compulsion existed. Under Section 8.05(c), compulsion exists only if the threat would have rendered a person of reasonable firmness incapable of resisting the pressure. According to Section 8.05(d), if the defendant intentionally, knowingly, or recklessly placed himself in a situation in which it was probable he would be subjected to compulsion, the defense is not available. Finally, under Section 8.05(e), acting merely at the command of a spouse is not a defense, unless the defendant can also show he or she acted under the kind of compulsion that would render a person of reasonable firmness unable to resist.

Section 4: INTOXICATION

OVERVIEW

Section 8.04(a) of the Texas Penal Code

(a) Voluntary intoxication does not constitute a defense to the commission of crime.

Intoxication is voluntary if the defendant exercised independent judgment or will in taking the intoxicant. Any substance, both legal and illegal can cause intoxication. Although voluntary intoxication is not a defense to a crime, it may be relevant to the defendant's mens rea. It may also be relevant to show the defendant did not possess a required level of skill or physical ability to perform the crime charged against him.

Section 8.04(b) and (c) of the Texas Penal Code

(b) Evidence of temporary insanity caused by intoxication may be introduced by the actor in mitigation of the penalty attached to the offense for which he is being tried.
(c) When temporary insanity is relied upon as a defense and the evidence tends to show that such insanity was caused by intoxication, the court shall charge the jury in accordance with the provisions of this section.

Texas courts have ruled that proof of temporary insanity as the result of intoxication must be read in conjunction with Section 8.01 of the Penal Code concerning the insanity defense. This means that in order to obtain a mitigation instruction for the jury because of voluntary intoxication, there must be evidence that, as a result of intoxication at the time the crime was committed, the defendant did not know his conduct was wrong.

CASES

1. *Joiner v. State*, 814 S.W.2d 135 (Tex. App. - Houston [14th Dist.] 1991)
Section 8.04 of the Texas Penal Code

Joiner was convicted of injury to a 13-year old neighbor girl who he attempted to attack sexually. When she resisted his advances, he beat her. He claimed he had been drinking and taking L.S.D. throughout the day, and the child, who was the daughter of his friend, reminded him of his mother when she was intoxicated. He became angry and attacked the girl. After the attack, he went home, showered, and changed clothes. He ran back to the girl's house and told her father he had heard a strange noise from a neighboring yard. Joiner told the father he saw a man running across the street away from a deserted yard. Joiner and the father went over to the yard and discovered the girl lying in a corner naked from the waist down, bloody and bruised. The girl suffered permanent loss of sight in one eye and was in the hospital for three weeks after Joiner's attack.

Joiner appealed his conviction because the trial judge refused to give the jury an instruction about temporary insanity by intoxication. The appeals court upheld his conviction, ruling:

The appellant knowingly and deliberately put himself in an intoxicated condition. Now he seeks to use that condition to mitigate against a penalty for consciously perpetrating a horrible assault against another person. This cannot be sanctioned. Voluntary intoxication will not allow him to avoid responsibility for the rights and well being of others. Intoxication alone does not give the defendant the right to a mitigating instruction. Since there is no evidence that appellant did not know that his conduct was wrong, he was not entitled to any mitigating instruction under TEX.PENAL CODE ANN. Section 8.04 (Vernon Supp. 1990).

2. *Torres v. State*, 585 S.W.2d 748 (Tex. Crim. App. 1979)
Section 8.04 of the Texas Penal Code

There is no statute in Texas that recognizes *involuntary* intoxication as a defense. Texas courts, however, have held that when a defendant can establish he or she exercised no independent will or judgment in taking the intoxicant, it can be used as a defense in conjunction with Section 8.01.

Helen Torres was convicted of aggravated robbery. She claimed at the time of the crime she was involuntarily intoxicated. Helen and Robert Miranda broke into the victim's house, held her at gun point, stole her property, forced her to accompany them to her bank and cash several checks made payable to them. At the bank, the victim was able to notify the security officer that something was wrong, and the two robbers were apprehended after an exchange of gunfire.

Miranda testified at Torres's trial that he had slipped thorazine tablets into an alka selzer drink he prepared for her because she felt sick. The Texas Court of Criminal Appeals ruled that involuntary intoxication is a defense in Texas even though it is not mentioned in the Penal Code. The insanity defense under section 8.01 also applies to involuntary intoxication: as a result of being involuntarily intoxicated, the defendant did not know her conduct was wrong or was unable to conform her conduct to the requirements of the law (*Torres* was decided prior to the change in the insanity defense in 1983). The court ruled that Helen Torres was entitled to a jury instruction on involuntary intoxication.

In another case, *Hanks v. State*, 542 S.W.2d 413 (Tex. Crim. App. 1978), the court ruled a defendant can not rely on involuntary intoxication as a defense if he suspected he was being subjected to an intoxicant but consumed it anyway.

Section 5: ENTRAPMENT

OVERVIEW

Section 8.06 of the Texas Penal Code

(a) It is a defense to prosecution that the actor engaged in the conduct charged because he was induced to do so by a law enforcement agent using persuasion or other means likely to cause persons to commit the offense. Conduct merely afforded a person an opportunity to commit an offense does not constitute entrapment.
(b) In this section "law enforcement agent" includes personnel of the state and local law enforcement agencies as well as of the United States and any person acting in accordance with instructions from such agents.

As a defense, the burden of persuasion is on the prosecution to convince the jury there was no entrapment beyond a reasonable doubt.

CASE

***England v. State*, 887 S.w.2d 902 (Tex. Crim. App. 1994)**
Section 8.06 of the Texas Penal Code

In 1994, the Texas Court of Criminal Appeals significantly changed the test of entrapment in Texas in a 5-4 en banc decision. Prior to *England*, the court had decided the Texas legislature enacted a purely objective test for entrapment. Once the defendant showed he had been the target of persuasive police conduct, regardless of whether he was actually persuaded to commit the offense by the police behavior, the court's focus was directed to the police conduct. The question was whether the persuasion used by the law enforcement agent was such as to cause a hypothetical person - an ordinary law abiding person of average resistance - to commit the crime. There was no need to examine the defendant's proclivities or predisposition to engage in criminal activity. The defendant's prior criminal history or reputation was not admissible unless it went to the issue of whether the police had used persuasion versus provided the defendant with an opportunity.

The *England* court reanalyzed the entrapment defense and the wording of Section 8.06. It determined that the legislature actually enacted a mixed objective/subjective test for entrapment. On the subjective side of the mixed test, a defendant must produce evidence that he was actually induced to commit the crime because of police conduct. Evidence of predisposition and prior criminal history is relevant to the issue of whether the defendant was induced by law enforcement or whether he was predisposed to engage in crime. The objective part of the standard still requires the defendant prove the police used such persuasion as to induce a hypothetical person of ordinary law abiding nature to commit the offense.

England demonstrates how powerful courts are in defining the criminal law. Their interpretive powers can be as important as the wording of the statute itself. For many years, Texas used an objective standard for entrapment, based upon the court's understanding of Section 8.06. In 1994, the same Texas court (obviously with different judges), interpreting the same statute, decided the state legislature had intended something quite different. The case is also interesting because the court's opinion reviews the federal and Model Penal Code entrapment standards and discusses the status of the law in other jurisdictions.

Two examples of cases where law enforcement inducement was held sufficient to establish an entrapment defense: *Gifford v. State*, 740 S.W.2d 76 (Tex. App. - Fort Worth 1987) in which a false representation by an agent that the conduct was legal was considered entrapment as matter of law; and *Gobin v. State*, 684 S.W.2d 802 (Tex. App. - Fort Worth 1985) in which the informant's threat to withhold rent money was considered entrapment.

An example of a case where law enforcement inducement was held insufficient to establish an entrapment defense: *Sebesta v. State*, 783 S.W.2d 811 (Tex. App. - Houston [1st Dist.] 1990) held that annoying telephone calls by a government informant were not sufficient to cause a person to commit a crime.

Section 6: MISTAKE OF FACT

OVERVIEW

Section 8.02(a) of the Texas Penal Code
(a) It is a defense to prosecution that the actor through mistake formed a reasonable belief about a matter of fact if his mistaken belief negated the kind of culpability required for the commission of the offense.

A reasonable belief means a belief that would be held by an ordinary and prudent person in the same circumstances as the defendant. Mistake of fact is a defense as opposed to an affirmative defense. As explained in Section 2.03(d) of the Penal Code, this means that a reasonable doubt on the issue requires the defendant be acquitted.

CASES

1. *Wages v. State*, 703 S.W.2d 736 (Tex. App. - Houston [14th Dist.] 1985)
Section 8.02 of the Texas Penal Code

Donna Wages was convicted of writing bad checks. The trial testimony showed she and her husband were small business owners, and he wrote several insufficient fund checks to her on the business account that she cashed. Her husband testified that his wife did not know the financial status of the business and nor that the checks were worthless. He intentionally kept his wife in the dark. The court refused Donna Wages' request for a mistake of fact jury instruction because other than her husband's testimony, there was nothing in evidence showing she was not aware the checks were worthless. She did not testify at trial so there was no evidence of what she believed to be the facts. In addition, there was evidence that the business received many bank notices about the dishonored checks. The question was raised as to whether a reasonable person would have believed there was sufficient money in the business bank account to cover the checks made payable to Ms. Wages. The court decided that a jury instruction concerning mistake of fact was not warranted by the evidence.

2. *Beggs v. State*, 597 S.W.2d 375 (Tex. Crim. App. 1980)
Section 8.02 of the Texas Penal Code

Alberta Beggs was convicted of injury to a child under Section 22.04 of the Penal Code. She argued on appeal that the jury should have been provided a mistake of fact instruction. She and her stepdaughter were charged with burning her granddaughter in hot bath water. Beggs admitted to helping her stepdaughter punish her granddaughter by administering the bath that scolded the child. Her defense was she did not know the bath water was hot enough to cause injury. Her stepdaughter had drawn the water before she came into the bathroom to help bathe the child. She assumed the water temperature was normal because the child hated to bathe and a normal bath would have been punishment to her.

The appellate court ruled in her favor, finding that testimony about mistakenly thinking the water temperature was normal, was sufficient to entitle her to an instruction on the mistake of fact issue. Remember, the Court of Criminal Appeals only decided that on remand to the trial court, the judge should give the jury a mistake of fact instruction. It will be up to the jury to assess the evidence.

Section 7: MISTAKE OF LAW

OVERVIEW

Section 8.03 of the Texas Penal Code

(a) It is no defense to prosecution that the actor was ignorant of the provisions of any law after the law has taken effect.

It is an affirmative defense, however, if the actor reasonably believed his conduct was not a crime based upon a written, official statement of the law from an administrative agency or public official charged with the responsibility for interpreting the law, or a written opinion of a court of record interpreting the law.

CASE

***Gallegos v. State*, 828 S.W.2d 577 (Tex. App. - Houston [1st Dist.] 1992)**
Section 8.03 of the Texas Penal Code

Richard Gallegos raised the mistake of law defense after he was convicted of bail jumping and failing to appear for trial. He had appealed an earlier Texas conviction for possession of marijuana. According to the terms of his appeal bond, he was permitted to live in Louisiana, but in the event his appeal was affirmed, he was required to return to Chambers County, Texas. Gallegos's conviction was affirmed, but he failed to appear at a court setting. His excuse for missing the hearing was that his Louisiana attorney advised him not to appear. The Texas Court of Appeals ruled that Gallegos was not entitled to a mistake of law defense because his decision not to return was not based on an official statement or interpretation of law by a court or an administrative agency. The court also ruled he was not entitled to argue mistake of fact, stating that a defendant who relied on another's mistake of law cannot claim a mistake of fact.

REVIEW

6. Harriet sold drugs to an undercover law enforcement officer after he begged and pleaded, saying that if he didn't get the drugs he was going to commit suicide. Harriet and he had been "dating" for several months. Harriet pled entrapment. Under Texas test, Harriet must show:
    a. the officer's persuasion would have induced a hypothetical law abiding person to sell him drugs.
    b. the officer's persuasion actually induced her to sell him drugs.
    c. that Harriet had never sold drugs before.
    d. a and b

7. Joey was 14 ½ years old when he recklessly caused the death of a neighbor as a result of running over him with his skateboard. The neighbor was a healthy 23-year-old woman who fell to the ground and suffered a concussion. Joey had been in juvenile court for several other skateboard-related accidents, none of which, however, had led to a death. The D.A. was considering petitioning the Family Court to transfer Joey to the adult court. Is this possible?
   a. Yes, Joey was over 14 and can be certified as an adult.
   b. Yes, Joey's prior juvenile history allows the D.A. to petition for transfer.
   c. No, Joey has to be facing at least a first-degree felony to be transferred.
   d. No, because no juvenile under 15 can be transferred to the adult courts in Texas.

8. Duress or coercion in Texas can only be pled for nonviolent felony cases.
   a. True
   b. False

9. Involuntary intoxication is a defense to criminal prosecution defined in section 8.04 of the Penal Code.
   a. True
   b. False

10. Henry spent the evening drinking and snorting cocaine. During the early morning, he stopped at a convenience store to purchase cigarettes. The clerk had a bad night and was rude to Henry who he suspected was intoxicated. Henry pulled out his handgun and shot the clerk dead. Henry has no previous criminal history and argued temporary insanity as a result of intoxication. To argue that defense successfully in Texas, Henry must:
    a. establish he was intoxicated involuntarily.
    b. establish he was not a chronic substance abuser.
    c. establish he did not know the nature of his actions or right from wrong.
    d. establish he tried to reason with the clerk before he shot him.

11. Harriet was a drug dealer before she sold the drugs to the undercover officer; however, she had turned over a new leaf and for eight months had been out of the drug selling business. Is that relevant evidence in Texas to her entrapment defense?
    a. Yes, because it goes to whether Harriet was actually induced by the officer's pleas.
    b. No, because the entrapment test is only concerned with the officer's behavior.
    c. No, because Harriet's prior history is not admissible.
    d. Yes, because it shows Harriet was a changed woman.

12. The Texas entrapment defense is:
    a. an objective test.
    b. a subjective test.
    c. a mixed objective/subjective test.
    d. the law is not clear.

FINAL COMMENTS ON EXCUSE DEFENSES

Although excuse defenses raise a lot of public criticism, they are seldom successful. Like many states, Texas has tightened the range of behaviors for which the excuse defenses are available. A stricter insanity defense was legislated in 1983 with the elimination of the irresistible impulse test. In 1994, the Texas Court of Criminal Appeals created a more difficult entrapment defense by introducing a subjective component to a previously objective standard. Effective 1996, youths as young as 14 years old who commit certain serious offenses became eligible for transfer to the adult criminal court system, a reduction from the age of 15. Time will determine whether more changes are in the offing.

Chapter Nine

Crimes Against Persons I: Criminal Homicide

INTRODUCTION

Murder cases intrigue us. They get more media coverage than other types of crimes, and murder is the favorite topic of television crime dramas and mystery novels. Murder statutes have a higher public profile than other criminal statutes, especially in those state that have the death penalty. This chapter examines the Texas murder statute with a special emphasis on capital punishment. Texas receives national and international recognition because of its generous use of the death penalty. It is especially important that any discussion about murder in this state spend substantial time on understanding how capital punishment law has developed and why. Texas death penalty law is different than death penalty law in any other jurisdictions. Could these differences explain why Texas sends more people to death row than any other state? Obviously, there are many contributing factors, but perhaps one factor is the unique Texas death penalty statute.

Section 1: MURDER

OVERVIEW

Texas no longer uses the first and second-degree murder scheme. Its murder statute is located in Chapter 19 of the Texas Penal Code and is based largely on the Model Penal Code.

Section 19.01 of the Texas Penal Code

(a) A person commits criminal homicide if he intentionally, knowingly, recklessly, or with criminal negligence causes the death of an individual.

(b) Criminal homicide is murder, capital murder, manslaughter, or criminally negligent homicide.

"Individual" is defined in Section 1.07 of the Penal Code as a human being who is alive, including an unborn child at every stage of gestation from fertilization until birth.

An offense under Section 19.01 is a first-degree felony unless the defendant proves he committed what used to be called voluntary manslaughter, in which case the offense is a second-degree felony.

Murder with Provocation

In 1993, the Texas legislature repealed the voluntary manslaughter statute that was located in Section 19.04, and placed the act of voluntary manslaughter into the murder statute, Section 19.01. The traditional elements of voluntary manslaughter are now located in:

> **Section 19.02(d) of the Texas Penal Code**
> At the punishment phase of the trial, the defendant may raise the issue as to whether he caused the death under the immediate influence of sudden passion arising from adequate cause. If the defendant proves the issue in the affirmative by a preponderance of the evidence, the offense is a felony of the second degree.
>
> What constitutes adequate cause and sudden passion under Section 19.02(d) are defined in:
>
> **Section 19.02(a)(1) the Texas Penal Code**
> (a)(1) "Adequate cause" means cause that would commonly produce a degree of anger, rage, resentment, or terror in a person of ordinary temper, sufficient to render the mind incapable of cool reflection.
>
> **Section 19.02(a)(2) of the Texas Penal Code**
> (a)(2) "Sudden passion" means passion directly caused by and arising out of provocation by the individual killed or another acting with the person killed which passion arises at the time of the offense and is not solely the result of a former provocation.

This means that voluntary manslaughter is no longer a separate homicide offense in Texas. It is considered a murder that can be reduced to a second-degree felony if the defendant introduces evidence that convinces the jury during the punishment phase by a preponderance of the evidence that he or she killed in sudden passion arising from adequate cause.

Sudden passion arising from adequate cause are fact issues a jury decides. Appellate courts are reluctant to overturn a jury's decision on these issues if there was evidence to support its conclusion. An accused is entitled to a jury instruction on the issue of murder committed in the heat of passion if there was any evidence supporting it no matter how strong, weak, contradicted, unimpeached, or even unbelievable the evidence may be.

CASE

***Perez v. State*, 940 S.W.2d 820 (Tex. App.- Waco 1997)**
Section 19.02 of the Texas Penal Code

Perez offered evidence that showed he killed his friend during an argument. He suspected his friend was having an affair with his wife and believed his friend carried a weapon. During the argument he saw his friend reach underneath his seat for something. Suspecting that he was reaching for a gun, Perez testified he became afraid and shot and killed the victim. His fear alone did not present evidence of killing in sudden passion, but if fear rendered him incapable of deliberate reflection, sudden passion could be argued. Perez had been convicted after first claiming self-defense during the guilt/innocence stage of his trial. The jury rejected that claim, after which Perez argued that he committed murder in the heat of passion.

This case demonstrates how defendants can rely on more than one legal theory to prove their innocence or at least to mitigate their guilt. Depending on the facts, self-defense cases often combine heat of sudden passion arguments in a two-prong approach to the prosecution's case. It is easy to see how a self-defense claim can sometimes include facts that suggest the murder was committed with adequate cause. The appeals court ruled the jury should have been instructed to consider the issue of provocation and sudden passion during the punishment phase.

Manslaughter and Criminally Negligent Homicide

With the voluntary manslaughter statute repealed, what had previously been termed involuntary manslaughter was re-identified as manslaughter. It is a second-degree felony. "Criminally negligent homicide" is also a separate offense and is punished as a state jail felony.

The difference between the culpable mental states for manslaughter and criminally negligent homicide is the appreciation of the risk. Recklessness for a manslaughter charge requires proof that the defendant perceived the risk and disregarded it. In criminal negligence, the evidence must show the defendant did not perceive a risk that an ordinary person would have recognized.

Section 19.04 of the Texas Penal Code
(a) A person commits an offense if he recklessly causes the death of an individual.

Section 19.05 of the Texas Penal Code
(a) A person commits an offense if he causes the death of an individual by criminal negligence.

CASE

***Trepanier v. State*, 940 S.W.2d 827 (Tex. App. - Austin 1997)**
Section 19.04 of the Texas Penal Code

Trepanier was convicted of manslaughter for killing a bicyclist while driving an automobile. The court refused to disrupt the jury's verdict that the appellant was reckless. Evidence showed that Trepanier was driving at an inappropriate speed in heavy traffic and attempted to pass a truck by driving on the shoulder of the road. The appellant argued he had a history of seizures and had forgotten to take his medication. The court concluded there was sufficient evidence that appellant voluntarily created a substantial and unjustifiable risk and consciously disregarded the risk of killing the bicyclist.

Section 2: CAPITAL PUNISHMENT TEXAS STYLE

OVERVIEW

In *Furman v. Georgia*, 408 U.S.238 (1972), the United States Supreme Court held the Georgia death penalty statute violated the Eighth Amendment prohibition against cruel and unusual punishment. The *Furman* decision actually involved three separate cases that the Supreme Court consolidated into the *Furman* case. One of the other two cases also originated in Georgia. The third case challenged the constitutionality of the Texas death penalty statute. In that case, *Branch v. State*, 477 S.W.2d 932 (Tex. Crim. App. 1969), the appellant had been convicted of "rape by force" and sentenced to death. At the time of Branch's conviction, Texas was one of a few states that allowed the death penalty to be assessed for crimes other than murder.

The *Furman* case did not rule that the death penalty per se violated the Constitution. The Court, in a 5-4 decision that is famous for its lack of clarity and clear direction, ruled the death penalty statutes violated the Eighth Amendment because they failed to provide guidance to juries who make decisions about who is sentenced to death and who is not. This lack of guidance can too easily lead to capricious and arbitrary sentences. The *Furman* decision in effect struck down all the death penalty statutes in the United States at that time because none of them had provisions to guide a jury's discretion in making the ultimate decision of who should live and who should die.

Like lawmakers in many states, the Texas legislature went to the drawing board in the wake of *Furman* and re-drafted the capital sentencing law to respond to the Supreme Court's concerns. It was not an easy task because the Court offered few suggestions as to how states could rewrite their laws to pass constitutional muster. States took essentially one of two different approaches. One type of statute provided a mandatory death penalty for certain designated capital offenses, thereby eliminating the need for juries to exercise any discretion. The other approach was to require the jury to consider specific criteria, written in the statute, during the sentencing decision. In 1976, the U.S. Supreme Court considered five death penalty cases involving new capital punishment statutes. The Court ruled that mandatory death penalty laws were unconstitutional but that guided discretion statutes were constitutional.

One of the statutes ruled constitutional in 1976 was the newly revamped Section 19.03 of the Texas Penal Code in the case *Jurek v. State*, 428 U.S. 262 (1976). Section 19.03(a) restricts the class of crimes for which the death penalty can be assessed to intentionally or knowingly committing a murder in eight situations:

Section 19.03(a) of the Texas Penal Code

(1) the person murders a peace officer or fireman who is acting in the lawful discharge of an official duty and who the person knows is a peace officer or fireman;
(2) the person intentionally commits the murder in the course of committing or attempting to commit kidnapping, burglary, robbery, aggravated sexual assault, arson, obstruction or retaliation, or terroristic threat under Section 22.07(a)(1), (3), (4), (5), or (6);
(3) the person commits the murder for remuneration or the promise of remuneration or employs another to commit the murder of remuneration or the promise of remuneration;
(4) the person commits the murder while escaping or attempting to escape from a penal institution;
(5) the person, while incarcerated in a penal institution, murders another:
(A) who is employed in the operation of the penal institution; or
(B) with the intent to establish, maintain, or participate in a combination or in the profits of a combination;
(6) the person:
(A) while incarcerated for an offense under this section or Section 19.02, murders another, or

(B) while serving a sentence of life imprisonment or a term of 99 years for an offense under Section 20.04, 22.021, or 29.03, murders another;
(7) the person murders more than one person:
(A) during the same criminal transaction; or
(B) during different criminal transactions but the murders are committed pursuant to the same scheme or course of conduct; or
(8) the person murders an individual under six years of age.

The State Legislature has amended the list of capital murders several times since the statute was originally enacted. In 1993, it added language to 19.03(a)(5) that makes it a capital murder for an inmate to kill another person with the intent to establish, participate or maintain a combination. The Legislature was concerned about the number of murders committed in Texas prisons and jails by prison gang members. Subsection (6) was also added in 1993 to deal with the growing problem of prison violence. Subsection (7) was added in 1985 to include multiple murders. Subsection (8) was added in 1993 to make the murder of a child under six a capital crime.

Provisions in the Texas Code of Criminal Procedure complete the law of capital punishment. Under this statute, as it was originally enacted, the same jurors who convicted the defendant had to answer three questions during the punishment phase of the trial:

Article 37.071(b) the Texas Code of Criminal Procedure (before revision)
(1) Whether the defendant's conduct that caused the death of the deceased was committed deliberately and with the reasonable expectation that the death of the deceased or another person would result;
(2) whether there is a probability that the defendant would commit acts of violence that would constitute a continuing threat to society;
(3) if raised by the evidence, whether the conduct of the defendant in killing the deceased was unreasonable in response to the provocation, if any, of the deceased.

If the jury found unanimously beyond a reasonable doubt that the answer to all three questions was "yes," the court was required to impose the death sentence. However, if ten jurors returned a negative answer to any issue, the court was required to issue a life sentence. Jurors could not be informed about the consequences of their votes.

Unlike the other capital punishment laws that were declared constitutional in 1976, the Texas statute was not based on the Model Penal Code. In fact, the Texas death penalty law differs significantly from capital punishment laws in most states. Under the Model Penal Code and in states with statutes like Georgia and Florida, which were also declared constitutional in 1976, during the punishment phase the jury hears evidence in mitigation of the offense and evidence in aggravation of the offense. A jury must find beyond a reasonable doubt that a certain number (depending on the jurisdiction) of aggravating factors exist before a death sentence can be imposed. In some statutory schemes jurors must weigh the aggravating factors against the mitigating factors. The Model Penal Code's aggravating factors track the list of eight types of capital murder found in Section 19.03 of the Texas Penal Code. The mitigating factors include such items as:

- the defendant had no significant prior criminal history;
- the murder was committed while the defendant was under the influence of extreme emotional stress or disturbance;
- the victim participated in the homicidal act or consented to it;
- the murder was committed under circumstances which the defendant believed to provide moral justification;
- the defendant was an accomplice with another and his involvement was relatively minor;
- the defendant acted under duress or domination;
- the defendant's judgment was impaired because of a mental disease or intoxication;
- the defendant was a young person.

In *Jurek v. State*, the Supreme Court decided that the constitutionality of the Texas law turned on whether the three questions presented to the jury allowed it to consider mitigating factors in favor of granting the defendant a life sentence. The Court had ruled in *Woodson v. North Carolina*, 428 U.S. 280 (1976) that a death penalty statute must allow the jury to consider mitigating circumstances surrounding the crime and the offender. The Court concluded that the second question outlined in the Texas Code of Criminal Procedure concerning future dangerousness required a jury to consider mitigating factors. The U.S. Supreme Court also relied on assurances provided by the Texas Court of Criminal Appeals when it ruled on the constitutionality of the new state law in *Jurek v. State*, 522 S.W.2d 934 (Tex. Crim. App. 1975). The Court of Criminal Appeals stated in its opinion that it intended to interpret the second question about future dangerousness so as to allow a defendant to bring mitigating circumstances to a jury's attention. The Supreme Court declared the Texas statute constitutional.

Following *Jurek*, the Court of Criminal Appeals addressed several challenges that article 37.071 violated the Eighth Amendment by failing to instruct the jury sufficiently about the need to consider mitigating evidence. In each of the cases, the Texas court ruled that the Eighth Amendment does not require a separate jury instruction concerning mitigating evidence. In 1989, the U.S. Supreme Court decided *Penry v. Lynaugh*, 492 U.S. 302 (1989) which involved a Texas death sentenced inmate who had presented evidence that he was mentally retarded, suffered from organic brain damage resulting in poor impulse control, had an inability to learn from experience, and was seriously abused as a child. At the punishment phase of his trial for capital murder, the trial judge submitted the three statutory questions required by article 37.071 but refused Penry's request for an additional jury instruction about his mitigating evidence. The U. S. Supreme Court held the Texas sentencing scheme unconstitutional, as applied to Penry, because jurors were not provided a vehicle to consider his mitigation evidence. Penry's evidence went beyond the scope of the three questions, making it difficult for the jury to consider mitigation adequately in deciding life or death.

In 1993, the Texas Legislature responded to the *Penry* decision by revising article 37.071. The revision affects capital murder cases for crimes committed after September 1, 1991. An already complicated set of instructions on punishment became even more complicated. In the new scheme, the jury is presented *two* questions to answer during punishment deliberations:

Article 37.071(b) the Texas Code of Criminal Procedure

(1) whether there is a probability that the defendant would commit criminal acts of violence that would constitute a continuing threat to society; and

(2) in cases where the jury charge at the guilt or innocence stage permitted the jury to find the defendant guilty as a party under Sections 7.01 and 7.02, Penal Code, whether the defendant actually caused the death of the deceased or did not actually cause the death of the deceased but intended to kill the deceased or another or anticipated that a human life would be taken.

Article 37.071(d) requires the court charge a jury that it should consider all the evidence submitted during both the guilt/ innocence and punishments stages, including evidence of the defendant's background or character or the circumstances surrounding the crime that militates for or mitigates against the imposition of death. The jury cannot answer "yes" to the two questions unless it agrees unanimously. A "no" answer requires a vote of at least ten jurors.

Finally, and most importantly in terms of complying with the *Penry* case, if the jury answers in the affirmative to both of the two questions, it must answer a third question:

Article 37.071(e)(1) the Texas Code of Criminal Procedure

Whether, taking into consideration all of the evidence, including the circumstances of the offense, the defendant's character and background, and the personal moral culpability of the defendant, there is a sufficient mitigating circumstance or circumstances to warrant that a sentence of life imprisonment rather than a death sentence be imposed.

The jury cannot answer "no" to the third question unless it agrees unanimously and may not answer "yes" unless ten or more jurors agree. The judge must sentence the offender to death if the jury responded "no" to the third issue and to life if the jury responded "yes." The Texas Court of Criminal Appeals automatically reviews a conviction and sentence to death.

The 1999 Texas Legislature amended article 37.071(e), to require a judge, upon request from defense counsel, to tell the jury that if it should decide the circumstances warrant a life sentence, the defendant will not become eligible for release on parole until the actual time he or she serves equals 40 years, without consideration of good time credits. Eligibility for parole does not guarantee that parole will be granted.

Felony-Murder Doctrine

According to the Texas capital punishment statute, murders committed during or fleeing from the commission of certain serious felonies can be punished by death. Murders committed during the commission of or fleeing from the scene of felonies that are not listed in Section 19.03(a)(2) are punished as first-degree felonies. From a defendant's perspective, it is very important to clearly define the scope of the felony murder doctrine, especially for those defendants who face a death sentence. Since many felony murders in Texas can be categorized as capital crimes, cases that have contributed to the development of the felony murder doctrine often involve defendants who are fighting for their lives.

In order for a murder to be committed during the course of a robbery, under Section 19.03(a)(2), the murder must have occurred during a theft involving the use of force or threats of serious bodily injury. The *intent* to rob the victim must have been formed *before or concurrent* with the murder. The robbery itself need not have occurred before the murder. It may have occurred during the murder or in immediate flight from the murder. The prosecution's job is to convince the jury beyond a reasonable doubt that the defendant intended to rob the victim before or during the time he killed the victim. The same is true for other capital felony murders: the intent to kidnap, commit burglary, sexually assault, rob, commit arson, obstruction, or retaliation must have been formed before or at the time of the murder. The actus reus of the felony underlying the capital murder charge did not have to occur before or during the victim's murder. Sometimes the jury has a difficult decision to make.

CASES

1. *Santellan v. State*, 939 S.W.2d 156 (Tex. Crim. App. 1997)
Section 19.03 of the Texas Penal Code

Santellan argued he was not guilty of capital murder because there was insufficient evidence that he intended to kidnap his victim/girlfriend before he murdered her. Santellan went to his girlfriend's place of employment to say goodbye. He ended up shooting her. Unclear in his mind as to whether she was alive or dead, he put her in his car, and drove her to a motel where he sexually abused her corpse. He claimed he intended to kill her but never intended and did not kidnap her. For Santellan, the difference was a first-degree felony punishable by 5 to 99 years in prison (if there was no kidnapping) or a capital murder verdict punishable by death (if there was a finding of kidnapping). The Court of Criminal Appeals upheld his capital murder conviction and death sentence. This case is discussed at length in Chapter 6 of the Supplement.

2. *Alvarado v. State*, 912 S.W.2d 199 (Tex. Crim. App. 1995)
Section 19.03 of the Texas Penal Code

Alvarado was seventeen at the time of his offense. He claimed he had not intend to rob his victims before he killed them. The jury rejected his claims and sentenced him to death. The Court of Appeals upheld the verdict. The evidence showed that Alvarado and his accomplices felt cheated by the victims from whom they had purchased drugs. They armed themselves with knives and went to the victims' home with the intent of killing them. Immediately after the murders, they searched the house and stole items from the victims. The Court concluded there was sufficient evidence for a jury to find that Alvarado formed the intent to rob either before or during the murders.

3. *Gonzales v. State*, 905 S.W.2d 4 (Tex. Crim. App. 1995)
Section 19.03 of the Texas Penal Code

Gonzales went to the home of his victims with the intent to kill them. The victims' daughter admitted him into the home while the victims were asleep. She aided and encouraged the killing of her parents. Gonzales was convicted of killing his victims during the commission of a burglary because the court ruled the daughter did not have the authority to consent to Gonzales entering the home. The daughter's participation in the crime rendered her consent to entry ineffective. The underlying offense was burglary of a habitation under Section 30.02: a person commits a burglary if he enters a habitation without the effective consent of the owner with the intent to commit a felony or theft.

The impact of the felony murder doctrine is far reaching. The more "liberally" the courts interpret it, the wider the net of the death penalty statute. District attorneys decide how aggressively to pursue the doctrine in their counties. Many offenders on death row have been convicted of felony murders, making the doctrine an important legal issue in many capital felony prosecutions.

Other Capital Murder Issues

According to Section 19.03(a)(7)(A), a person commits capital murder if he intentionally or knowingly murders more than one person during the same criminal transaction. The Legislature did not define the term "same criminal transaction." Under 19.03(a)(7)(B), it is capital murder if the killings were accomplished during different criminal transactions but pursuant to the same scheme or course of conduct. Neither did the legislature define the meaning of "same scheme or course of conduct."

1. *Coble v. State*, 871 S.W.2d 192 (Tex. Crim. App. 1993)
Section 19.03(a)(7)(A) of the Texas Penal Code

Billie Coble argued that "same criminal transaction" requires a continuity of time and place. He was convicted of capital murder after murdering his ex-wife's brother and her parents over a span of three hours. The murders were committed in different locations but in the same neighborhood. The Court of Criminal Appeals concluded:

> In determining whether the evidence is sufficient to support the jury's finding that appellant committed the murders during the same criminal transaction, we "look to see whether the jury could *rationally* conclude appellant engaged in a continuous and uninterrupted process over a short period of time, of carrying on or carrying out murder of more than one person." *Rios v. State*, 846 S.W.2d at 314 (emphasis added). Given that the three murders occurred in close proximity to each other, on the same road, within a few hours of each other, in a continuous and uninterrupted series of events, a jury could have *rationally* concluded beyond a reasonable doubt that appellant murdered Karen Vicha's father, brother, and mother during the "same criminal transaction."

2. *Corwin v. State,* 870 S.W.2d 23 (Tex. Crim. App. 1993)
Section 19.03(a)(7)(B) of the Texas Penal Code

Corwin was convicted of murdering more than one person pursuant to different criminal transaction but pursuant to the same course of conduct or scheme. He abducted, sexually assaulted, and killed two women over the course of nine months. During those nine months, he had also attempted to abduct a third woman, and when he could not, he killed her. Corwin claimed that the term "same scheme or course of conduct" was so indefinite he could not tell whether his conduct in killing more than one person during different criminal transactions was a capital offense. The Texas Court of Criminal Appeals reviewed the legislative history of the penal provision and concluded in its opinion that the Legislature intended to target serial murders. The Court agreed there will be some difficult fact situations as time and distance between murders increases, but in Corwin's case, the court found the jury had sufficient evidence that he killed as part of the same scheme or course of conduct.

3. *Underwood v. State*, 853 S.W.2d 858 (Tex. App. - Fort Worth 1993)
Section 19.03(a)(3) of the Texas Penal Code

The court defined "remuneration" in Section 19.03(a)(3) to include more than pecuniary gain. Underwood offered to kill someone for the offeree if the offeree would kill someone for him. "Remuneration" includes any benefit or compensation received because of the killing. A wife can be found guilty of murder for remuneration for killing her husband for the proceeds of his life insurance benefits. An actor's unilateral conduct in killing for gain or benefit can lead to a capital murder charge under 19.03(a)(3), *Beets v. State*, 767 S.W.2d 711 (Tex. Crim. App. 1987).

4. *Cameron v. State*, 925 S.W.2d 246 (Tex. App. – El Paso 1995)
Sections 19.03(a)(2) and 7.02 of the Texas Penal Code

An important aspect of Texas death penalty law is the law of parties and how it applies to capital murder. In order to impose culpability on a defendant as a party to the crime of capital murder, the State must prove that one party committed the murder, and that the defendant, with the intent to promote or assist the murder, aided, encouraged, or solicited the other party. The evidence must show that at the time of the crime, the parties were acting together, each doing some part of the execution of their common purpose. Persons convicted under the law of parties can also be sentenced to death.

David Cameron was convicted of capital murder for his participation in the robbery and murder of two victims. The evidence showed Cameron agreed with his friends to rob the victims, brought knives to the scene of the crime, at one point wrestled with one of the murder victims, and robbed the victims after the murders were completed. The evidence did not show Cameron had actually committed the murders. The court concluded there was sufficient evidence that Cameron intended to facilitate the murders. His conviction for capital murder was upheld.

REVIEW

1. In Texas, the capital murder statute states that the State must prove at least one aggravating factor and disprove any mitigating factors in order to establish a capital murder.
   a. True
   b. False

2. The capital punishment law in Texas is similar to capital punishment statutes in other states.
   a. True
   b. False

3. The Texas Legislature revised the questions that jurors are required to answer during the sentencing phase, after they have convicted a defendant of capital murder in:
    a. *Jurek v. Texas*
    b. *Furman v. Georgia*
    c. *Branch v. State*
    d. *Penry v. Lynaugh*

4. Hector was discharged from prison and flagged down a cabdriver to drive him from Huntsville to Dallas. Hector realized he was not able to pay the full fair. When they arrived in Dallas, Hector decided to assault the cabdriver. He didn't want to kill the cabby, just do enough harm to get away without paying the fair. Unfortunately, the cabby was a hemophiliac. Hector's blow left him to bleed to death. Hector is guilty of:
    a. murder
    b. capital murder because he killed the cabby during a robbery.
    c. capital murder because he attacked a man with serious health problems, making the murder particularly heinous.
    d. manslaughter because he recklessly created a risk but never intended a murder.

5. Wally decided the members of his prison gang needed discipline. He "requested" Rocky Hardnose to "rub out" a dissident gang member. Rocky dutifully complied. Wally is guilty of:
    a. no crime, he did not commit the murder.
    b. murder.
    c. capital murder.
    d. manslaughter.

6. A Texas jury is not advised when they begin deliberations on punishment in a capital murder trial about the consequences of the questions they must answer under the Code of Criminal Procedure.
    a. True
    b. False

7. The 1976 Texas capital punishment case that was reviewed by the U.S. Supreme Court when the Court decided the Texas statute passed constitutional muster was:
    a. *Gregg v. Texas.*
    b. *Jurek v. Texas.*
    c. *Proffitt v. Texas.*
    d. *Furman v. Texas.*

8. Prosecutors are required under the law in Texas to ask for the death penalty in every capital murder case.
    a. True
    b. False

9. Louise decided to knock-off her wealthy husband in hopes of inheriting his fortunes. She decided to commit the murder herself and not hire a hit man. She successfully murdered her husband. Louise is guilty of:
    a. capital murder for remuneration.
    b. murder because the money was adequate provocation.
    c. capital murder as a felony-murder, she murdered intending to steal his money.
    d. murder because she intentionally killed her husband.

10. Jerry was out late at night driving drunk. He has had several DWI convictions. He pulled into the McDonald's parking lot and went inside to order. He forgot to put his emergency break on, and the car rolled down a noticeable incline onto the street. It plowed into another car, killing the driver. Jerry is guilty of:
    a. criminally negligent homicide.
    b. manslaughter.
    c. murder.
    d. vehicular homicide.

11. The crime of voluntary manslaughter has been totally eliminated in Texas.
    a. True, there are no provisions recognizing murders committed with adequate provocation and in the heat of passion.
    b. True, all murders are equal.
    c. False, voluntary manslaughter is no longer a separate crime but evidence of the elements of voluntary manslaughter can be introduced during the punishment phase of a murder trial in mitigation of punishment.
    d. False, manslaughter has now been redefined to include both voluntary and involuntary manslaughter.

12. Tony decided it was time to eliminate his rival in the waster management industry. One night he followed his rival to his favorite pizza parlor. As his rival was leaving, Tony shot him with his gun. Tony looked over the dead body and noticed a large gold and diamond ring on his rival's pinky finger – similar to a ring that Tony's father used to wear. Tony leaned over and took the ring. Did Tony commit a capital murder?
    a. No, it was not a stranger-on-stranger homicide.
    b. Yes, it all happened within the same criminal transaction.
    c. No, theft cannot be used to elevate a murder to a capital felony murder status.
    d. Yes, a violent murder with a gun is a capital murder.

FINAL COMMENTS ON THE MURDER STATUTES

Before debating the death penalty, it's important to understand the law of capital murder. What distinguishes a first-degree felony murder from a capital murder? How do jurors decide punishment for someone they've convicted of capital murder? The *process* by which a person is sentenced to death or life is a key component in the debate. No process is full proof. How a jury answers the special questions during the punishment phase depends on how they interact, communicate, and compromise. It is a complex exchange, and a life is in the balance. We can question whether the state should have the power to take away a person's life. For those who decide there are circumstances that warrant a death sentence, the issue becomes whether the process by which a person is sentenced to death is fair, and, if it isn't, how can it be made better. How fair must the process be? Are there parts of the process that will remain problematic no matter what we do to improve them?

Chapter Ten

Crimes Against Persons II: Criminal Sexual Conduct, Bodily Injury and Personal Restraint

INTRODUCTION

This chapter looks at the crimes of sexual assault and assault. After homicide, assault crimes are considered the most dangerous offenses. Sexual assault, in particular, is a difficult crime to prosecute. It is a complicated criminal statute that is supplemented by various articles from the Texas Code of Criminal Procedure. The crime of assault in Texas consolidates the common law crimes of assault and battery into one statute. Both sexual assault and assault can be aggravated into more serious offenses if certain specific statutory elements were present at the time the crimes were committed.

Section 1: SEXUAL OFFENSES

OVERVIEW

Penal Code sections 22.011 and 22.021 govern the offenses of sexual assault and aggravated sexual assault. They are among the most complex statutes in the Code, in part because the State Legislature has amended them so frequently. When it comes to reviewing the cases that have interpreted these two statutes, it is sometimes difficult to know which court opinions construe which statutes.

History of Texas Rape Laws

The amendments to the sexual assault statutes reflect how society's awareness and perspective have changed. When the Texas Penal Code was totally revamped in 1974, the statutes were labeled rape and aggravated rape. At that time, rape was defined as intercourse with a woman other than the defendant's spouse without her consent. The statute required proof that the force used against the victim overcame what earnest resistance might reasonably be expected under the circumstances. Rape of a child was defined as intercourse with a female child who was not the defendant's wife and was under the age of 17. Lack of consent was not an element of the crime because children were deemed unable to consent. Aggravated rape was defined as rape or rape of a child plus certain aggravating factors. In 1974, the Texas Legislature created the separate crimes of sexual abuse and aggravated sexual abuse. Sexual abuse was essentially defined as deviate sexual intercourse with any non-consenting partner. Deviate sexual intercourse included acts of sodomy.

As they interpreted the 1974 rape and sexual abuse statutes, Texas courts focused primarily on the nature and strength of the force or threats used to compel a victim to submit. In *Rucker v. State*, 599 S.W.2d 581 (Tex. Crim. App. 1979), the Texas Court of Criminal Appeals ruled that a victim who was badly beaten by her attacker *after* he raped her did not suffer an aggravated rape because there was no evidence that her attacker used force or a threat of serious bodily injury or harm to compel her to submit. The court decided that the aggravating element of threatening death, serious bodily injury, or kidnapping could be satisfied only if it was used to compel the victim to submit to the act. That decision was highly controversial and was followed by significant legislative amendments to the statutes in both 1981 and 1983.

In 1981, the rape statutes were amended to permit conviction if the defendant compelled a victim to submit by any threat, communicated by actions, words, or deeds, that would prevent a woman of ordinary resolution from resisting, under the same or similar circumstances, because she reasonably feared harm. Language was eliminated that the force must have been sufficient to overcome such earnest resistance as might reasonably be expected. The aggravated rape statute, which already permitted conviction for serious bodily harm, was amended to permit conviction because of acts, words, or deeds that placed the victim in fear that death, serious bodily injury or kidnapping would be inflicted upon *anyone* if she did not submit. These amendments allowed juries and judges to consider not only the injuries and express verbal threats that victims suffered but also the defendant's overall conduct as manifested by his acts, words, and deeds. Prior to 1981, the defendant's violence had to compel the victim's submission. After 1981, if a rape occurred and there was violence, the crime was aggravated rape, regardless of whether the violence was used to compel submission or for some other reason. The 1981 amendments added an additional factor that could aggravate rape – using or exhibiting a deadly weapon during the crime.

The 1983 legislature continued to pass significant amendments. It combined rape and sexual abuse into one statute and changed its title to sexual assault. Aggravated rape and sexual abuse were combined into one aggravated sexual assault statute. The Legislature amended the provisions that addressed threats used to compel submission to include threats of force that a victim believed the defendant had the ability to execute. This change went further than the 1981 amendment that required a threat to meet the level that would prevent resistance by a woman of ordinary resolution. The 1983 statute replaced the objective standard of a person of ordinary resolution with the victim's subjective belief in the attacker's ability to execute the threat. The amendments also created a gender-neutral statute. Both men and women can commit sexual assault, and both men and women can be victims of sexual assault.

Recognizing that nonconsensual sexual activity is inherently violent, the 1981 and 1983 changes refocused the crime of sexual assault away from an emphasis on how much force was used against the victim to the nonconsensual nature of the offense. The statute evolved quickly as society learned more about the nature of sexual violence. In 1991, the Texas statute was amended to eliminate the marital exemption provision, so spouses can be convicted of sexually assaulting their mates.

The Elements of Modern Texas Rape Law

Section 22.011(a) of the Texas Penal Code

(a) A person commits an offense if the person:
(1) intentionally or knowingly
(A) causes the penetration of the anus or female sexual organ of another person by any means, without that person's consent;
(B) causes the penetration of the mouth of another person by the sexual organ of the actor, without that person's consent; or

(C) causes the sexual organ of another person, without that person's consent, to contact or penetrate the mouth, anus, or sexual organ of another person, including the actor; or

(2) intentionally or knowingly

(A) causes the penetration of the anus or sexual organ of a child by any means;

(B) causes the penetration of the mouth of a child by the sexual organ of the actor;

(C) causes the sexual organ of a child to contact or penetrate the mouth, anus, or sexual organ of another person, including the actor;

(D) causes the anus of a child to contact the mouth, anus, or sexual organ of another person, including the actor;

(E) causes the mouth of a child to contact the anus or sexual organ of another person, including the actor.

The mens rea for the crime of sexual assault is intentionally *or* knowingly. The State is not required to prove the defendant both intentionally and knowingly had intercourse and intentionally and knowingly compelled the victim to submit. If force or violence was used to compel submission, the State does not need to prove or allege the defendant used any specific level of force or physical violence. The State only has to show the defendant used force or violence that was directed at the victim.

Lack of consent is determined by eleven statutory conditions, one of which must be proved beyond a reasonable doubt before there can be a conviction.

Section 22.011(b) of the Texas Penal Code

(b) A sexual assault under Subsection (a)(1) is without the consent of the other person if:

(1) the actor compels the other person to submit or participate by the use of physical force or violence;

(2) the actor compels the other person to submit or participate by threatening to use force or violence against the other person, and the other person believes that the actor has the present ability to execute the threat;

(3) the other person has not consented and the actor knows the other person is unconscious or physically unable to resist;

(4) the actor knows that as a result of mental disease or defect the other person is at the time of the sexual assault incapable either of appraising the nature of the act or of resisting it;

(5) the other person has not consented and the actor knows the other person is unaware that the sexual assault is occurring;

(6) the actor has intentionally impaired the other person's power to appraise or control the other person's conduct by administering any substance without the other person's knowledge;

(7) the actor compels the other person to submit or participate by threatening to use force or violence against any person, and the other person believes that the actor has the ability to execute the threat;

(8) the actor is a public servant who coerces the other person to submit or participate;

(9) the actor is a mental health services provider or health care services provider who causes the other person, who is a patient or former patient of the actor, to submit or participate by exploiting the other person's emotional dependency on the actor;

(10) the actor is a clergyman who causes the other person to submit or participate by exploiting the other person's emotional dependency on the clergyman in the clergyman's professional character as spiritual advisor; or

(11) the actor is an employee of a facility where the other person is a resident, unless the employee and resident are formally or informally married to each other under Chapter 2, Family Code.

CASES

1. *Suarez v. State*, 901 S.W.2d 712 (Tex. App. - Corpus Christi 1995)
Section 22.011(b)(3) of the Texas Penal Code

This case involved charges of sexual assault against a midwife who assaulted his patient during a pelvic examination. The evidence showed that during the examination, while the patient was on the table and her heels in the stirrups, Suarez used his fingers to touch her female sexual organs inappropriately while telling the patient he was conducting a thorough exam. The patient was pregnant and feared Suarez might harm her baby if she moved or protested. The patient did not tell Suarez to stop because she was frozen with fear. In her testimony, she claimed she did not consent to his actions. An exam that should have taken less than a minute took about 30 minutes. A nurse was not in the room, and the door was closed. Suarez argued there was no evidence that the victim was physically unable to resist. She was not tied to the table. He made no threats and used no violence. He had no weapon. The appellate court affirmed his conviction because it found there was sufficient evidence that the victim was physically unable to resist. She was pregnant on an examination table with her legs in stirrups, which made it difficult for her to sit up with Suarez standing over her, and she was concerned about the safety of her unborn baby.

If lack of consent is based on evidence that the actor knew the victim was physically unable to resist, the State is not required to show the actor used or threatened force, nor that the victim resisted. The State only needs to prove the actor knew the victim was physically impaired and not able to resist.

2. *Garcia v. State*, 661 S.W.2d 96 (Tex. Crim. App. 1983)
Section 22.011(b)(4) of the Texas Penal Code

If the defendant knew the victim suffered from a mental disease or defect and was unable to appraise the situation or resist, the act is also considered nonconsensual. Garcia's conviction was reversed by the Court of Criminal Appeals because there was insufficient evidence he knew the victim was mentally retarded and unable to appraise the act of sexual intercourse or resist it. The evidence showed the victim did not appear to be mentally retarded. She testified that many people did not realize that she was mentally retarded and she had not informed the defendant of such. Garcia did not have much contact with the victim prior to the incident.

Child Sexual Assault

As stated in Section 22.022(a)(2), there is no need to prove lack of consent when the victim to a sexual assault is a child because children are unable to consent according to law. Section 22.011(c)(1) defines a child as a person under 17 years old who is not the spouse of the actor. It is not necessary that the defendant knew the child was under 17. There is no mistake of fact defense in Texas, according to *Jackson v. State,* 889 S.W.2d 615 (Tex. App. - Houston [14th Dist.] 1994).

There are two important defenses to a charge of sexual assault against a child.

Section 22.011(d) of the Texas Penal Code
It is a defense to prosecution under Subsection (a)(2) that the conduct consisted of medical care for the child and did not include any contact between the anus or sexual organ of the child and the mouth, anus, or sexual organ of the actor or third part.

This defense was unnecessary under the 1974 version of the law because that statute required proof that the actor intended to arouse or gratify the victim sexually. Again, it is apparent how the law has changed to reflect society's more sophisticated understanding of what constitutes a sexual assault. The mens rea requirement no longer requires evidence that the defendant intended to arouse or gratify the victim.

The other defense to a charge of sexual assault against a child is found in:

Section 22.011(e) of the Texas Penal Code
It is an affirmative defense to prosecution under Subsection(a)(2) that:
(1) the actor was not more than three years older than the victim at the time of the offense:
(2) was not required under Chapter 62, Code of Criminal procedure, as added by Chapter 668, Acts of the 75th Legislature, regular Session, 1997, to register for life as a sex offender; or
(3) was not a person who under Chapter 62 had a reportable conviction or adjudication for an offense under this section; and
(2) the victim was a child of 14 years of age or older.

The age difference for this defense was originally only two years but was extended to three in 1993. The defense is only available to a defendant if he or she was not required at the time of the offense to register for life as a sex offender and was not a person who had a reportable conviction or adjudication for an offense under the sexual assault statute.

A third defense to a charge of sexual assault against a child is no longer available because the Texas legislature repealed the provision in 1993. Prior to 1993, a defendant could introduce evidence of a child victim's promiscuity, as long as the victim was over 14 years old and the acts of promiscuity occurred prior to the charge against the defendant. Texas courts had interpreted the defense to require more than a few prior sexual experiences. The term was defined to mean a variety of sexual behaviors over a reasonable period of time with a variety of partners. The promiscuity defense proved troublesome for the courts. Critics of the provision argued it was out of step with the direction Texas law had been heading and behind legal developments in the rest of the country. The defense was repealed by the same Legislature that raised the age difference defense to three years.

Aggravated Sexual Assault

Section 22.021 defines the crime of aggravated sexual assault. It begins by incorporating all of the requirements of sexual assault and adding certain specified aggravating factors. Any one of these factors can aggravate an assault, and it can occur at any point during the assault. It does not have to compel submission to the attack. If an aggravating factor occurs at the beginning of the assault but does not continue throughout, the offense is still considered an aggravated crime. In *McAfee v. State*, 624 S.W.2d 776 (Tex. App. - Houston [14th Dist.] 1981), the appellant argued that he should not be convicted of aggravated rape because his threats to kill the victim were made 30 to 45 minutes before he actually raped her. The appellate court rejected his argument, finding that his threats and actions were all a part of an episode that culminated in an aggravated rape.

An aggravated sexual assault occurs:

Section 22.021(2) of the Texas Penal Code
(2) if:
(A) the person:
(i) causes serious bodily injury or attempts to cause the death of the victim or another person during the same criminal episode;
(ii) by acts or words places the victim in fear that death, serious bodily injury, or kidnapping will be imminently inflicted on any person
(iii) by acts or words occurring in the presence of the victim threatens to cause the death, serious bodily injury, or kidnapping of any person;
(iv) uses or exhibits a deadly weapon in the course of the same criminal episode;
(v) acts in concert with another who engages in conduct described by Subdivision (1) directed toward the same victim and occurring during the course of the same criminal episode; or
(vi) administers or provides flunitrazepam, otherwise known as rohypnol, gamma hydroxybutyrate, or ketamine to the victim of the offense with the intent of facilitating the commission of the offense;
(B) the victim is younger than 14 years of age; or
(C) the victim is an elderly individual or a disabled individual.

The Legislature amended the statute in 1999 to provide that a sexual assault is aggravated if the defendant administered or provided rohypnol or gamma hydroxybutrate (GHB) (also known as "date rape" drugs) to the victim with the intent of facilitating the crime of sexual assault.

A sexual assault is also automatically aggravated if the victim was under the age of 14 years of age, elderly, or disabled. In these cases, requirements listed in Subsection (2)(A) are not necessary elements for the offense to be elevated from a sexual assault to an aggravated sexual assault.

CASE

***Seek v. State*, 646 S.W.2d 557 (Tex. App. - Houston [1st] 1982)**
Section 22.021(2)(A)(ii) of the Texas Penal Code

Acts or words that threaten do not have to be express or verbal. Threats can be inferred from the totality of the circumstances, including a defendant's words, acts, and deeds. The issue is whether given all that transpired, was the victim placed in fear of imminent serious bodily injury, death, or kidnapping. Seek argued he was not guilty of aggravated rape because he did not use a weapon or suggest that he had one, nor did he compel submission by an express verbal threat. The evidence showed that Seek threw the victim to the floor, hit her in the face and choked her with his hands. The victim testified she feared for her safety. The court concluded that by his acts, words, and deeds, the appellant put the victim in fear for her life and committed the crime of aggravated rape. A jury could infer from the totality of circumstances that Seek's acts and deeds placed the victim in fear.

Another aggravating factor involves threats of future death, serious injury, or kidnapping to any person. There is no requirement that the threats be of imminent harm; however, the threats must be made in the victim's presence.

The Outcry Statement

Because the only witnesses to sexual assault crimes are often the victim and the offender, the law is concerned about the need to substantiate or corroborate a lone victim's allegations. Article 38.07 of the Texas Code of Criminal Procedure provides that a conviction under Sections 22.011 or 22.021 can be supported on the uncorroborated testimony of the victim if the victim informed any person, other than the defendant, of the offense within one year after the date on which the offense occurred. The one-year reporting period went into effect in 1993 and expanded what was previously a six-month reporting period.

That requirement is waived if at the time of the offense the victim was younger than 17 years old, older than 65 years, or 18 years or older and by reason of age or physical or mental disease, defect, or injury was unable to satisfy the need for food, shelter, medical care, or protection from harm. This evidentiary requirement is called the *outcry statement*. The Legislature raised the maximum age for which no corroboration is required from 14 to 18 years old in 1993. In 2001, the Legislature waived the requirement for persons over 65 and for mentally and physically ill persons who are unable to take care of their own basic needs.

If the victim makes a report within a year of the offense, there is no need for corroborating evidence. If a report was not made, article 38.07 requires some kind of corroboration. Without it, there can be no conviction. Corroborating evidence only needs to connect the defendant to the offense. In *Nemecek v. State*, 621 S.W.2d 404 (Tex. Crim. App. 1980), the appellant admitted to having sexual intercourse with a 13 year old child but alleged it was with the child's consent. The child did not make an outcry statement within the time period specified in article 38.07 so that corroborating evidence was necessary to support Nemecek's conviction. The court concluded that Nemecek's own admissions were sufficient corroboration of the victim's testimony.

Article 38.071 of the Texas Code of Criminal Procedure protects children who are victims of sexual assault. Under certain circumstances, it allows a videotape of a child's statement to be introduced into evidence in lieu of the child testifying in court. It also allows a child to be questioned by closed circuit television as opposed to appearing live in the courtroom.

Victim's Past Conduct

Another very important evidentiary matter in sexual assault cases concerns the admissibility of evidence about the victim's prior sexual conduct. Rule 412 of the Texas Rules of Criminal Evidence governs the admissibility of such evidence. It provides that reputation or opinion evidence about the victim's past sexual behavior is inadmissible. Evidence of specific instances of a victim's prior sexual behavior is also inadmissible except under certain narrow circumstances, and only if the court first determines that the probative value of the evidence outweighs any danger of unfair prejudice to the victim.

To be admissible under one of the two narrow exceptions, evidence of specific past instances might be necessary to rebut or explain scientific or medical evidence offered by the State. For instance, if the State introduces evidence concerning tears and lacerations to the victim's vagina on the theory they were caused by the defendant, the defendant could introduce evidence of an alternative cause of the injuries. Prior sexual conduct is also admissible if the conduct was with the accused and the accused raises consent as a defense. The evidence is admissible only if it exposes the victim's bias or a motive to testify falsely. Decisions about the admissibility of evidence about a victim's prior sexual conduct are made outside the presence of the jury in a hearing before the judge, closed to the public. The record of that hearing is sealed from public view and is only for review by the appellate court, if necessary. The rule is strictly enforced. Rule 412 minimizes the embarrassment and humiliation suffered by sexual assault victims and seeks to encourage victims to report sexual assaults to authorities.

Read two other important Texas Penal Code provisions dealing with sexual misconduct: Section 21.11 Indecency with a Child and Section 25.02 Prohibited Sexual Conduct. Notice how those statutes address different but related types of behavior compared to Sections 22.011 and 22.021.

Sex Offender Registration

State Legislatures throughout the country have examined sexual assault statutes in recent years to find ways to better protect communities. The U.S. Congress passed legislation in 1994, 1995, and 1996 that requires states to create registries of certain sex offenders and establish community notification programs. As of 1996, all fifty states require sex offenders to register with local law enforcement agencies when they are on community supervision.

The Texas Sex Offender Registration Program, found in Chapter 62 of the Texas Code of Criminal Procedure, was originally enacted in 1991 and has been amended many times. In 1997, the registration requirements were made retroactive to convictions or adjudications that occurred on or after September 1, 1970. It is a multi-agency program that is administered by the Texas Department of Public Safety.

There are ten categories of sex crimes that carry a requirement to register. Convictions, adjudications, deferred adjudications, or adjudications of delinquent conduct for any offense in these categories, including attempt, conspiracy or solicitation result in registration. Offenders who commit sex crimes that are listed as sexually violent must register for the remainder of their lives. Other sex offenders must continue to register for ten years after their release or discharge from supervision or incarceration, whichever arrives first.

The categories of sex crimes that require registration are listed in Article 62.01 of the Texas Code of Criminal Procedure:

- Indecency with a Child – Compelling Prostitution;
- Sexual Assault – Aggravated Sexual Assault;
- Prohibited Sexual Conduct – Sexual Performance by a Child;
- Aggravated Kidnapping with Intent to Violate or Abuse the Victim Sexually;
- Burglary of a Habitation with Intent to Commit a Felony Sexual Offense;
- A second conviction for Indecent Exposure;
- Unlawful Restraint, Kidnapping, or Aggravated Kidnapping if the judgment contains a finding that the victim was a child under 17;
- Any substantially similar offense committed under the laws of another jurisdiction;
- Any offense that results in a condition of parole, release on mandatory supervision, or community supervision requiring registration as a sex offender.

The violent sex crimes requiring lifetime registration are:

- Indecency with a Child by Contact;
- Compelling Prostitution of a Minor;
- Sexual Assault and Aggravated Sexual Assault, regardless of the victim's age;
- Prohibited Sexual Conduct;
- Sexual Performance by a Child;
- Possession or Promotion of Child Pornography;
- Aggravated Kidnapping with Intent to Violate or Abuse the Victim Sexually;
- Burglary of a Habitation with Intent to Commit a Felony Sexual Offense.

Sex offenders who fall within the requirements must register their address with the appropriate local law enforcement agency. They must notify authorities about any change of address. Offenders must verify their registration with local law enforcement annually, on their birthday. If the offender has two or more violent sex offender convictions, they must verify their registration every ninety days. Offenders who fail to comply with any of the registration requirements face punishment ranging from a state jail felony for those who are not required to register for a lifetime to a third-degree felony for those who must register annually for life. Offenders who must register every ninety days face a second-degree felony.

Local law enforcement agencies send registration information to the Department of Public Safety who up-date the state registry. All sex offender registration information is considered public and must be released by local law enforcement agencies upon written request, including information on adult and juvenile offenders. The public information includes the offender's name, address, offense, and his or her photograph. Information about offenders whose victims were under age 17, and whose case was dispositioned on or after September 1, 1995, is subject to publication in newspapers or on a website. Public and private schools are provided information about all offenders who live in the school district and whose victims were under age 17.

REVIEW

1. To convict a person of the crime of sexual assault in Texas, there must be evidence that:
    a. the victim resisted the attacker to the utmost.
    b. the accused used physical force against the victim.
    c. the accused made threats of force and the victim believed the accused had the present ability to execute the threats.
    d. either b and c.

2. The only exception to the marital exemption for sexual assault in Texas is if the husband and wife are living separately.
    a. True
    b. False

3. If the actor did not know that the victim was incapable of appraising the nature of the act because of a mental disease, the actor is still guilty of the crime of sexual assault.
    a. True
    b. False

4. If the actor, 22 years old, did not know that the victim was 16 years old and can show that the victim looked much older and lied about her age, he can be still found guilty of sexual assault in Texas.
    a. True
    b. False

5. By arguing that he was not aware of her age, the defense offered by the actor is:
    a. mistake of law.
    b. mistake of fact.
    c. the victim was promiscuous.
    d. he was overwhelmed and acted in self-defense.

6. A victim's uncorroborated testimony can be used against a defendant in a sexual assault case if the:
    a. victim made an outcry statement within one year of the crime.
    b. defendant made a confession to the crime.
    c. defendant had a prior history of sexual assault.
    d. victim's outcry statement specifically identifies the defendant as the actor.

7. A victim's prior sexual conduct can be introduced into a trial of a sexual assault crime if:
    a. under no condition; it is never admissible.
    b. the State introduces medical evidence and evidence of the victim's prior sexual conduct can rebut or explain it.
    c. it relates to past sexual conduct with the accused that relates to the issue of consent.
    d. b and c.

8. If Jack was 18 years old when he had consensual sexual relations with Lily who is 15 years old, he can still be found guilty of sexual assault because Lily is a child under section 22.011. Jack has no prior convictions.
    a. True
    b. False

9. Jack slipped some GHB into Sara's beer without her knowing it. Later that night, he had sexual intercourse with Sara while she was under the influence of the GHB. Jack has:
    a. been deceptive and is a jerk, but not a criminal. Women should be careful about who they meet at bars.
    b. committed the crime of sexual assault.
    c. committed the crime of extortion.
    d. commited the crime of aggravated sexual assault.

Section 2: ASSAULT

OVERVIEW

Texas law does not separate the common law crimes of assault and battery into different statutes. There are two primary assault statutes: Sections 22.01 and 22.02. The crime of assault is defined in Section 22.01 of the Penal Code and includes behavior that could be categorized as battery.

Section 22.01 of the Texas Penal Code
(a) A person commits an offense if the person:
(1) intentionally, knowingly, or recklessly causes bodily injury to another, including the person's spouse;
(2) intentionally or knowingly threatens another with imminent bodily injury, including the person's spouse;
(3) intentionally or knowingly causes physical contact with another when the person knows or should reasonably believe that the other will regard the contact as offensive or provocative.

The mens rea requirement for causing bodily injury is intentionally, knowingly, or recklessly. The mens rea requirement for threatening to cause injury or causing offensive or provocative contact is intentionally or knowingly. A person cannot recklessly threaten or cause offensive contact.

An offense under Subsection (a)(1) is a Class A misdemeanor. It is a third-degree felony if it was committed against a public servant while the servant was discharging his or her official duties or in retaliation for an action taken by a public servant in the performance of official duties. It is also a third-degree felony if it was committed against a family member and the defendant had previously been convicted of an offense against a family member.

Section 22.02 of the Texas Penal Code

(a) A person commits an offense if the person commits assault as defined in Section 22.01 and the person:

(1) causes serious bodily injury to another, including the person's spouse; or

(2) uses or exhibits a deadly weapon during the commission of the assault.

A conviction under Section 22.02 is a second-degree felony unless it was committed against a public servant while he or she was performing official duties or in retaliation for performing those duties, which would make it a first-degree felony. It is a first-degree felony if it was committed in retaliation against or on account of service as a witness, prospective witness, informant, or against a person who reported a crime to the authorities. It is also a first-degree felony if it was committed against a security officer while performing his or her duties.

CASES

1. *Powell v. State*, 939 S.W.2d 713 (Tex. App. - El Paso 1997)
Section 22.02(a)(2) of the Texas Penal Code

What can be considered a deadly weapon is important in an aggravated assault charge. Powell was convicted of aggravated assault after repeatedly kicking a police officer with his foot. The Penal Code defines a deadly weapon in section 1.07 as anything that in the manner of use or intended use is capable of causing death or serious bodily injury. A foot is not usually considered a deadly weapon, but the court concluded it might become a deadly weapon if used in such a way that it could cause death or serious injuries. The evidence showed Powell's foot caused serious injuries. A medical expert testified that Powell's blows to the victim's head with his foot were serious and could have killed the officer. The aggravated assault conviction was affirmed. In *Gibbs v. State*, 932 S.W.2d 256 (Tex. App. - Texarkana 1996), the appellate court affirmed Gibb's aggravated assault conviction for using his truck as a deadly weapon. The evidence showed Gibbs used his truck to back into several victims and ran forward over another victim.

2. *Melonson v. State*, 942 S.W.2d 777 (Tex. App. - Beaumont 1997)
Section 22.02(a)(2) of the Texas Penal Code

The Court of Appeals upheld the aggravated assault conviction of Isaac Melonson who argued he did not participate in the use of a deadly weapon against the victim who had been beaten with a baseball bat. Melonson admitted hitting the victim and being present during the baseball bat beating but claimed he was only guilty of assault. The court relied on the law of parties to affirm his conviction for aggravated assault on the grounds that he was aware his crime partners were using a baseball bat against the victim and he did not attempt to stop the attack. He had also agreed to attack the victim in order to steal his truck. The court concluded that Melonson was acting with the other attackers, and encouraged and participated in the aggravated assault even though he did not use the bat himself.

Other Important Assault Statutes

In addition to the assault and sexual assault statutes already discussed in this chapter, there are several other important assault-related statutes. If a person *recklessly* puts another person in imminent danger of serious bodily injury, he or she can be charged with **Deadly Conduct - Section 22.05**. Deadly conduct also includes knowingly discharging a firearm at or in the direction of other people or a habitation, building, or vehicle and being reckless as to whether those structures are occupied. Recklessness and danger are presumed if the defendant knowingly pointed a firearm in the direction of another person whether or not the defendant believed the firearm was loaded.

Section 22.04 - Injury to a Child, Elderly Individual, or Disabled Individual makes it a crime to intentionally, knowingly, recklessly, or with criminal negligence cause bodily injury, serious bodily injury, or serious mental deficiency, impairment, or injury to a child, an elderly person, or a disabled person. The actus reus includes acts of omission if the defendant had a legal or statutory duty to act or assumed care for the injured person. A child is a person 14 years old or under. An elderly individual is 65 years or older. A disabled individual is a person who because of age or physical or mental disease, defect, or injury is unable to protect himself or to provide food, shelter, or medical care for himself.

Section 22.015 - Coercing, Soliciting, or Inducing Gang Membership was added to the Penal Code in 1999. The statute makes it a separate crime to threaten a child or cause a child injury with the intent to coerce, induce, or solicit a child to actively participate in street gang activities. Threatening injury results in a state jail felony. Causing injury results in a third-degree felony.

Also added to the assault statutes in 1999 was **Section 22.11- Harassment by Persons in Certain Correctional Facilities,** which makes it a third-degree felony for persons who are incarcerated in secure correctional facilities or in the Texas Youth Commission to cause another person to contact blood, seminal fluid, vaginal fluid, saliva, urine, or feces with the intent to harass, alarm, or annoy them. This statute is aimed at a significant problem in correctional institutions: prisoners who throw blood, urine, and feces at correctional officers.

Section 22.07 - Terroristic Threat statute was amended during the most recent Texas legislative session to include Subsections (5) and (6). This is a very comprehensive statute and the newest amendments obviously reflect many of society's concerns about terrorist activities. Remember, however, that Subsection (a)(2) also extends the reach of this statute to an individual who uses threats of violence to put his ex-wife, supervisor, next door neighbor, friendly used car dealer, etc. in fear of imminent serious bodily harm!

Section 22.07 of the Texas Penal Code

(a) A person commits an offense if he threatens to commit any offense involving violence to any person or property with intent to:

(1) cause a reaction of any type to his threat by an official or volunteer agency organized to deal with emergencies;

(2) place any person in fear of imminent serious bodily injury;

(3) prevent or interrupt the occupation or use of a building; room; place of assembly; place to which the public has access; place of employment or occupation; aircraft, automobile, or other form of conveyance; or other public place;

(4) cause impairment or interruption of public communication, public transportation, public water, gas, or power supply or other public service;

(5) place the public or a substantial group of the public in fear of serious bodily injury; or

(6) influence the conduct or activities of a branch or agency of the federal government, the state, or a political subdivision of the state.

REVIEW

10. Margaret Jones was the Director of Public Parks for a medium sized city. She told the owner of a small business that did work for her department that unless he had sexual relations with her, she would make public that he had overcharged the city in a number of different transactions. The businessman submitted but afterwards decided to report the incident to the police. Jones can be found guilty of:
    a. nothing, the businessman was not threatened with force or violence and no weapons were used by Jones. He consented.
    b. he can sue her in civil court for sexual harassment but there is no criminal charge.
    c. sexual assault under section 22.011(b)(8).
    d. extortion.

11. The crime of assault can be committed in Texas if a person:
    a. intentionally, knowingly or recklessly threatens another person with imminent bodily harm.
    b. intentionally threatens another with imminent bodily harm.
    c. intentionally or knowingly threatens another person with imminent bodily harm.
    d. recklessly threatens a person with imminent bodily harm.

12. In order for an assault to be aggravated, it must have resulted in serious injury to the victim.
    a. True
    b. False

13. Assault of an elderly person can be elevated to a Class A misdemeanor if it occurred:
    a. intentionally only.
    b. intentionally and knowingly.
    c. intentionally, knowingly and recklessly.
    d. by mistake.

14. Although no one was injured, Joe knowingly fired a firearm into a building he assumed was unoccupied because business hours had ended. Joe can be charged with:
    a. aggravated assault.
    b. deadly conduct.
    c. threatening the public.
    d. assault.

15. Tommy was angry with his boss. Tommy wanted to scare his boss, so he took his unloaded pistol to his place of employment and waived it around while he yelled at his boss and threatened to harm him. Tommy never laid a hand on his boss. Tommy can be charged with:
    a. assault only, no injuries occurred and the gun was not loaded.
    b. aggravated assault, the fact that there were no injuries and the gun was not loaded is not relevant.
    c. no crime, this was a disagreement only and Tommy never intended harm.
    d. deadly conduct for bringing a pistol into a building and exhibiting it.

FINAL COMMENTS ON SEXUAL ASSAULT AND ASSAULT

Sexual assault statutes have undergone tremendous reform during the last two decades. The law is a living presence. It is shaped by what we think is inappropriate behavior. It evolves as we evolve. The study of criminal law is much more than the study of statutes and legal analysis. It is the study of how society changes to meet new challenges, and how the sensibilities of human beings develop over time. Sexual assault laws are a good example of how what happens in the legislature and in the courtroom reflects what is happening in the hearts and minds of ordinary men and women.

Chapter Eleven

Crimes Against Property

INTRODUCTION

This is an ambitious chapter. We look at the many criminal offenses against property. Some of those crimes involve violence against persons as well. Chapter 31 of the Penal Code, which defines theft offenses, is by far the broadest, most comprehensive set of statutes in the Code. Some of the theft offenses are based on the value of the property taken. Others focus on the type of property taken, and others on the manner in which the property was taken. Robbery, which is as much a crime of violence as an offense against property, is defined in Sections 29.02 and 29.03. Fraud, including forgery crimes, is defined in Chapter 32.

Many of us have been the victims of a burglary. We may even be blasé about burglary to the point of not bothering to report a crime when the value of the stolen items was below the amount of the insurance deductible. We don't expect the police to capture the burglar much less recover our property. Criminal trespass and criminal mischief are also crimes we may chose to ignore if the damage was not significant. On the other hand, a house burglary, especially, can seriously undermine our sense of security. A large industry caters to that insecurity: house and car alarm systems, gates, burglar bars, and breeders of large German Shepherds! These types of crimes have residual effects that extend far beyond the actual damage done or loss incurred. This chapter also examines the Texas laws that address burglary, criminal trespass, arson, and criminal mischief.

Section 1: TAKING OTHER PEOPLE'S PROPERTY

OVERVIEW OF THEFT

Prior to 1974, Texas courts spent a considerable amount of time in theft cases deciding exactly what type of theft occurred and whether the State charged the defendant with the correct crime. The legislature addressed those problems when it created a consolidated theft statute. In Section 31.02, the lawmakers made it clear that theft is theft is theft in Texas. All theft crimes were consolidated into one main statute. No longer are larceny, shoplifting, embezzlement, false pretenses, extortion, receiving or concealing stolen property, or conversion by a bailee defined as different offenses. There were only two exceptions made in 1974. The Legislature created a separate statute for theft of services and for the unauthorized use of an automobile.

Section 31.03 of the Texas Penal Code

(a) A person commits an offense if he unlawfully appropriates property with intent to deprive the owner of property.

(b) Appropriation of property is unlawful if it:

(1) It is without the owner's effective consent;

(2) the property is stolen and the actor appropriates the property knowing it was stolen by another; or

(3) property in the custody of any law enforcement agency was explicitly represented by any law enforcement agent to the actor as being stolen and the actor appropriates the property believing it was stolen by another.

The mens rea of the crime of theft is the intent to deprive the owner of property. Section 31.01 defines the terms whose definitions are essential for understanding the crime of theft.

Section 31.01(2) of the Texas Penal Code

(2) "Deprive" means:

(A) to withhold property from the owner permanently or for so extended period of time that a major portion of the value or enjoyment of the property is lost to the owner;

(B) to restore property only upon payment of a reward or compensation; or

(C) to dispose of property in a manner that makes recovery of the property by the owner unlikely.

Intent to deprive often becomes an issue if a defendant asserts he exercised control over the property for only a short while. Prior to 1974, the statute required that the defendant permanently intend to deprive the owner of property. Under the consolidated statute, the State can now show the owner was deprived for a period of time in a manner that interfered with using or enjoying the property. It is the defendant's intent at the time the property was taken that must be established. If a defendant takes property with the intent of keeping it permanently and later decides to return it, he or she can still face theft charges.

The actus reus of theft is to unlawfully appropriate someone else's property.

Section 31.01(4) of the Texas Penal Code

(4) "Appropriate"means:

(A) to bring a transfer or purported transfer of title to or other nonpossessory interest in property, whether to the actor or another; or

(B) to acquire or otherwise exercise control over property other than real property.

The Texas Court of Criminal Appeals interpreted the meaning of "intent to deprive" in *McClain v. State*, 687 S.W.2d 350 (Tex.Crim.App. 1985). The court ruled that if a defendant exercised control over the owner's property knowing they did not have the owner's consent and with the intent to deprive the owner, the defendant committed theft. The crime of theft is accomplished *without regard to how the defendant acquired the property.* This ruling has made it easier for the State to establish both the mens rea and actus reus elements of theft.

Section 31.06 of the Penal Code permits the presumption that the defendant intended to steal property or services if he or she obtained them by issuing or passing a check when there were insufficient funds on deposit with the bank for the full payment of the check. This presumption operates under one of two conditions: if the defendant had no account at the bank at the time he or she issued the check or payment was refused by the bank because of insufficient funds and the defendant failed to pay the holder of the check within 10 days after receiving notice.

Receiving Stolen Property

Prior to 1974, receiving stolen property and concealing stolen property were two separate offenses. The new Code consolidated those offenses into the general theft offense in Section 31.03(b)(2). Technically, there is no offense of receiving stolen property. The crime is appropriating property that the defendant knows is stolen. In Section 31.03(c)(1), the statute provides that evidence of similar and recent offenses to the current charge can be admitted in order to establish knowledge that the property was stolen. An accomplice's uncorroborated testimony can be introduced to establish both knowledge and intent, pursuant to Section 31.03(c)(2).

Finally, Section 31.03 permits certain presumptions to be made. A person who is in the business of selling used merchandise is presumed to know the property was stolen if he or she pays more than $25.00 for it and fails to record the seller's name, address, physical description or identification number, fails to record a complete description of the property, including serial number or fails to obtain a warranty from the seller that the seller has the right to possess the property. Legal presumptions are governed by Section 2.05 of the Penal Code. Presumptions are a powerful leverage for the State. If there is sufficient evidence of the facts required to establish a presumption, the issue is submitted to the jury. The jury, however, is instructed that the facts establishing the presumption must be proved beyond a reasonable doubt, and that they are not obligated to accept the presumption.

Punishment

The value of the stolen property is the primary determinant of punishment for a theft crime. Punishment can range from a Class C misdemeanor to a first-degree felony. Punishment ranges are amended by the legislature periodically. Section 31.08 provides the standards by which value is to be calculated.

In some instances, the character of the property determines the punishment range. Theft of livestock is determined by both the value of the livestock and the number of animals stolen. Theft of property from another person or from a human corpse or grave is a state jail felony, regardless of the property's value. Stealing from a person using force or violence would be a robbery, not a theft. Picking pockets and purse snatching, however, are covered by the theft statute. *Cook v. State*, 706 S.W.2d 775 (Tex. App. – Houston [14th Dist.] 1986). If the stolen property was a firearm, it is also punished as a state jail felony. If a public servant appropriated property by virtue of his or her status as a public servant, punishment is increased to the next higher category.

Section 31.09 allows the State to aggregate a number of thefts together and prosecute them as one criminal offense. As long as the State can show that the thefts resulted from one scheme or continuing course of conduct, the conduct can be considered one crime and the amounts stolen can be aggregated for determining punishment.

CASE

***Hardesty v. State*, 656 S.W.2d 73 (Tex.Crim.App. 1983)**
Section 31.03 of the Texas Penal Code

The Court of Criminal Appeals ruled that if a defendant is found in possession of stolen property and offers no reasonable explanation for his or her possession, a jury might infer that the defendant stole the property. If the inference is used, there must be evidence the property found with the defendant is the same as the stolen property. The property must be in the defendant's exclusive possession and had to be recently stolen. The *Hardesty* inference is not available for crimes involving receiving stolen property where it must be established that the defendant knew the property was stolen.

Theft of Service

Section 31.04 of the Texas Penal Code

(a) A person commits theft of service if, with intent to avoid payment for service that he knows is provided only for compensation:

(1) he intentionally or knowingly secures performance of the service by deception, threat, or false token;

(2) having control over the disposition of services of another to which he is not entitled, he intentionally or knowingly diverts the other's services to his own benefit or to the benefit of another not entitled to them;

(3) having control of personal property under a written rental agreement, he holds the property beyond the expiration of the rental period without the effective consent of the owner of the property, thereby depriving the owner of the property of its use in further rentals; or

(4) he intentionally or knowingly secures the performance of the service by agreeing to provide compensation and, after the service is rendered, fails to make payment after receiving notice demanding payment.

Service is generally anything that would be provided for compensation that would not be considered property, such as labor, professional services, and rental of property. Labor is not always a service if it was primarily the property the defendant was seeking to gain. There are situations that are mixed service/property transactions. Are you purchasing food - property, or service - food preparation - in a restaurant? Courts typically apply the theft of service statute when some service was intended. Restaurant food and hotel rooms are considered services. *Chance v. State*, 579 S.W.2d 471 (Tex.Crim.App. 1979).

Theft of service can occur in three ways if the defendant intended to avoid payment for service he knew were provided for compensation:

Section 31.04(b) of the Texas Penal Code

(b) For purposes of this section, intent to avoid payment is presumed if:

(1) the actor absconded without paying for the service or expressly refused to pay for the service in circumstances where payment is ordinarily made immediately upon rendering the service, as in hotels, campgrounds, recreational vehicle parks, restaurants, and comparable establishments;

(2) the actor failed to return the property held under a rental agreement or failed to make payment under a service agreement within 10 days after receiving notice demanding return; or

(3) the actor returns property held under a rental agreement after the expiration of the rental agreement and fails to pay the applicable rental charge for the property within 10 days after the date on which the actor received notice demanding payment; or
(4) the actor failed to return the property held under a rental agreement:
(A) within five days after receiving notice demanding return, if the property is valued less than $1500; or
(B) within three days after receiving notice demanding return, if the property is valued at $1500 or more.

If the State attempts to show the defendant absconded without making payment under Section 31.04(b)(1), there must be evidence that he or she left clandestinely or furtively. It is not sufficient that he or she simply left without making payment. The importance of the deception element was emphasized in *Bullet v. State*, 538 S.W.2d 785 (Tex.Crim.App. 1976). In that case the maid, who had been instructed not to make long distance telephone calls on her employer's phone, was found not to have committed theft of service by accepting a collect call on that phone because there was no showing of deception.

Chapter 31 of the Penal Code includes several other theft offenses that have been added by the Texas Legislature over the years.

Section 31.05 - Theft of Trade Secrets
Section 31.11 - Tampering with Identification Numbers
Section 31.12 - Theft of or Tampering with Multichannel Video or Information Services
Section 31.13 - Manufacture, Distribution, or Advertisement of Multichannel Video or Information Services
Section 31.14 – Sale or Lease of Multichannel Video or Information Services Device
Section 31.15 - Possession, Manufacture, or Distribution of Certain Instruments Used to Commit Retail Theft

Unauthorized Use of a Vehicle

Unauthorized use of a motor vehicle is defined in Section 31.07. Included as motor vehicles are automobiles, trucks, boats, airplanes, and any other motor-propelled vehicle. The section makes it unlawful intentionally or knowingly to operate another person's motor vehicle without their consent. There are limits on the extent to which circumstantial evidence can be used to show operation.

CASES

1. *Anthony v. State*, 628 S.W.2d 151 (Tex. App. - Houston [14th Dist.] 1982)
Section 31.07 of the Texas Penal Code

In this case, the court held that even though Anthony was seen exiting the driver's seat in a car and fleeing the scene when he was approached by a police officer who testified the car could not have been turned off for more than two minutes, there was insufficient evidence of unauthorized use of the vehicle.

2. *Denton v. State*, 880 S.W.2d 255 (Tex. App. – Fort Worth 1994)
Section 31.07 of the Texas Penal Code

In this case, the court upheld the defendant's conviction for unauthorized use of a motor vehicle. Denton attempted to steal a truck that would not run until it had warmed up for at least five minutes. The truck owner stopped the defendant before the truck had warmed up. The court concluded the defendant had exerted enough power, influence and control over the truck to constitute operation.

REVIEW

1. Sally operated a pawnshop in Houston and regularly purchases items from Tommy. She was suspicious but liked the merchandise he sold her. She failed to get a warranty from him that he had the right to possess the property he sold. The police visit Sally one day after Tommy is busted for burglary and selling the property he stole.
    a. She has nothing to worry about because she has no proof the merchandise was stolen.
    b. Sally faces a legal presumption that she knew the property was stolen.
    c. She has no problems because she was not a part of a burglary ring.
    d. She has problems only if Tommy implicates her.

2. The neighborhood Gang of Vandals forced small business owners on their block to pay them protection money. Failure to pay the money put the businesses at risk for being vandalized by gang members. The Vandals were apprehended by the Dallas police and charged with:
    a. extortion.
    b. theft.
    c. robbery.
    d. larceny.

3. Kevin "borrowed" his uncle's car because his car was in the shop. Unfortunately, Kevin did not request permission from his uncle, nor did he inform his uncle that he borrowed his car. Kevin intended to return the car that evening. Kevin has committed:
    a. theft of automobile.
    b. there was no crime because it involved another family member.
    c. unauthorized use of a motor vehicle.
    d. larceny.

4. Mary gave Larry an expensive sound system that she took from Terry, without Terry's consent. Larry knew the sound system was stolen, but he had absolutely no involvement in stealing it or planning to steal it. Neither did he encourage Mary to steal it. Larry loves the system and installs it in his apartment. Is Larry guilty of the crime of theft?
    a. No, he had no involvement in stealing the system from Terry.
    b. No, it was a gift from Mary.
    c. Yes, he appropriated the system, knowing it was taken without Terry's consent
    d. Yes, his actions are immoral.

5. Will was driving home from a camping weekend with his two small children in a crowded VW bug. He pulled into a gas station to fill up. After he filled the tank, he was distracted by one of the kids who was waving his arms outside the window. Exasperated, Will reprimanded his son, got in the VW and drove off without paying for the gasoline. Will has:
    a. committed the crime of theft of service.
    b. embarrassed himself but committed no crime because he didn't intend not to pay
    c. committed the crime of theft of property .
    d. two children who need better discipline!

OVERVIEW OF FRAUD

Chapter 32 defines crimes involving fraudulent conduct. Common to all the offenses in the chapter is fraudulent intent. Crimes of fraud do not require a victim who has suffered harm. If a defendant engages in fraudulent conduct with the intent defined in the statute, the defendant can be prosecuted even if no one has suffered loss. Section 32.01 defines the terms common to the fraud crimes, including "financial institution," "property," "service," and "steal." Section 32.02 sets out the manner for determining the value of stolen property. Section 32.03 allows for the aggregation of amounts of property stolen as part of the same scheme or continuing course of conduct.

Forgery

Section 32.21 of the Texas Penal Code

(a) For purposes of this section:
(1) "Forge" means:
(A) to alter, make, complete, execute, or authenticate any writing so that it purports:
(i) to be the act of another who did not authorize that act;
(ii) to have been executed at a time or place or in a numbered sequence other than what was in fact the case; or
(iii) to be a copy of an original when no original existed;
(B) to issue, transfer, register the transfer of, pass, publish, or otherwise utter a writing that has been forged within the meaning of Paragraph (A); or
(C) to possess a writing that is forged within the meaning of Paragraph (A) with intent to utter it in a manner specified by Paragraph (B).

In short, forgery is making a forged instrument, passing a forged instrument, or possessing a forged instrument with the intent to utter. Depending on the nature of the forged writing, punishment for forgery can range from a Class A misdemeanor to third-degree felony.

The mens rea required by the statute is defined in Section 32.21(b): intent to defraud or harm another person. Texas law prior to 1974 required only intent to defraud. By adding intent to harm as a second mens rea element, the Legislature expanded the scope of the statute. According to *Landry v. State*, 583 S.W.2d 620 (Tex.Crim.App. 1979), the State no longer needs to establish that the defendant obtained property or received some benefit for the forged writing. If there was intent to harm someone, that is sufficient to satisfy the mens rea element. Under prior law, without a showing of harm, the case would be one of attempted forgery.

What constitutes a "writing" is broadly defined. Under prior Texas law, the forged instrument must have resulted in a pecuniary loss or somehow affected property. Since 1974, under Section 32.21(a)(2) writings also include symbols of value, right, privilege, or identification along with instruments and items that involve pecuniary obligations. Under the prior law, the forged instrument had to appear so genuine on its face that it would deceive a person under ordinary observation. The current statute is focused entirely on the defendant's intent. If the intent was to defraud, *it does not matter that the forged instrument did not appear genuine.* Also, it is the document's deceptive appearance, even if it does not appear genuine, that creates forgery, not false statements made within the document. *Sales v. State*, 628 S.W.2d 796 (Tex.Crim.App. 1982).

Criminal Simulation

Criminal simulation, defined in Section 32.22, is almost the same as a forgery offense except it addresses objects and not writings. The mens rea is the same as forgery: intent to defraud or harm another person. The actus reus is to make or alter objects so that they appear to have value because of age, antiquity, rarity, source, or authorship. Like forgery, the actus reus element can be satisfied by possessing such an object with the intent to sell or pass it. It can also be satisfied by authenticating or certifying such an object as genuine or as different from what it is. There is no requirement that the defendant receive anything of value for the crime to have been committed.

Chapter 32 defines many other fraud offenses:

Section 32.31 - Credit Card or Debit Card Abuse
Section 32,32 - False Statement to Obtain Property or Credit
Section 32.33 - Hindering Secured Creditors
Section 32.34 - Fraudulent Transfer of a Motor Vehicle
Section 32.35 - Credit Card Transaction Record Laundering
Section 32.41 - Issuance of Bad Check
Section 32.42 - Deceptive Business Practices
Section 32.43 - Commercial Bribery
Section 32.44 - Rigging Publicly Exhibited Contest
Section 32.441 - Illegal Recruitment of an Athlete
Section 32.45 - Misapplication of Fiduciary Property or Property of Financial Institution
Section 32.46 - Securing Execution of Document by Deception
Section 32.47 - Fraudulent Destruction, Removal, or Concealment of Writing
Section 32.48 - Simulating Legal Process
Section 32.49 - Refusal to Execute Release of Fraudulent Lien or Claim
Section 32.50 - Deceptive Preparation and Marketing of Academic Product
Section 32.51 - Fraudulent Use or Possession of Identifying Information

REVIEW

6. Rocky Heartless promised elderly Mrs. Smith that he would repair her roof for only $15,000.00, one-half of her life savings. He told her the roof would cave in if she did not act quickly. Mrs. Smith paid the money. As it turned out, the roof did not need any repair. Heartless is guilty of:
   a. nothing, let the buyer beware.
   b. extortion.
   c. false pretenses.
   d. deceptive business practices.

7. Hanna Heartless, Rocky's sister told Mrs. Smith that the armoire she purchased from Hanna dated from the early 1700s. In reality, the armoire dated to 1955. To be guilty of a crime, there must be proof that Hanna:
   a. Knew Mrs. Smith was vulnerable.
   b. bought the armoire from someone else who altered it.
   c. recklessly suggested the armoire was older than it really was.
   d. authenticated the armoire as from the 1700s with the intent to defraud Mrs. Smith.

8. Leroy created false passports for his friends so they could take a quick trip to South America. He was not compensated by them, but provided his services as a favor. Leroy is guilty of a:
   a. third-degree felony.
   b. first-degree felony.
   c. Class A misdemeanor.
   d. b or c.

9. Rocky Heartless not only ripped off Mrs. Smith but several other homeowners in her neighborhood, all within the same month for about $15,000 each. The D.A.can aggregate all the amounts involved in the fraud to determine Heartless's punishment.
   a. True
   b. False

10. Dr. Tricky forged the medical degree diploma that he had hanging in his front office. Dr. Tricky graduated from a dental college in Iowa. The diploma, however, was "purportedly" from the Dental School at Harvard University. Dr. Tricky is:
    a. not guilty of a crime because he does have a dental degree from an accredited school
    b. not guilty because his conduct doesn't harm his patients; he is an excellent dentist.
    c. is guilty of forgery because he created a false document that was intended to give his patients a false impression.
    d. only guilty if the false degree looks very authentic.

11. Deceptive business practices violate the civil statutes and put a business at risk of lawsuit; however, they can never be considered criminal offenses. Buyer beware!
    a. True
    b. False

OVERVIEW OF ROBBERY

Robbery and aggravated robbery are defined in Chapter 29. Robbery is a crime of violence and case law emphasizes the violent nature of the act. Robbery is a second-degree felony, and aggravated robbery is a first-degree felony.

Section 29.02 of the Texas Penal Code

(a) A person commits an offense if, in the course of committing theft as defined in Chapter 31 and with intent to obtain or maintain control of the property, he:

(1) intentionally, knowingly, or recklessly causes bodily injury to another; or

(2) intentionally or knowingly threatens or places another in fear of imminent bodily injury or death.

CASE

***Lane v. State*, 763 S.W.2d 785 (Tex.Crim.App. 1989)**
Section 29.02 of the Texas Penal Code

If the evidence shows the defendant was reasonably certain that his or her conduct was likely to cause injury or they disregarded a known risk that their conduct would cause injury, the State has satisfied the requirements of (1). Lane snatched a purse off the arm of an undercover police officer posing as a stranded motorist. A struggle ensued over the purse, Lane twisted the officer's wrist, and the officer sustained a bruise. The defendant argued he did not intentionally or knowingly injure the officer. The Court of Criminal Appeals ruled that in struggling with the officer and twisting her arm to obtain the purse, there was sufficient evidence that he was reasonably certain he would cause her injury. It is not necessary that the defendant inflict serious harm to a victim. The severity of the violence is not important as long as the victim suffered some physical pain, illness, or any impairment of physical condition.

Injury and Threats

To prove a defendant committed a robbery with threats of injury or death requires the State to prove the victim feared imminent injury and the fear was produced either intentionally or knowingly. The evidence must show that the victim was afraid because of the defendant's acts, conduct, or words. The defendant's acts, conduct, or words must be such that they would induce an ordinary person to part with their property.

CASES

1. *Patterson v. State*, 639 S.W.2d 695 (Tex.Crim.App. 1982)
Section 29.02(a)(2) of the Texas Penal Code

The threat of imminent injury does not have to be verbal. Acts can threaten; such as displaying a weapon or causing the victim to believe the attacker has a weapon. Patterson created the impression that he had a gun by holding his hand across his waist, as if the conceal it. The court found sufficient evidence that the defendant created an environment of fear in order to induce the victim to hand over his property

2. *Hernandez v. State*, 656 S.W.2d 630 (Tex. App. – San Antonio 1983)
Section 29.02(a)(2) of the Texas Penal Code

Hernandez's victim testified at trial that he was not afraid during the attack, even though the defendant stabbed him in order to accomplish the theft. The court upheld the robbery conviction and found that despite the victim's testimony the defendant's conduct was so violent that only an unreasonable person would not have been afraid.

3. *Birl v. State*, 763 S.W.2d 860 (Tex.Crim.App. 1982)
Section 29.02(a)(2) of the Texas Penal Code

Birl walked alongside the victim and displayed a knife. The victim screamed and ran away, dropping her purse along the way. The defendant chased after her, picked up her purse, and returned to his car. The victim sustained no injuries. After Birl retrieved the purse off the ground he left the victim alone. The court found the threats sufficient for a robbery conviction.

4. *Yarbrough v. State*, 656 S.W.2d 200 (Tex. App. – Austin 1983)
Section 29.01(2) of the Texas Penal Code

The injuries or threats must have been committed during the course of committing the theft. Section 29.01(1) defines "in the course of committing theft" as conduct that occurs in an attempt to commit, during the commission, or in immediate flight after the attempt or the commission of theft. Prior to 1974, the Penal Code required a completed theft in order to prove the crime of robbery. The definition of "in the course of committing theft" broadens the crime considerably. The violence, which is now the focus of the offense, can occur at any point during the criminal episode. It is not relevant whether the theft was completed or the property abandoned after it was taken.

In the *Yarborough* case, the court found that a robbery had been committed because Yarborough kicked the victim while trying to escape even though he had abandoned all attempts to secure the property. In *Thomas v. State*, 708 S.W.2d 580 (Tex. App. – Eastland 1986), Thomas was arrested for shoplifting. Fifteen or twenty minutes later, she tried to escape and inflicted injuries on a security guard in the process. The court concluded there was sufficient evidence of robbery.

Aggravated Robbery

Section 29.03 of the Texas Penal Code

(a) A person commits an offense if he commits robbery as defined in Section 29.02, and he:
(1) causes serious bodily injury to another;
(2) uses or exhibits a deadly weapon; or
(3) causes bodily injury to another person or threatens or places another person in fear of imminent bodily injury or death, if the person is:
(A) 65 years or age older; or
(B) a disabled person.

It is not necessary that the defendant display the entire weapon, nor that the victim actually see the weapon. The court upheld an aggravated robbery conviction in *Benavidez v. State,* 670 S.W.2d 297 (Tex. App. – Amarillo 1983), based on facts that showed the defendant poked something into the victim's back that felt like a gun.

REVIEW

12. Sydney brandished a toy gun during his robbery of a convenience store. He had no other weapon with him, caused no injury, and never threatened verbally to hurt the store clerk who was the only other person in the store. Sydney cannot be convicted of aggravated robbery because the gun was not real.
    a. True
    b. False

13. The store clerk in the convenience store testified at trial that she knew the gun was a toy because her son has one just like it. She testified she was not afraid that Sydney would harm her. The clerk's testimony does not affect the aggravated robbery case against Sydney.
    a. True
    b. False

14. The store clerk was 70 years old. Sydney's arguments against aggravated robbery are unaffected by that fact.
    a. True
    b. False

15. Tony hands a note to the bank teller telling him to put all of his money in a bag and give it to Tony or Tony will hurt someone in the bank. The experienced teller presses a panic button underneath his station and the police appear within seconds to arrest Tony. Tony is guilty of:
    a. attempted robbery because he didn't exhibit a weapon
    b. attempted aggravated robbery because he threatened harm
    c. attempted theft
    d. stupidity

16. Nelson wants Bo's expensive backpack, but he doesn't want to harm or scare Bo. Nelson is well-known as a gentle, quiet young man. Nelson sees his chance to steal Bo's pack while Bo is out of the room. He grabs it quickly and starts to run, but Bo's girlfriend walks in and realizes what is happening. She lunges after Nelson who flings his arm at her to keep her away, not intending to hit her. He does hit her, and she falls to the ground with a broken jaw.
    a. Nelson has just committed an aggravated robbery
    b. Nelson has committed a robbery – he never intended to harm the girlfriend.
    c. Theft, the harm he caused was accidental.
    d. Theft because the girlfriend "forced" him to fling his arm.

Section 2: DAMAGING AND DESTROYING OTHER PEOPLE'S PROPERTY

OVERVIEW OF ARSON

Prior to 1974, a building had to be damaged for the crime of arson to occur. Since 1974, the starting of a fire or causing an explosion is sufficient. There need be no actual damage. It makes no difference if the property was constructed of inflammable material. If the defendant intended to do damage, the crime has been committed.

Section 28.02 of the Texas Penal Code

(a) A person commits an offense if the person starts a fire, regardless of whether the fire continues after ignition, or causes an explosion with intent to destroy or damage:

(1) any vegetation, fence, or structure on open-space land; or

(2) any building, habitation, or vehicle:

(A) knowing that it is within the limits of an incorporated city or town;

(B) knowing that it is insured against damage or destruction;

(C) knowing that it is subject to a mortgage or other security interest;

(D) knowing that it is located on property belonging to another;

(E) knowing that it has located within it property belonging to another; or

(F) when the person is reckless about whether the burning or explosion will endanger the life of some individual or the safety of the property of another.

The law prohibits starting a fire or setting an explosion with intent to destroy or do damage to any building, habitation, or vehicle. A recent amendment to the arson statute recognizes that setting a fire to agricultural land can cause economic damage. Arson now includes setting a fire to destroy or damage any vegetation, fence, or structure on open-space land. Open-space land is real property undeveloped for human habitation.

Subsection (a)(2)(A) recognizes that intentionally setting a fire inside a city's limits can be more dangerous than setting a fire in more remote areas. Under (a)(2)(B), the State must prove the fire was set for the purpose of collecting the insurance benefits. Subsection (a)(2)(E) protects a person who owns property located on premises he or she does not own. The statute also makes clear that an owner, under certain specific circumstances, can set fire to his or her own property and be guilty of arson.

Arson is a second-degree felony unless injury or death occurs because of the offense, in which case it is a felony of the first-degree. In many cases, a death that occurs because of an arson offense can be prosecuted as a felony capital murder. The difference between a capital murder charge and first-degree felony arson is that in capital murder the State must prove the defendant knew the existence of a potential victim. This is because the State must show the defendant committed an act clearly dangerous to human life while in the course of committing an underlying felony. With arson, a defendant can be convicted of first-degree felony without having to be aware that someone could be killed or was killed. If he or she committed arson to collect the insurance proceeds without knowing that someone was inside the premises, they are guilty of first-degree felony arson.

OVERVIEW OF CRIMINAL MISCHIEF

Section 28.03 defines the crime of criminal mischief. When it was enacted in 1974, it replaced forty separate offenses. It addresses the *intentional and knowing* destruction of property. Section 28.04, Reckless Damage or Destruction, is aimed at *reckless* destruction of property. The two offenses combined forbid all damage to property, except arson, regardless of how it was inflicted or the nature of the property harmed.

Criminal mischief and reckless damage include damaging or destroying property, tampering with property and causing pecuniary loss or substantial inconvenience to the owner, and making markings, slogans, drawings, or paintings on property. The punishment range for the crime is based on the value of the property that was damaged or its cost of repair.

- Class C misdemeanor - damage of $50 or less;
- Class B misdemeanor - damage of $50 to $500;
- Class A misdemeanor - damage of $500 to $1500;
- State jail felony - damage of $1500 to $20,000;
- Third-degree felony - damage of $20,000 to $100,000;
- Second-degree felony - damage of $100,00 to $200,000;
- First-degree felony - damage of $200,000 or more.

The Texas legislature frequently adjusts these value limits and adds special provisions to protect specific kinds of property. The statute makes it a crime to impair, interrupt, or divert public communications, transportation, water, gas, power supply, or any public service. It is also a state jail felony to damage or destroy a place of worship, human burial grounds, a public monument, or a community center and the loss is less than $20,000. The 2003 Texas Legislature added a new provision that makes it a first-degree felony to introduce mad cow disease into livestock.

The reckless damage or destruction of property is a Class C misdemeanor, regardless of the amount of reckless damage or the cost of repair.

Section 28.06 in the Penal Code explains how the amount of pecuniary loss is calculated for the crime of arson, criminal mischief, and reckless damage of property. This can become an important issue in a case because the seriousness of the punishment is based on these calculations. The statute is careful to outline criteria for determining loss. It is up to the State and the defense to argue the details. Issues involving the amount of loss may require the testimony of experts whose profession it is to appraise the value of property. The statute only protects against pecuniary loss. Emotional and psychological are not included in the criminal arena; however, a conviction for criminal mischief does not preclude a civil lawsuit for damages.

REVIEW

17. Johnny, 17 years old, was caught scribbling graffiti on the outside walls of his high school. It cost $155.00 to remove the graffiti. Johnny can be charged with:
    a. he can be expelled, but no criminal charges can be brought against him.
    b. a Class A misdemeanor because it was a public building.
    c. a Class B misdemeanor.
    d. state jail felony.

18. Mr. Grumble posted signs all over his house and yard telling people to stay off his property. Some of his less mature neighbors decided to teach him a lesson. They threw basketballs into his yard on a regular basis to annoy him. The balls did no damage to his yard, but he had to retrieve them. He went to the D.A. and filed a complaint. The D.A. explained that:
    a. the neighbors can be charged with criminal trespass.
    b. the neighbors cannot be charged with criminal trespass because they did not enter his property.
    c. the neighbors can possibly be charged with criminal mischief.
    d. both b and c.

19. Johnson decided to burn down an old shed on his property outside of town. He doused it with gasoline and it burned. Unfortunately, the wind was blowing wildly, and the shed was close to his barn. The barn burned down also. The barn was subject to a bank mortgage. Can Johnson be found guilty of arson?
    a. Yes, he was reckless and property was destroyed that the bank had an interest in.
    b. No, you cannot be guilty of arson for destroying your own property.
    c. No, the property was located outside town limits.
    d. Yes, he was intentionally destroyed his shed and that intent is transferred to his barn.

20. Tony set fire to Angela's house because she had a grand piano that had belonged to Tony's famous pianist father. Angela won the piano from Tony in a poker game. Tony was heartbroken and decided that if he could not have the piano; no one should have it. He did not intend to destroy Angela's house. His intent was to destroy the piano by setting fire to it. Luckily, the fire was stopped before any damage was done to Angela's home. Is Tony guilty of arson?
    a. No, he did not intend to destroy the house.
    b. No, because there was no damage to the home.
    c. Yes, he intended to start a fire and did start a fire.
    d. Yes, Angela's house was in the city limits.

21. Tony decided to break into Angela's house and destroy the piano with a sledgehammer. He attended a party at her home but failed to leave after all the other guests left. Angela went to bed, thinking everyone had gone home. Tony was secreted in a closet. While Angela slept, he destroyed the piano. Tony is guilty of:
    a. criminal mischief only.
    b. burglary.
    c. criminal trespass and reckless damage to property.
    d. criminal trespass.

22. Before Tony acted on his design to destroy Angela's newly won piano; he went to a psychotherapist who convinced him not to take revenge. He attended a party at Angela's home and got very intoxicated. He leaned against the famous piano against Angela's warnings to stay away from it. In his drunken stupor, he pounded on the keyboard and damaged several keys. It was expensive to repair. Tony can be charged with:
    a. nothing, let Angela sue him in civil court.
    b. reckless damage or destruction to property.
    c. criminal mischief.
    d. no crime because the damage cannot be calculated.

23. Tony is obsessed with his father's piano. He broke into Angela's home one evening while she was not there to play the piano for several hours. He left Angela a note thanking her for a wonderful evening. Angela was furious because she had told Tony repeatedly to stay away from her home. Tony can be charged with:
    a. burglary, hc broke into Angela's home.
    b. criminal mischief.
    c. criminal trespass.
    d. give him a break, he's a sad guy.

Section 3: INVADING OTHER PEOPLE'S PROPERTY

OVERVIEW OF BURGLARY

Prior to 1974, burglary was categorized into distinct offenses based on the burglar's time of entry. Under the former Code, burglary of a private residence at night was a separate offense, which was penalized more severely than ordinary burglary. If the accused was charged with a daytime burglary, entry had to be effected by an actual breaking or by entry at an unusual place. If the charge was a nighttime burglary, evidence of an actual breaking was not essential, and proof of entry by force, threat, or fraud was sufficient. The 1974 Code eliminated any distinction between daytime and nighttime burglary and omitted the breaking requirement.

Burglary is now defined as:

Section 30.02(a) and (b) of the Texas Penal Code

(a) A person commits an offense if, without the effective consent of the owner, the person:

(1) enters a habitation or a building (or any portion of a building) not then open to the public, with intent to commit a felony, theft, or an assault; or

(2) remains concealed, with intent to commit a felony, theft, or an assault, in a building or habitation; or

(3) enters a building or habitation and commits or attempts to commit a felony, theft, or an assault.

(b) For purposes of this section, "enter" means to intrude:

(1) any part of the body; or

(2) any physical object connected with the body.

The punishment range for burglaries depends on the type of premises the burglar entered. If the premises were a habitation, it is a second-degree felony. Entry into a building is a state jail felony. Two circumstances can elevate a second-degree burglary of a habitation to a first-degree felony. If any party entered the habitation with the intent to commit a felony other than theft or committed or attempted to commit a felony other than felony theft, the punishment is first-degree.

"Effective consent" is defined in Section 1.07(19) as consent by a person legally authorized to act for the owner. Consent is not effective if it is based on fraud, force or threats. Effective consent cannot be given by someone who the defendant knows does not have authority because of age, mental disease or defect, or intoxication that has impaired his or her ability to make a decision.

Mens Rea of Burglary

The crime of burglary is completed once the burglar enters the premises, whether or not any theft, felony, or assault was committed after the entry. The felony or theft does not have to be from the burglarized structure or from the owner of the structure. The State only needs to show that there was a clear connection between the unauthorized entry and the felony or theft. This is much broader than the common law of burglary that required the theft or felony be from or occur in the burglarized premises. For example, in *Robles v. State*, 664 S.W.2d 91 (Tex.Crim.App. 1984), the defendant broke into a home and forced the owner to accompany him to a bank where the owner obtained money for the intruder. Robles' burglary conviction was affirmed.

The 1999 Legislature added assault to the list of offenses that a burglar can intend to commit upon gaining entry to a habitation or building. Until Texas courts have the opportunity to address cases that raise tricky issues about what connection must exist between an unauthorized entry and an assault, prior cases law suggests the assault did not have to occur on the premises for a burglary to have been committed.

Entry must be accompanied with intent to commit a felony, theft, or assault when the offender enters a habitation or building under Section 30.02(a)(1) and (2). The circumstances surrounding a case are used to prove mens rea. The courts in Texas have ruled it permissible to infer that a nighttime entry included intent to commit a theft, felony, or assault. The State cannot rely on this inference in front of a jury, but a jury is permitted to make the inference according to *Browning v. State*, 720 S.W.2d 180 (Tex.Crim.App. 1986). In *Ortega v. State*, 626 S.W.2d 746 (Tex.Crim.App. 1981), the court ruled that an entry was affected when the defendant entered into a part of the house between the screen door and the wooden door. Where a defendant dug a hole though a roof with an automobile wrench, the intrusion of the wrench was considered an unlawful entry in *Hayes v. State*, 656 S.W.2d 926 (Tex. App. - Eastland 1983).

Intent to commit a felony, theft, or assault is also required for a burglary committed by a surreptitious remaining. The intent must be present at the time of entry. If a defendant forms the intent after entering the premises, it is not a burglary.

If a defendant is charged under Section 30.02 (a)(3), there is *no* requirement that the entry was made with the intent to commit a felony, theft, or assault if the felony, theft, or assault was actually committed. All that is required is that the defendant enter the premises without the owner's consent and attempt to commit or commit a felony, theft, or assault. In *Davila v. State*, 547 S.W.2d 606 (Tex.Crim.App. 1977), the Texas Court of Criminal Appeals ruled that an unauthorized entry under subsection (a)(3) must be done intentionally or knowingly.

Habitations and Buildings

Section 30.01 of the Texas Penal Code

In this chapter:

(1) "Habitation" means a structure or vehicle that is adapted for the overnight accommodation of persons, and includes:

(A) each separately secured or occupied portion of the structure or vehicle; and

(B) each structure appurtenant to or connected with the structure or vehicle.

The Court of Criminal Appeals concluded in *Jones v. State*, 532 S.W.2d 596 (Tex.Crim.App. 1976) that a habitation had to have been adapted for overnight accommodation prior to the burglary and still have been used for that purpose at the time of the offense. The *Jones* court ruled that a new home with no previous occupants, no furniture, and no utilities was not a habitation. In *Moss v. State*, 574 S.W.2d 542 (Tex.Crim.App. 1978), the Court of Criminal Appeals ruled that a furnished home which had been rented in the past but was unoccupied at the time of the burglary was a habitation. The court also ruled, however, that a house with past tenants and no utilities and which was being used for storage was not a habitation. In 1989, the Court of Criminal Appeals acknowledged it needed to clarify the statute. It decided that the nature of the premises is defined by how an ordinary person would reasonably perceive it. In *Blankenship v. State*, 780 S.W.2d 198 (Tex.Crim.App. 1988), the court ruled a structure that had once been occupied, was rented occasionally, had functional rooms, connected utilities and was being used to store household items was a habitation for purposes of the burglary statute.

Garages and carports are considered parts of habitations because they are appurtenant to them. It does not matter whether they were opened or closed at the time of the burglary. Court cases have decided that appurtenant means any structure connected to the use and enjoyment of a habitation, including unattached garages, storage sheds, and other outbuildings. *Jones v. State*, 690 S.W.2d 318 (Tex. App. - Dallas 1985).

Section 30.01(2) of the Texas Penal Code

(2) "Building" means any enclosed structure intended for use or occupation as a habitation or for some purpose of trade, manufacture, ornament, or use.

In *Day v. State*, 534 S.W.2d 681 (Tex.Crim.App. 1976), the Court of Criminal Appeals considered a building that was made of concrete blocks, had three entries that could not be closed, and was surrounded by a fence. Because the structure was not enclosed, was not designed to secure its contents, and was permanently open, the court did not consider it a building. Being enclosed by something else, such as a fence, did not change the character of the structure.

Enclosed areas that are not open to the public are also considered buildings for purposes of the crime of burglary. If a defendant enters a public area but makes his way to a storage area or office that is closed to the general public with the intent to commit a felony, theft, or assault he or she is guilty of burglary.

Other Burglary Statutes

Section 30.04(a) of the Texas Penal Code

(a) A person commits an offense if, without the effective consent of the owner, he breaks into or enters a vehicle with intent to commit any felony or theft.

According to Section 30.04, a crime is committed if without the effective consent of the owner, a person breaks into or enters a vehicle or any part of a vehicle with the intent to commit any felony or theft. Intent to commit assault is not included. To enter means to intrude any part of the body or any physical object connected to the body. There is no requirement that the vehicle not be open to the public. Unlike burglary of a habitation or building, burglary of a vehicle still requires a breaking and entering. A use of force is necessary to establish the offense. Steeling tires, hubcaps or ornamentation on the outside of an automobile does not constitute burglary of a motor vehicle.

Section 30.03 defines the crime of Burglary of Coin-Operated or Coin Collection Machines. For purposes of the entry requirement, any entry without the effective consent of the owner is sufficient.

Probably the best and most interesting way to learn about the crime of burglary is to read actual cases decided by Texas courts.

CASES

***Rogers v. State*, 929 S.W.2d 103 (Tex. App. - Beaumont 1996):** there was sufficient circumstantial evidence that the defendant entered a habitation to uphold his burglary conviction, based on his unexplained possession of recently stolen property and the circumstances of that possession. There was no evidence that anyone was ever seen entering or leaving the home, and no direct identification evidence.

***Lawhorn v. State*, 898 S.W.2d 886 (Tex.Crim.App. 1995):** defendant was convicted of burglary of a habitation with intent to commit felony escape. The Court of Criminal Appeals overturned the burglary conviction by finding it was legally impossible for the defendant to have intended to commit the crime of escape when he unlawfully entered a habitation. The escape occurred when he left the custody of the police officer.

***Soto v. State*, 782 S.W.2d 17 (Tex. App. - San Antonio 1989):** a locked toolbox bolted to the bed of a truck constituted "any part of the vehicle" and satisfied that element of burglary of a vehicle.

***Mack v. State*, 928 S.W.2d 219 (Tex. App. - Austin 1996):** on the night of the burglary, the defendant's girlfriend had a greater right to possession of the apartment for which the two of them had signed a lease. She was the owner of the apartment within the meaning of the burglary statute. Defendant had moved out and stopped paying rent. A new roommate was paying rent, and the defendant had agreed not to visit the apartment unless he first called for permission.

***Richardson v. State*, 888 S.W.2d 822 (Tex.Crim.App. 1994):** an individual who reaches into the open bed of a pickup trick with the intent to remove property breaks into the close of the vehicle and enters part of the vehicle under Section 30.04.

***Van Dalen v. State,* 789 S.W.2d 334 (Tex. App. - Houston [14th Dist.] 1990):** the fact that a truck was without a motor or rear wheels did not destroy its character as a vehicle under Section 30.04.

***Jones v. State*, 899 S.W.2d 25 (Tex. App. - Tyler 1995):** evidence that missing property was found in defendant's truck on the same day it was taken and when confronted, the defendant did not offer to explain his possession or return the property, was sufficient for burglary of a habitation. His vehicle matched the description of a vehicle seen earlier on the day of the crime.

REVIEW

24. Simon decided to burglarize a local video store and steal his favorite movies. He drove his truck into the front window of the store. The police found him in his truck passed out from the collision before he could enter the store. The truck shattered the window. Simon argued he is not guilty of burglarizing the store because he never entered it. Valid defense?
    a. Yes, he never entered the store.
    b. No, his truck entered the store sufficiently for the crime of burglary.
    c. Yes, he never stole items from the store.
    d. No, he satisfied the burglary statute's breaking requirement.

25. The thief who tried to steal Carrie's expensive car sound system ($2500 cost) was caught and convicted. Luckily Carrie had an alarm, but the damage to the sound system was extensive - at least $1500. The would-be thief had no prior offenses. He faced a Class A burglary misdemeanor charge.
    a. True
    b. False

26. Two roommates shared an apartment with the understanding that their bedrooms were totally off limits to each other. One of the roommates came home to find the other roommate in his bedroom, looking through his dresser drawers. In his pocket, he had an expensive ring he had found in the dresser drawer. Can the snoopy roommate be charged with burglary?
    a. No, they share an apartment together.
    b. No, the bedrooms are not separate habitations.
    c. Yes, the bedrooms are separately occupied and the entry was without consent.
    d. No, he had not yet left the apartment with the ring.

OVERVIEW OF CRIMINAL TRESPASS

An unauthorized entry into another person's premises, including an aircraft, is the crime of criminal trespass. It is almost identical to the crime of burglary except there is no intent to commit a felony, theft, or assault. Also unlike burglary, criminal trespass requires entry of the entire body. Entry of a part of the body or a physical object connected to the body is insufficient.

Section 30.05 of the Texas Penal Code

(a) A person commits an offense if he enters or remains on or in property, including an aircraft or other vehicle, of another without effective consent or he enters or remains in a building of another without effective consent and he:
(1) had notice that the entry was forbidden; or
(2) received notice to depart but failed to do so.
(b) For purposes of this section:
(1) "Entry" means the intrusion of the entire body.
(2) "Notice" means:
(A) oral or written communication by the owner or someone with apparent authority to act for the owner;
(B) fencing or other enclosure obviously designed to exclude intruders or to contain livestock;
(C) a sign or signs posted on the property or at the entrance to the building, reasonably likely to come to the attention of intruders, indicating that entry is forbidden;
(D) the placement of identifying purple paint marks on trees or posts on the property, provided the marks are:
(i) vertical lines of not less than eight inches in length and not less than one inch in width;
(ii) placed so that the bottom of the mark is not less than three feet from the ground or more than five feet from the ground; and
(iii) placed at locations that are readily visible to any person approaching the property and not more than:
(a) 100 feet apart on forest land; or
(b) 1000 feet apart on land other than forest land; or
(E) the visible presence on the property of a crop grown for human consumption that is under cultivation, in the process of being harvested, or marketable if harvested at the time of entry.

The 1999 Texas Legislature added a provision, Section 30.05(e), which makes it criminal trespass to enter or remain on agricultural land without the express consent of the owner or other legal authorization. To be guilty of the crime, the offender must have been on notice that entry was forbidden or fail to depart when asked to and be on the land when apprehended or within 100 feet of the land's boundary.

It is a defense to prosecution that at the time of the entry, the actor was a fire fighter or emergency medical service personnel acting according to official duties. The 2003 Legislature added a second defense to a trespass charge. If the basis for forbidding entry on property, land, or in a building is that entry with a handgun is forbidden, it is a defense if the person was carrying a concealed handgun as long as they also had a license allowing them to carry it.

Criminal trespass is a Class B misdemeanor unless it was committed in a habitation, shelter center or a Superfund site, or if the defendant carried a deadly weapon during the criminal trespass. In those cases, it is a Class A misdemeanor.

FINAL COMMENTS ON CRIMES AGAINST PROPERTY

Crimes against property constitute a considerable portion of the work of law enforcement agencies and district attorneys' offices. They are complex crimes to define. The Texas theft statute is long and involved. Over the years, the Legislature has added new theft crimes to address special circumstances. Changes in how we live and do business are evident in the evolution of property offenses.

Fraud crimes are also complex. The mens rea element is often difficult to prove beyond a reasonable doubt. For that reason, many fraudulent schemes are more easily handled as civil fraud. The victim sues the perpetrator of the fraud in civil court for civil damages. In civil court, proof is based on a preponderance of the evidence. The perpetrator is not subject to criminal punishment, but he or she can be ordered to make the victim whole and, in some circumstances, pay a punitive judgment beyond the amount of the victim's injuries.

In most respects, robbery is not a crime against property. It is a crime of violence against other persons committed during a theft. Since 1974, the Texas robbery statutes have treated robbery as a violent offense, more in the nature of assault, than as a property offense.

The offenses of burglary, arson, and criminal trespass cover a wide range of conduct. They have become more and more inclusive over the centuries as our style of living has changed. Homes are enhanced with garages, storage sheds, and barns. We spend significant time in our vehicles where we keep valuable personal property. There is little difference between daytime and nighttime in a society that functions 24 hours a day. Our property is often insured and mortgaged, giving persons other than owners a financial stake in its well-being.

Chapter Twelve

Crimes Against Public Order and Morals

INTRODUCTION

This chapter looks primarily at crimes against public order as defined by the Texas Penal Code, which are found in Chapters 42. Public order offenses account for a high percentage of local law enforcement's workload, however, they generate few appellate court opinions. Sentenced for misdemeanors, persons convicted of crimes of public order generally do not appeal their cases. Many of these state offenses also have counterparts in city and county ordinances.

Section 1: Individual Disorderly Conduct

OVERVIEW

Section 42.01 is a collection of diverse offenses under the label of disorderly conduct. The legislature periodically amends the list of acts that make up the offense. They constitute the actus reus of the offense:

Section 42.01 of the Texas Penal Code

(a) A person commits an offense if he intentionally or knowingly:

(1) uses abusive, indecent, profane, or vulgar language in a public place, and the language by its very utterance tends to incite an immediate breach of the peace;

(2) makes an offensive gesture or display in a public place, and the gesture or display tends to incite an immediate breach of the peace;

(3) creates, by chemical means, a noxious and unreasonable odor in a public place;

(4) abuses or threatens a person in a public place in an obviously offensive manner;

(5) makes unreasonable noise in a public place other than a sport shooting range, as defined by Section 250.001, Local Government Code, or in or near a private residence that he has no right to occupy;

(6) fights with another person in a public place;

(7) discharges a weapon in a public place other than a public road or a sport shooting range, as defined by Section 250.001, Local Government Code;

(8) displays a firearm or other deadly weapon in a public place in a manner calculated to alarm;

(9) discharges a firearm on or across a public road; or

(10) exposes his anus or genitals in a public place and is reckless about whether another may be present who will be offended or alarmed by his act; or

(11) for a lewd or unlawful purpose:

(A) enters on the property of another and looks into a dwelling on the property through any window or other opening in the dwelling;
(B) while on the premises of a hotel or comparable establishment, looks into a guest room not the person's own through a window or other opening in the room; or
(C) while on the premises of a public place, looks into an area such as a restroom or a shower stall or changing or dressing room that is designed to provide privacy to a person using the area.

The mens rea of disorderly conduct is intentionally or knowingly engaging in one of the behaviors identified by the statute. All the acts constitute Class C misdemeanors, except for discharging a firearm in a public place and displaying a firearm or deadly weapon in a public place. They are punished as Class B misdemeanors.

CASES

1. *Blanco v. State*, 761 S.W.2d 38 (Tex. App. - Houston [14th Dist.] 1988)
Sections 42.01(a)(5) and 42.04 of the Texas Penal Code

Section 42.04 provides an important defense to prosecution under 42.01(a)(5) - creating unreasonable noise. The same defense is available for prosecution under Section 42.03 - obstructing a highway or other passageway. The defense provides that if conduct which would otherwise violate one of these statutes consists of speech or communication or gatherings to listen to speech or communication for the purpose of social protest, authorities must order defendants to move prior to arresting them if they have not yet harmed someone else's interests. If no such order was given or if the order was unreasonable, defendants must be exonerated

Joe Blanco was convicted of disorderly conduct for intentionally making unreasonable noise in a public place. He had positioned the stereo speakers on his apartment porch so the sound of his music was directed toward the swimming pool area of the apartment complex. He had refused requests to turn down the stereo volume from his neighbors, the apartment management, and a police officer. He was arrested under Section 42.01(a)(5) of the Penal Code. Blanco challenged the provision of the statute as overbroad and vague. The Court of Appeals affirmed Blanco's conviction by noting that the State's police powers include the right to protect the tranquility, quiet enjoyment, and well-being of a community. The only limit on that power is an individual constitutional right, such as the First Amendment right to free speech. In his case, the court concluded that the statute did not infringe on the right to free speech because Section 42.04 restricts the reach of the unreasonable noise provision when constitutionally protected speech is involved and sufficiently protects an individual's rights. The court found that Blanco's conduct clearly fell within the proscribed activity, and he failed to show the statute was unconstitutional as applied to him.

2. *State v. Rivenburgh*, 933 S.W.2d 698 (Tex. App. - San Antonio 1996)
Section 42.01(a)(2) of the Texas Penal Code

The appellate court reviewed Rivenburgh's conviction for driving while intoxicated which started as a stop for the crime of disorderly conduct. The arresting officer testified Rivenburgh was stopped at a red light, and when the light turned green, other motorists honked their horns because she was holding up traffic. The officer observed Rivenburgh make a vulgar gesture with her middle finger and mouth an obscenity in her rear view mirror. In his experience as a police officer, he testified that such gestures often cause fights, so he proceeded to stop her for disorderly conduct. The court had to clarify whether the officer had the right to arrest Rivenburgh without a warrant for disorderly conduct in order to establish the legality of her arrest for driving while intoxicated.

Section 42.01(a)(2) provides that a person can be arrested for disorderly conduct if he or she intentionally makes an offensive gesture in a public place, which tends to incite an immediate breach of the peace. According to Texas courts, the offensive gesture or display must amount to fighting words that plainly tend to excite people to breach the peace. Harsh and insulting language does not generally rise to the fighting words level. Whether a particular gesture amounts to fighting words is a question of fact. The Court of Appeals upheld the trial judge's decision that Rivenburgh's gesture and the obscenity she mouthed were fighting words.

3. *Nixon v. State*, 928 S.W.2d 212 (Tex. App. - Beaumont 1996)
Section 42.01(c) of the Texas Penal Code

Section 1.07(a)(40) defines "public place" as any place to which the public or a substantial group of the public has access, not limited to streets, highways, the common areas of schools, hospitals, office and apartment buildings, transport facilities and shops. In the *Nixon* case, the issue was whether a person's backyard could be considered a public place under the disorderly conduct statute. Nixon was arrested in the backyard of his private residence for disorderly conduct. Cocaine was found on his person during a search incident to that arrest. He challenged the right of the police to arrest him for disorderly conduct on his own property, hoping to establish that his arrest was unlawful, and, therefore, that the search was unlawful. The court concluded that a residential backyard was a public place because a crowd of 50 or so persons gathered when the defendant became loud and abusive toward the police officer. A place is or is not public according to the facts and circumstances of a particular case.

As is evident in the *Rivenburgh* and *Nixon* cases, law enforcement often uses the right to arrest a person for disorderly conduct as a means to investigate more serious offenses. Is this an appropriate use of the statute? It is legal, but can discretion be abused? What advantages are there for police in having authority to use a crime like disorderly conduct to dig deeper into the facts of a suspicious situation?

Other sections of Chapter 42:
Initiating or Communicating a False Alarm - Section 42.06
Silent or Abusive Calls to 9-1-1 - Section 42.061
Harassment by Telephone or Written Communication - Section 42.07
Stalking - Section 42.072
Abuse of Corpse - Section 42.08
Cruelty to Animals - Section 42.09
Dog Fighting - 42.10
Destruction of Flag - Section 42.11
Discharge of Firearm in Certain Municipalities - Section 42.12
Use of Laser Pointers - Section 42.13

You can refer to your local city or county ordinances to locate those sections that address many of the same or similar offenses defined in Chapter 42. For example, Chapter 23 section 8 of the Fort Worth Municipal Code declares that any unreasonably loud, disturbing, unnecessary noise that causes material distress, discomfort, or injury to people with ordinary sensibilities is a nuisance and prohibited. The ordinance then goes on to specifically prohibit playing the radio, phonograph, or a musical instrument in such a manner between 10 p.m. and 7 a.m.

City ordinances also address conduct that is not addressed by state law. Houston City Ordinance Chapter 28 section 46 prohibits aggressive panhandling. The ordinance, which defines a panhandler as a solicitor and the person they are panhandling from the solicitee, provides:

> Immediately upon any request from a solicitee to a solicitor, a solicitor who is in a public place (that is a street, sidewalk or other place that is open to the public) at the moment the request is made shall discontinue the solicitation until there is a space of at least eight feet between the solicitor and the solicitee or, in the alternative, discontinue all efforts to engage in the solicitation if within eight feet proximity to a requesting solicitee.

The San Antonio Municipal Code, Chapter 21 section 7, makes it illegal to climb pecan trees in any public park or street within the city or to throw sticks, stones, or other missiles in order to gather pecans. Common city code ordinances prohibit such relatively innocuous behavior nowadays as spitting in public places. Check your city's code. Notice that although there is a lot of overlap, city codes cover a lot of circumstances not covered by state statute.

Section 2: GROUP DISORDERLY CONDUCT

OVERVIEW

Section 42.02 of the Texas Penal Code
For the purposes of this section, "riot" means the assemblage of seven or more persons resulting in conduct which:
(1) creates an immediate danger of damage to property or injury to persons;
(2) substantially obstructs law enforcement or other governmental functions or services; or
(3) by force, threat of force, or physical action deprives any person of a legal right or disturbs any person in the enjoyment of a legal right.

The State must plead and prove that a defendant performed one of the enumerated acts. It is a defense to prosecution that the assemblage started lawfully and when one of the participants expressed intent to engage in riotous conduct, the defendant left the assembly. It is not a defense to prosecution that a person who was a part of the riot was acquitted, not arrested, prosecuted or convicted, was convicted of another offense, or was immune to prosecution.

The courts have ruled that the riot statute does not violate the First Amendment because it does not proscribe participation in a lawful assembly. By requiring knowing participation, the State must show the defendant participated knowing the assembly was resulting in unlawful activity. Mere presence at the scene of a riot does not make a person a party to a riot.

Section 42.03 prohibits obstructing highways or other passageways. It can be committed intentionally, knowingly, or recklessly. The actus reus includes obstructing streets, sidewalks, railways, waterways, elevators, aisles, hallways, entrances, or exits to which the public has access. It does not matter how the obstruction was created or whether the defendant was acting alone or with others. Passage must be blocked in such a way as to render it unreasonably inconvenient or hazardous. Merely slowing down passage or momentarily impeding passage does not violate the statute. In *Haye v. State*, 634 S.W.2d 313 (Tex. Crim. App. 1982), the defendant's conviction was upheld because he refused to allow pedestrians to use the sidewalk and forced them to walk in mud on the street. The court affirmed the defendant's conviction for parking his truck across a ditch along the highway right-of-way and forcing a road crew to stop and leave their vehicle in *Brightbill v. State*, 734 S.W.2d 733 (Tex. App. – Amarillo 1987).

A second way to commit an offense under Section 42.03 is to fail to obey a reasonable request or order to move by a peace officer, fireman, or person with the authority to control the premises. The State does not have to show that there was obstruction, it only needs to show that a defendant failed to obey an order designed to prevent obstruction.

CASES

1. *Lauderback v. State*, 789 S.W.2d 343 (Tex. App. – Fort Worth 1990)
Section 42.03 of the Texas Penal Code

Edna Louise Lauderback was convicted of obstructing a highway or other passageway after she had a disagreement with Olney Savings in Gainesville, Texas. She picketed the bank on foot for approximately five weeks. She then borrowed a wheel chair, attached a sign to it that stated "Olney Savings cripples women" and placed the wheelchair in a lane of traffic on a street in front of the bank. The street was busy and narrow with no parking available on it. The police received angry telephone calls from citizens who complained that the sign and chair obstructed the street. Lauderback refused a police officer's requests to move. She argued that public highways are open to everyone and where there are no sidewalks, a pedestrian can use the roadway. There was conflicting evidence as to whether Lauderback was handicapped. The court, however, affirmed her conviction, handicapped or not. The evidence showed that she obstructed a highway. It was not necessary that she actually cause a hazard. It was reasonable for police to ask her to move based on a potential hazard or the inconvenience she caused motorists. The court concluded that the statute did not abridge Lauderback's right to free speech because she could have picketed on the sides of the bank or on its parking lot.

2. *Morehead v. State*, 807 S.W.2d 577 (Tex. Crim. App. 1991)
Section 42.05 of the Texas Penal Code

Section 42.05 proscribes intentionally preventing or disrupting a lawful meeting, procession, or gathering through physical actions or verbal utterances. Gardell Morehead was convicted of disrupting a lawful meeting. Gardell attended a national conference of a sorority at the Dallas Convention Center where civil rights leader Jesse Jackson was the speaker. Halfway through Rev. Jackson's speech, Morehead rose from his seat and began walking down the center aisle of the auditorium toward the podium. He yelled loudly that Jackson was a liar. Morehead continued yelling and interrupted Jackson's speech. Morehead was arrested after refusing an officer's request to leave.

The issue again was whether the Texas statute violated Gardell's right to free speech. The Court of Criminal Appeals overturned Gardell's conviction because the jury was not properly instructed on the limits of Section 42.05. The statute should be construed to criminalize only physical acts or verbal utterances that substantially impair the ordinary conduct of lawful meetings and thereby curtail the exercise of other people's First Amendment rights. The jury was not informed about the limits of the statute. The court's concern was that Section 42.05 not be constructed too narrowly so as to criminalize all disturbances to lawful meetings. Some impairment of meetings is the price we pay to maintain the freedom of political expression under the Constitution. Individuals and groups who propose change sometimes engage in aggressive conduct. Some of that conduct must be considered constitutionally protected speech.

REVIEW

1. The Texas disorderly conduct statute makes it illegal to carry a weapon in a public place even if it is placed in an appropriate carrying case and not being waived or brandished to the public.
    a. True
    b. False

2. It is not illegal to use indecent or profane language in public as long as the language does not tend to incite an immediate breach of the peace.
    a. True
    b. False

3. Noise is unreasonable if it exceeds 85 decibels after a peace officer notifies the person making the noise that it's a public nuisance.
    a. True
    b. False

4. A person who unwittingly gets caught up in a riot, not intending, wanting, or knowing that what started as a peaceful assembly is now disturbing another person's legal rights is not guilty of the crime of riot.
    a. True
    b. False

5. Riot statutes need to be interpreted with which constitutional protection primarily in mind:
    a. the Fourth Amendment protection against an unreasonable arrest
    b. the Second Amendment protection to bear arms
    c. the First Amendment protection to assemble and free speech
    d. the Fourteenth Amendment requirement for due process.

Section 3: OTHER PUBLIC MORAL CRIMES

Public intoxication is defined by Section 49.02 of the Penal Code.

Section 49.02 of the Texas Penal Code
A person commits an offense if the person appears in a public place while intoxicated to the degree that the person may endanger the person or another.

The danger does not have to be immediate and the arresting officer does not have to specify an identifiable danger. In *Bentley v. State*, 535 S.W.2d 651 (Tex. Crim. App. 1976), the court found it sufficient that in the officer's opinion the defendant would have attempted to drive an automobile were he not arrested. It is a defense to prosecution if a licensed physician administered the alcohol or substance for therapeutic purposes as part of treatment.

Chapter 43 of the Penal Code provides for two sets of crimes involving public indecency. The first set (Sections 43.01 through 43.05) addresses prostitution, promoting prostitution, and compelling prostitution. The second set (Sections 43.21 through 43.26) addresses obscenity: its definition, obscene display or distribution, promoting obscenity, the sale, distribution or display of harmful material to a minor, sexual performance by a child, employment harmful to children, and possession or promotion of child pornography. Some of these offenses are also addressed in city ordinances.

Chapter 46 of the Code addresses weapons offenses (Sections 46.01 through 46.15) including unlawful possession of a firearm, prohibited weapons, places where weapons are prohibited, hoax bombs, penalty for an offense committed in a weapon-free zone, and making a firearm accessible to a child.

Illegal gambling is defined in the Chapter 47 offenses. In addition to defining public intoxication, Chapter 49 defines the driving while intoxicated offenses and intoxication manslaughter.

FINAL COMMENTS ON CRIMES AGAINST PUBLIC ORDER AND MORALS

This chapter focused on crimes against public order. Although they can involve less serious criminal behavior, these offenses raise interesting issues. Authorities often use crimes like disorderly conduct as pretexts to investigate more serious criminal conduct. There are frequent allegations from many communities that public order statutes are used to harass citizens rather than to keep peace. Some public order crimes raise First Amendment free speech issues. It is easy to dismiss public order crimes as minor. As the first line of offenses imposing criminal sanctions, however, public order statutes affect large numbers of people and leave lasting impressions about the workings of law enforcement agencies and the courts. Out of necessity, they are broadly written and give police wide discretionary powers.

Chapter Thirteen

Crimes Against the State

INTRODUCTION

Chapter Thirteen is the shortest chapter in this Supplement for a reason. Crimes of treason, disloyalty, sedition, sabotage, and espionage are federal offenses. The crime is committed against the United States and prosecuted under the appropriate section of the federal criminal code. The Texas Penal Code has no comparable offenses.

If the conduct involved also includes violations of a Texas Penal Code provision, it can be prosecuted under that provision, whatever the motives of the actors might be. If the conduct violates a Code section, it is subject to prosecution in Texas. If during the course of and as part of committing espionage against the U.S., an offender engages in the unauthorized use of an automobile in Texas, he or she can be prosecuted for that crime, separate and apart from the federal espionage charge. In addition, there are several interesting and important state crimes found in our Penal Code that can be used to prosecute offenders involved in "terroristic" activities in the Texas courts. It does not violate the Double Jeopardy Clause of the Fifth Amendment in the U.S. Constitution when a person is prosecuted by different jurisdictions, under their respective criminal statutes, for the same or similar criminal conduct. It is conceivable that an offender would be prosecuted under federal law for a crime against the United States and also be prosecuted under state law for an offense that is not defined as a crime against the government but that nevertheless is illegal.

Listed below are several sections scattered throughout the Texas Penal Code that address conduct of particular concern to law enforcement officials who are on alert for terrorist activities. This is not intended to be an exhaustive list. It only highlights certain Code sections of interest.

Section 22.07 of the Texas Penal Code
Terroristic Threat, discussed in Chapter 10, now includes a provision that makes it illegal to threaten to use violence to place the public in fear of serious bodily injury or to try to influence the conduct of an agency of the federal, state, or local government.

Section 28.02 of the Texas Penal Code
The arson statute, discussed at length in Chapter 11, includes causing an explosion with intent to destroy or damage property as offense.

Section 28.03 of the Texas Penal Code
Criminal Mischief, also discussed in Chapter 11, has specific punishment categories for impairment or interruption of the public water supply, public communication, transportation, gas or power supply.

Section 28.07 of the Texas Penal Code
Interference with Railroad Property has a specific Penal Code provision.

Section 32.51 of the Texas Penal Code
Fraudulent Use or Possession of Identifying Information makes it illegal to use the identifying information of another person without consent to harm or defraud someone.

Section 34.02 of the Texas Penal Code
Money Laundering

Section 37.10 of the Texas Penal Code
Tampering With Governmental Record

Section 42.03 of the Texas Penal Code
Obstructing Highway or Other Passageway

Chapter 46 of the Texas Penal Code
Addresses weapons offenses

Section 71.02 of the Texas Penal Code
Engaging in Organized Criminal Activity

The federal government takes the lead in prosecuting crimes against the government. State Penal Codes, however, have provisions that may be applicable to certain types of activities. Dual prosecution may be possible. That's a judgment call made by the authorities based on strategic and evidentiary issues.

Appendix
Review Question Answers

Chapter One
Q1:c; Q2:d; Q3:c; Q4:d; Q5:c; Q6:c; Q7:d; Q8:a; Q9:d; Q10:d
Q11: a; Q12:c; Q13: a; Q14:b; Q15: b.

Chapter Two
Q1:a; Q2:d; Q3:c; Q4:a; Q5:d; Q6:d; Q7:b; Q8:b; Q9:d; Q10:b;
Q11:b; Q12:c; Q13:b; Q14:b; Q15:b; Q16:a; Q17:d; Q18:a; Q19:a

Chapter Three
Q1:d; Q2:a; Q3:c; Q4:b; Q5:c; Q6:b; Q7:c; Q8:b; Q9:a; Q10: c;
Q11:b; Q12:b; Q14:c; Q14:c; Q15:c; Q16: a; Q17:a

Chapter 4
Q1:a; Q2:c; Q3:a; Q4:a; Q5:c; Q6:b; Q7:a; Q8:d; Q9:d; Q10:b;
Q11:b

Chapter 5
Q1:b; Q2:a; Q3:c; Q4:b; Q5:c; Q6:a; Q7:b; Q8:c; Q9:a: Q10:b;
Q11:b

Chapter Six
Q1:b; Q2:c; Q3:d; Q4:a; Q5:b; Q6:b; Q7:c; 8:c; Q9:a; Q10:b;
Q11:b; Q12b; Q13b; Q14:c

Chapter Seven
Q1:b; Q2:b; Q3:c; Q4b; Q5:d; Q6:c; Q7:d; Q8:c; Q9:a

Chapter Eight
Q1:c; Q2:d; Q3:b; Q4:b; Q5:a; Q6:d; Q7:c; Q8:b; Q9:a; Q10:c;
Q11:a; Q12:c

Chapter Nine
Q1:b; Q2:b; Q3:d; Q4:a; Q5:c; Q6:b; Q7:b; Q8:b; Q9:a; Q10:b;
Q11:c; Q12:c

Chapter Ten
Q1:c; Q2:b; Q3:b; Q4:b; Q5:b; Q6:a; Q7:d; Q8:b; Q9:d; Q10:c;
Q11:c; Q12:b; Q13:d; Q14:b; Q15:b

Chapter Eleven
Q1:b; Q2:b; Q3:c; Q4:c; Q5:b; Q6:d; Q7:d; Q8:a; Q9:a; Q10:c;
Q11:b; Q12:b; Q13:b; Q14:b; Q15:a; Q16:a; Q17:d; Q18:d; Q19:a;
Q20:c; Q21b; Q22:b; Q23c; Q24:b; Q25:a; Q26c

Chapter Twelve
Q1:b; Q2:a; Q3a; Q4:a; Q5:c